Sarah ... across ... including ... was the edito... magazines *Sta... returned ...p of the ...s*, for w...ed she interviewed man, high-profile stars including Justin Timberlake, Britney Spears, Jennifer Ellison and Craig David. Alongside her celebrity writing, Sarah also works for a number of specialist music publications (*Mixmag, B&S, Echoes, IDJ, M8, DJ*). Her recent publications include biographies of Sienna Miller, Lindsay Lohan, Jennifer Aniston and Fern Britton as well as upmarket travel books on Berlin and Lisbon for the *Hedonist Guide 2* series. Sarah lives in London.

# DANIEL
# CRAIG

SARAH MARSHALL

# DANIEL CRAIG

## THE BIOGRAPHY

JOHN BLAKE

Published by John Blake Publishing Ltd,
3 Bramber Court, 2 Bramber Road,
London W14 9PB, England

www.johnblakebooks.com

www.facebook.com/johnblakebooks [f]
twitter.com/jblakebooks [t]

First published as a hardback in 2007
Previously published as a paperback in 2011
This edition published in 2015

ISBN: 978 1 78418 812 2

British Library Cataloguing-in-Publication Data:

A catalogue record for this book is available from the British Library.

Design by www.envydesign.co.uk

Printed in Great Britain by CPI Group (UK) Ltd

1 3 5 7 9 10 8 6 4 2

Papers used by  Publishing are natural, recyclable products made from wood
grown in sustainable forests. The manufacturing processes conform to the
environmental regulations of the country of origin.

Every attempt has been made to contact the relevant copyright-holders,
but some were unobtainable. We would be grateful if the
appropriate people could contact us.

For Sheila Fitzpatrick – a most beautiful
and inspirational woman

# CONTENTS

# CHAPTER 1

# HUMBLE BEGINNINGS

It was hardly a plush mansion but Tim and Carol Olivia Craig (later known simply as Olivia) were extremely proud of their humble house at 41 Liverpool Road in Chester. It hadn't been easy for them and for years they had struggled to save enough money to purchase their own property. A former merchant seaman, Tim now worked as a pub landlord. (In later years he was to manage more exotic bars in the Caribbean.) The work was hard and the income often unrewarding, but Tim was happy. He enjoyed socialising and always made customers feel welcome. Occasionally he had to deal with difficult and cantankerous old men, but a few stern words usually put them in their place. He would often come home in the early hours of the morning with just a few pounds in his pocket, but at least he was making an honest living. And even though Carol loved her job as an art teacher, she had never expected to make a million. Many years previously the couple had resigned themselves to a life of financial restraints and, aside from the odd final demand that dropped through their letterbox, they were happy.

When Carol discovered she was pregnant, the couple were overjoyed. Even the logistical considerations of finding the money to feed another did little to dampen their spirits. They already had a daughter, Lea, but Tim reassured his wife that somehow they would cope. At work, his bosses had hinted that some overtime might be available to him and if the situation became really bad then he could always take on a second job. A traditional northerner, he prided himself on being the breadwinner. Carol and their newborn baby would want for nothing and this was a promise he vowed to keep.

Neighbours in the area found the young couple extremely amenable. Tim was a traditional working-class male, a salt-of-the-earth character. Carol, meanwhile, was far more creative and somewhat idealistic in her views. She was involved in several theatre groups and her social circle comprised mostly of actors and writers. Although on the face of it the two seemed worlds apart, together they had forged a relationship that worked. Carol had always been attracted to Tim's honesty, not to mention his rugged good looks.

They made arrangements for a home birth at Carol's request. She had never been fond of hospitals and was keen to give birth to her child in a friendly, safe and familiar environment. That day came on Saturday, 2 March 1968. The couple had already been in touch with the midwife who was to oversee the birth. Carol coped with the birth remarkably well. Despite the river of sweat pouring from her brow, she refused to scream and complain. Instead she gripped her husband's hand tightly. At one point the pressure became so intense that he almost let out a blood-curdling wail. For days afterwards the nail marks were visible in his skin.

As it turned out, Carol and Tim were ill prepared for the birth, however. As the midwife cradled the new baby, she searched around for a towel or blanket in which to wrap him but there was nothing available. 'Here, use this,' said Tim, passing her an old piece of newspaper. And so Daniel Wroughton Craig was presented to his mother in an old newspaper. 'Just like a packet of chips!' he would later joke. There was, however, a scientific reason for swathing a baby in newspaper print. 'Midwifes used to lay newspaper down because it prints at such high temperatures that it's actually a sterile surface,' Daniel later explained. 'It's the same principle with fish and chips!'

Ironically, it was a foretaste of his future as an actor famed for his working-class sentiments and complete disregard for the trappings and luxuries of celebrity life. 'Perhaps I should lie in interviews and say it was a copy of *The Times Literary Supplement*,' he would laugh.

Recalling his son as a toddler, Tim insists that it was always obvious that Daniel would grow up to become an actor. The signs were plain to see. He recalls an incident in their family pub, the Ring O'Bells near Frodsham, Cheshire. 'I remember having some friends over and Daniel was just weaving in and out between their legs,' he says. 'One asked him what he was doing and what he was going to do when he grew up, and without breaking stride, he said, "Be an actor." I remember at the time blinking and doing a doubletake because he said it with such certainty and he was so small.'

Daniel himself later maintained that his interest in acting stemmed from a desire for 'dressing up and showing off… attention seeking mainly, I think. It's a great way to get rid of your insecurities,' he would joke. 'And find plenty of new ones!'

He made his stage debut aged six in a school production of *Oliver!* Peter Mason, headmaster of Frodsham Church of England Primary School, was impressed by the young lad's performance. 'Both Daniel and his older sister Lea were very good,' he enthused, years later. 'I could tell even then that Daniel was gifted. I was sorry when they left the school.'

Ironically Daniel's declaration of an ambition to act coincided with a rather difficult and sad time in his life. When he was just 'four, five, six' years old (he is vague on dates) his parents separated and subsequently divorced. He and Lea moved to Liverpool with their mother and they would later relocate again to the Wirral. Eventually Carol was to remarry when she met the painter Max Blond. Fortunately, Daniel survived the divorce relatively unscathed and even today he still

4

enjoys a close relationship with both his step-father and his biological dad.

'We're off to Dublin next weekend to watch the last game of the Six Nations,' he told one interviewer. A rugby fan since childhood, in later years Daniel has developed an obsession with the game. 'It's not the coolest thing in the world to like,' he shrugged. 'But I've been watching it since I was a kid.' As a little boy he would wonder why his father used to spend so many weekends in Dublin. As an adult it became apparently clear. 'Your feet don't touch the ground!' he grinned.

Now a single woman, Carol's social life was to centre round the prestigious Everyman Theatre in Liverpool, a hotbed of creative talent during the 1970s. Actors such as Julie Walters and Bernard Hill would regularly tread the boards. Carol had studied Art & Theatre Design at college and instantly warmed to the environment. She quickly befriended several set designers, who invited her to watch shows backstage. Daniel and his older sister Lea would frequently accompany their mother and it was during this period that he developed an obsession with the theatre. 'I knew what the back end of a theatre looked like from an early age and I think that rubbed off,' he says. 'I'd see the plays or I would be in the lighting box backstage and I knew that was what I wanted to do. It was as simple as that.' When asked to recall any specific productions, however, he shrugs and replies casually, 'Most of them involved walking around in the nude.'

At the time, the Everyman Theatre was one of the most

exciting venues in the area. 'It was the place to be. We'd spend a lot of time at the theatre and then I'd see actors in the bar afterwards, socialising, and I thought they were gods... I was a sucker for it all, the idea of being taken somewhere, being entertained... Then I found out many were drunks!'

But Daniel's interest wasn't restricted to the theatre – he also became a big fan of the cinema and every weekend he would beg Carol to take him to a show. 'I got the bug in the cinema when I was about six,' he grins. 'I just went and watched movies from *Quest For Fire* to *Blade Runner*. I had no idea what was happening but I knew then that I wanted to make movies. Seeing those guys' faces blown up on that huge screen, I thought, "I want to do that."'

Although he quickly settled into theatre circles he didn't have quite as much luck in school. Adam Brierley, an old school friend of his, described Daniel's loneliness to one magazine. 'Because he'd just moved in after his parents had separated he didn't have any friends. I invited him out to play football with us on the beach and we became mates.'

Fortunately, Daniel did manage to find several creative outlets at Hilbre High School in West Kirby. (Former students include cyclist Chris Boardman and pop stars The Coral and Orchestral Manouvres In The Dark.) He appeared in several productions, such as *Cats*, *Cinderella* and another version of *Oliver!* He was 14 at the time.

Brenda Davies, Daniel's former drama teacher at Hilbre High School in the Wirral, had to practically force the young boy to audition. He only went along to give his friend some moral support, but Miss Davies convinced him to have a go. 'Danny had tagged along with a friend who was auditioning for a part in *Oliver!*' she recalls. 'He just wanted to stay and watch his friend, and had no interest in auditioning. But I told him he could only stay if he auditioned too. He was adamant he wouldn't and eventually pulled such a face I told him he'd be perfect for the part of Mr Sowerberry. My jaw nearly hit the floor when he eventually got up on stage. He had such timing and range, and he had stage presence for a thirteen-year-old. I thought, "What have we got here?" After that first audition you could sense he had been bitten by the stage bug. From then on he'd tell everyone, "I'm going to be an actor." It was all he could think about.'

Daniel also played for Hoylake Rugby Club. School friend Adam recalls how his friend became a lead singer for his band Inner Voices. 'We needed a frontman as my voice was in the middle of breaking,' he says. 'Danny was always in shows and clearly had a good stage presence. He was always a big character and was quite tall for his age: fifteen at the time. He wasn't fazed by anyone, and he could sing. His style was like Mark Knopfler from Dire Straits. But he left the band when he decided he was better at acting.'

Another old school pal, Trudy Kilpatrick, recalls Daniel's ambitions in the 1980s. 'Way back then he had ambition and you knew he was going to go on and do something. People looked up to him because he was good. He didn't have a massive girl following but there were a few teenagers who fancied him because he was so obviously talented.' His former drama teacher Hilary Green was equally supportive of him. 'Good old Danny. For me he was absolutely superb. It's fantastic that his career has really taken off.'

Although Daniel shied away from academic work, Carol fed his imagination with works of literature. She encouraged him to read various novels and he remembers how he received a copy of Ted Hughes' *Crow* for his 10th birthday. He was to become quite a fan of the poet. One time he even sneaked into a girls' grammar school to hear Hughes read a selection of works but recalls his hero's voice as being disappointingly monotone.

Years later, at the height of Daniel's fame, one red-top paper ran a story claiming that at school his nickname had been 'Mr Potato Head'. Of course Daniel adamantly rubbished the claims as 'bullshit!' In fact, quite the opposite had been true. According to reports from old school pals, the brash northerner had actually been a classroom Casanova. 'He was always popular with the girls,' remembers Adam. 'He would always have new girlfriends and keep the relationship on an on-and-off basis. As well as being a good laugh, he was also quite a deep person, quite thoughtful and mature – and the girls liked that a lot.'

Although Daniel would never claim to be a genuine Scouser (his accent barely betrays his upbringing), he is extremely proud of his humble roots. He will always have a fondness for Liverpool and the 'bullshit debates' that went on at the Everyman Theatre. He recalls overhearing writers such as Alan Bleasdale make proclamations that were 'bang on the right end of socialism'. And of his hometown he says, 'People will shout fucking this and fucking that; they will just have a go at things. There is a need to get out, but also to understand where you're from, and people strike that balance there.'

Despite his fond memories of the city, he admits that during the 1970s and early 1980s Liverpool was a far from prosperous place. Early on he realised his future lay beyond the city boundaries. 'I was looking down here but I was always going to move to London,' he admits. 'By the time I left in 1984 the city was in an awful state. And it's amazing to go back and see it reawakening. It's had some European cash and it's coming alive again. Paul McCartney has built a school there and I really respect him for that – it was a great thing to do. It's being done up and I love it – it's such a beautiful city.

'I always wanted to be an actor. I had the arrogance to believe I couldn't be anything else,' he continues. With that thought in mind, he was never sufficiently motivated to become an academic high achiever. By his own admission he 'failed' at school and even English lessons failed to ignite his interest. 'It was like, Shakespeare, what the fuck do these words mean? And I'm still like that.' Having failed his 11-plus, Daniel also failed his O Levels and left school without completing his A Levels. 'I just drifted away,' he shrugs. He tried a foundation course but soon dropped out of that as well. At this stage, not wanting to see her son unemployed, his mother intervened.

'My mum wanted me to get an education but, when she realised that wouldn't happen, she encouraged my acting. I was lucky to have that,' Daniel concedes. 'Liverpool was a pit. It was depressed as fuck. She realised I wasn't going to get my exams and she was worried enough to want to get me out.

'I hated school. The only thing I ever wanted to do was to act. And when I was young I had this blind faith and ego that helped me believe I could do whatever I wanted to but, as I get older, I get more and more nervous. It's sort of reversing!'

Dutch courage helped him decide that a move to London was the necessary next step. Carol stumbled upon an advertisement for the National Youth Theatre and suggested that Daniel should give it a shot. Taking her advice he headed along to the regional Manchester auditions. 'She obviously thought, "Why won't this smelly eating machine leave my house!"' he jokes. In fact, she was extremely supportive of her son's career choice. Daniel later discovered that his mother had once secured a place at RADA but had never taken it up. 'It wasn't the thing for a young lady to do then,' he shrugs. 'The pressures of family life were different to now. I admire her for not applying her ambition to me.'

Amazed by the fact that his mother had sacrificed her ambitions for a family, Daniel understood his own position of privilege and so he became even more determined to succeed as an actor. 'This business is still as misogynistic,' he reflects. 'But then one of my mother's heroes is Judi

Dench and look what she's achieved.' Ironically, years later, he was to end up working alongside the acclaimed actress in *Casino Royale*. And he understood why his mother had held her in such high esteem. 'My mother had a picture of Judi as Puck [from *A Midsummer Night's Dream*]. She still looks like Puck now – her eyes sparkle.'

Daniel's mind was firmly made up – he was moving to London. Later, he would describe the move as a 'complete epiphany'. He packed his bags, bade an emotional farewell to his mother and headed for the Big Smoke. 'She advised me just to fuck off and go for it!' he beams. But unfortunately, the streets of London weren't quite so paved with the gold he'd initially imagined. Despite several determined attempts, he failed to land a place at RADA, LAMDA, The Young Vic or The Guildhall. He remains stoical about the situation and, looking back, he believes the knockbacks did him the power of good. 'It allowed me to just fuck about and be seventeen,' he says.

Fortunately he had much more success with his application for the National Youth Theatre and the experience he gained during his period of study there was to prove invaluable in later life. 'It was good for me,' he says. 'It's like a big youth club but it's also quite serious because they use professional crews and you quickly get involved with what real theatre is like.'

Although enjoyable, sadly his stint at the National Youth Theatre didn't open any doors for Daniel. Acting work failed to materialise and all he was left with were fond memories. Despite this, he refused to give up and was more determined than ever to pursue his dream career. Besides, he couldn't imagine doing anything else. After several more attempts Daniel finally won a place at the Guildhall School of Music and Drama in London. As it turned out he was in good company: Ewan McGregor, Joseph Fiennes and impressionist Alistair McGowan were all fellow students.

'It was a good move for a northern boy,' he laughs. 'I met people. I had no idea what the business was all about. But I knew it was the right place for me – I wanted to be there even more than in a pub or a nightclub.' Although he was glad to see the back of school, he now wishes that he'd put more effort into gaining an education. 'I have regrets about not being educated,' he admits. 'I'd love to be able to sit down to write a letter without panicking. I can't really write and that bothers me. I didn't acquire that essay thing; I just cannot sit down and write even half a page.'

Daniel did confess to writing the odd piece of poetry later in life, though. 'Just the sort of stuff you write when you get back from the pub. Pages of "What's life all about?" bollocks!' But at the time he couldn't have cared less about learning and the world of academia seemed alien and inaccessible. 'I was massively arrogant, my head firmly stuck up my arse. I thought nothing could touch me. I could have learned verse but I didn't. It was like, Shakespeare, what the fuck do these words mean? Now I'd love to do Shakespeare but I don't think I'm up to it. It's a big discipline and there's an awful lot of thinking going on. With Shakespeare you've got to leave your ego at the door and that's sort of scary.'

Funnily enough, his father Tim doesn't share his view of that time. Instead, he recalls seeing Daniel in a production by the Bard. 'I remember seeing him in his first National Youth Theatre production as Agamemnon in Shakespeare's *Troilus And Cressida*,' he says. 'I was sat next to his mother who had encouraged him every step of the way, like myself. It was pitch dark and out of the darkness comes this booming voice – it was Daniel. It was very good.'

Daniel would be the first to admit that in many ways his aversion to Shakespeare simply boiled down to an issue of class. Often he was to joke that his mother's teaching profession by default made him middle class. Surrounded by more privileged kids in drama school, however, he always felt like an outsider. 'I'm not scared of it,' he smiles, reflecting on his roots.

Associating costume dramas with the upper classes, this was an area of acting that he purposely steered clear of. 'I don't want to be dressing up in costumes and pansying around,' he spat with scorn. 'It doesn't appeal to me; it never did. When I left drama school, the only jobs were for boys with floppy fringes who went to Eton. I could fit in because I could do a slightly posh accent. I'm a bullshitter, I'm an actor, but I realised actually I can't be posh.'

Instead he gravitated towards the darker and more twisted roles, a character type with which he would famously become associated much later in his career. 'When I first started, villains were all I did,' he remembers. 'I'm blond and blue eyed, so they always gave me the part of the Nazi. When I started getting roles that were goodies, I didn't really know what to do with them – I just wanted to thump people!'

After a while he grew tired of being constantly cast as either the 'fascist or fop'. 'It was very much Merchant Ivory at the time. And it started to bother me, because I was getting all these parts of terribly posh boys and I'm not posh,' he recalls. 'It was a great lesson because I can't play posh. Posh is breeding. I'm not interested in that kind of stuff. It's lovely, and it may have relevance somewhere but it has no relevance to me whatsoever.'

Overall he has mixed feelings about his experiences at Guildhall. 'For three years you talk shit to each other,' he says. 'If it works, it keeps the sparks going and you hit the industry with lovely open eyes, not cynical.' But the training he received would hardly turn out to be instrumental in shaping his career. Surrounded by the type of luvvies that he still despises to this day, he always felt like an uncomfortable outsider. 'I'm not sure what I got out of it,' he sighs nonchalantly. 'Apart from the discipline of getting up in the morning... and [learning] not to shout when you're backstage.'

Now an established film star he frequently receives invitations to give talks at the Guildhall but he says that doesn't know what to tell students. 'I suppose my advice would be to stick with it and make something happen. I was lucky to do a bit of TV that paid the rent and a bit of theatre, which pays fuck all!' Although his comments may seem flippant, there is a large degree of truth in them.

Paying the bills was one of the greatest obstacles facing Daniel in those early years. Stumbling from one part-time job to another, he just about managed to make ends meet. Although ambitious and determined, he laughs at the suggestion that he was ever 'driven'. Distasteful of a cliché so often attached to successful actors he says, 'Driven at seventeen? Some seventeen-year-olds may be driven but I certainly wasn't! I was just like everybody else, living day to day, getting on with it... I was no Dick Whittington. At that age bravery doesn't come into it – you do what you do. You either come here and fall flat on your face, or you survive and become successful.'

One thing Daniel was determined to do, however, was to please his parents. 'They have always been very supportive,' he says. 'And what they think means a lot to me so I think they probably have influenced my choices. I have to prove to them I'm on the right track and not sleeping in a gutter somewhere.'

By his own admission, he led a rootless and nomadic existence. He never had a serious career plan and simply fell from one job to another. In between low-income roles he would work in restaurant kitchens and sleep on friends' floors. The need to survive made him unscrupulous. 'When you come here [London] you have to survive. You tend to end up being selfish. You have to live off people's floors and rent property, and you end up doing runners. I've done awful things to survive because I've had no money.'

The whole experience has imbued him with an

indispensible sense of humility. 'I was a jobbing actor, just doing what I could,' he reflects. 'I was out of work for seven or eight months but I wasn't penniless and starving. I had an overdraft – this is the modern world. I owed the bank a lot of money!' Years later, though, several of those embarrassing appearances would come back to haunt him. One fan website has even uploaded several voiceover recordings that Daniel made for various adverts. He can be heard extolling the virtues of alcohol emporium Beer Paradise: 'Open every day on the South Access Road, near the Crown Point retail park, Liverpool,' he announces. At the time any cash he did earn, however, was quickly frittered away.

Despite the hardships of being a struggling actor in his early twenties, this was a period of his life that he looks back on with fondness. He recalls landing roles in cities such as Valencia and Moscow. Jetting across Europe – albeit on a shoestring – his lifestyle was exhilarating. He thrived on the unexpected and took great pleasure in pursuing a career that circumvented the normal conventions of a 9–5 lifestyle. 'I'd come back from a job and be in the car coming from the airport, and I'd go to the driver, "Take me some-where else."' He smiles. 'I loved being nomadic.'

During this time as a free spirit exploring life, he was impossible to pin down. It was a fact that many of his early girlfriends would testify. Marina Pepper, now a Liberal Democrat councillor living in East Sussex, sold her story to a celebrity magazine. She came across Daniel during the 1980s when she was working as a Playboy model. The couple met in a trendy Notting Hill bar. At the time

Marina was 20, two years older than Daniel. She had thick, fiery red hair and a cleavage that always turned heads. Friends would later describe her as the very epitome of a buxom beauty.

'I was meeting a friend for drinks and Daniel was there,' she recalls. 'He was a bit younger than me but he had a great body, piercing blue eyes that looked right through you and an incredibly sexy presence.' The pair sparked up a conversation and, according to Marina, they went back to her nearby flat after closing time. 'He was irresistible and incredible in the bedroom!' she enthuses. 'He was an animal in bed!'

She went on to tell the magazine how Daniel had moved into her flat just two weeks later. 'He had a very healthy sexual appetite and we didn't get much sleep when we were in bed together – which was a lot of the time. He was a tough act to follow because of his sexual stamina and he was also very sensitive to a woman's body.' A large-breasted woman herself, Marina confirmed that Daniel was very much a 'boobs man too'.

At the time she was also struck by his drive to succeed. 'He was incredibly ambitious and always wanted to be the leading man.' But she was quick to point out that he was far from a workaholic. He made sure that there was plenty of time for social activities in his schedule. 'He was dedicated to his acting but he loved to party as well,' Marina remembers. Daniel would often invite her along to glamorous parties with his theatre pals.

Even though he was to vehemently refute her claims,

Marina revealed to the magazine that Daniel loved to spend hours preening himself in front of the mirror. 'I soon realised that his sexy ruffled look was actually the result of a lot of care and attention. My moisturiser started disappearing when he lived with me and he deliberately wouldn't shave for days to get that rough image.'

Although she enjoyed spending time with Daniel, their relationship was disappointingly short lived. Over time Marina grew sick and tired of her boyfriend's unexplained absences. Sometimes he would disappear for days on end. 'I'd arrange to meet him outside a phone box so he could get in touch if he needed to, but I'd still be waiting when the pubs began to close.'

Deep down she knew Daniel must be cheating on her. 'I suspected I wasn't the only girl in his life,' she sighs. 'But then he'd come back and his charm would win me over again.' Even his charms, however, couldn't last for ever. After one heated argument too many Marina asked him to pack his bags and leave. 'We parted on a sour note when I realised I wanted more than fantastic sex every night.'

This was the last time the couple would speak for a long time. It was only years later when Marina flicked on her TV set that she actually set eyes on Daniel again and she was amazed but not wholly surprised by his success. She always knew he had the talent and good looks to be a star. But that wasn't the end of the story. One day, while walking through Notting Hill, she bumped into Daniel again. Ironically, at the time she was wearing one of his old shirts. 'I'd popped out to the shops when I heard a voice say, "That's my shirt!" And there he was. I'd been wearing it to do some decorating.'

Stunned and slightly taken aback, she didn't know what to say. Realising he had taken her by surprise, Daniel smiled and made polite conversation. The pair shared pleasantries and then parted. Marina congratulated him on his acting success and made a joke about hanging onto his shirt. When Daniel waved goodbye, she was left speechless. Her heart still fluttering, she couldn't believe how handsome he remained. 'He still looked as sexy as ever,' she told the magazine. 'He's one of the sexiest men I've ever met.'

Immediately after graduating, Daniel scored his first big film break with a role in John Avildsen's *The Power Of One* (1992). Filmed in Zimbabwe, the plot took the flimsy premise of overcoming apartheid through boxing. An English-speaking orphan in South Africa is sent to an Africaans school, where he is bullied by a neo-Nazi clique. Tired of the beatings, he turns to a trainer, played by Morgan Freeman, and learns how to box. Daniel was cast as the former head bully, now a thuggish Afrikaner policeman. Panned by critics for being trivial, the film did little to set his career alight. 'I was a fish out of water; I didn't know what I was doing,' he admits.

At that point in his career, Daniel had extensive experience in the theatre and on various TV shows, but he felt completely out of place on a film set so there was still a lot for him to learn. 'After leaving drama school I was terrified. It made no sense to me whatsoever. On set people would call my name and I'd be like [sitting bolt upright], "Yes?" I wish I had someone say to me, "Relax, everything's fine. It's not the end of the world."'

Although the film was a flop at the box offices, he still has no regrets about taking on the job. For him it proved an invaluable opportunity to cut his acting teeth. 'It was the first job I ever did. It threw me into a bit of a spin; it was an experience. Suddenly I was on a shoot in Zimbabwe on huge sets. It didn't work out in the sense of propelling me forward – thankfully – because it wasn't the right time or place... Besides, it was a piece of shit and I'm glad! If it had worked I'd still be playing policemen beating people up.'

Financially, though, the next few months would prove to be difficult. Daniel jokes that 'unfortunately' he made enough money to keep himself drunk. Despite several setbacks, giving up on his dream was something he never considered. 'There is always that pessimistic optimism in actors because you deal with so much refusal... But I always had blind faith. I swore to myself I'd never go back to being a waiter. It was arrogance that made me stick at it,' he says.

Unlike many of his peers, he never had a clear career path in mind. Instead he fell into a series of jobs. Early on, he landed several TV roles, including an extended episode of *Young Indiana Jones* (1992). Initially intended for TV, the two-hour special 'Daredevils of the Desert' was eventually released on video. Its script was written by Frank Darabont, who would eventually become famous for *The Shawshank Redemption* (1994). The film also starred a young Catherine Zeta Jones.

Later in 1992, Daniel starred in *Covington Cross* (an entertaining series that relates the adventures and loves of the children of an English lord during the Middle Ages) and an episode of *Boon* – 'MacGuffin's Transputer'. He also returned to the stage with a play titled *No Remission*, with the Midnight Theatre Company at the Lyric Theatre in London. Billed as a tough prison drama, the script revolved around a bank robber, double murderer and a paratrooper that are all forced to share a cell. Daniel was cast as the soldier whose resolve only breaks when the other cellmates reveal that his girlfriend is nothing more than a common tart. The play was extremely successful and a review in the *Independent* newspaper even gave him a special mention, saying that he 'contains his violence like an unexploded mine'.

After spending so many hours in front of the TV cameras, he welcomed the opportunity to perform in front of a live audience. 'Theatre is the great casting couch,' he says, smiling. 'It generates something new. That's why Kevin Spacey comes over here and does it.'

Meanwhile, still more dramatic changes were afoot in Daniel's personal life. After years of flitting between different love interests, the restless actor shocked his friends and family when he settled down by marrying the Scottish actress Fiona Loudon. The couple met in Edinburgh when he was just 23. Fiona gave birth to Daniel's daughter Ella that same year but the pair were divorced in 1994.

Although Daniel has no regrets in life, with hindsight he wishes the situation could have been handled differently. 'I was twenty-three when I got married. I was too young. I don't know if it was a mistake exactly but it was not the right thing to do at the time. I thought it was the mature thing to do. I don't regret it, but I do wish I'd lived it in a different way. That relationship went badly pear shaped and I'm determined not to make the same mistake twice.'

The experience has in no way tainted his views on marriage, however. 'I do believe in marriage,' he says. 'I really do. I believe that getting together with somebody and making a public statement about it is a good thing. I just didn't really understand it before.' He confessed it was something that wasn't easy for him. 'Commitment is part of a life – the toughest part, probably.'

Initially, he found it tough to adapt to fatherhood. 'I'm a bad dad!' he once joked. But over time he came to cherish the role. 'My daughter is brilliant!' he was to once exclaim. 'And being a father is great. But I won't talk about it. I'll talk about my work because that's part of what I do but if you want to talk about myself, my personal life, forget it – it's nobody's fucking business!' But now he describes the whole experience as 'the most wonderful thing that'll ever happen to you. It's a constant struggle but very rewarding. When it happens it's like, "Oh my fucking God!" But you just have to enjoy it.'

Being a father also made him more wary of his own age. He would make light of his daughter's taste in music, joking that he had spent hours trying to convert her to The Rolling Stones, but that she was adamantly stuck on The Beatles. On several occasions he would also express concern about teenagers growing up too quickly. 'Nowadays free time seems to be ten times more complicated than it was,' he complained. 'There was less to think about for us. Although Sunday night was all about recording *The Chart Show* on the radio, it was a major technical deal… so it was probably just as stressful as downloading something from MySpace. It fills the same hole in your head, doesn't it?' Listening back to his own words, he realised how paternalistic he had reluctantly become.

As to whether Ella would follow in her father's acting footprints, he remained uncertain. 'I try to dissuade her from that!' he joked, before adding, 'Nah, she can do what she wants. Whatever she wants to do, I shall give her my full support. As long as it's not mass murder.'

Although there were predictions of success from certain critical circles, overnight fame failed to materialise for Daniel. Instead he continued to happily plod along with several TV appearances and well-chosen theatre productions. In 1993 he appeared in the acclaimed news satire *Drop The Dead Donkey*, the police corruption series *Between The Lines*, as well as the light-hearted Sunday evening drama *Heartbeat*. There were also two major TV dramas. *Sharpe's Eagle* was a continuation of Bernard Cornwell's war saga starring Sean Bean. Daniel played a belligerent officer determined to insult and undermine the hero Sharpe. After attacking Sharpe's girlfriend with a riding crop, he is challenged to a duel. Cast again in the role of brooding villain, Daniel did a fine job. By the end of the same year he would also star in the black comedy *Genghis Cohn*.

On stage he appeared in Tony Kushner's production of *Angels In America* at The National Theatre, in which he played a Mormon who decides to reveal his true sexuality. Critics commended his performance but, wishing to distance himself from the thespian world he so desperately detested, Daniel nonchalantly shrugged off his success. 'I never saw the original production,' he told reporters. Although he was involved in several productions, Daniel never claimed to be a fan of being in the audience at the theatre. 'Theatre passes me by,' he shrugged nonchalantly. 'If I hadn't been in it anyway, I probably wouldn't have had a clue.' More of a fan of having a drink in the interval than sitting through the performance itself, Daniel joked, 'I'm the worst audience in the world!'

But the following year he was to make another stage appearance with *The Rover*, a production for the Women's Playhouse Trust. It was a dark Restoration comedy about a group of mercenaries who set out to rape and pillage. Daniel starred alongside Dougray Scott and Andy Serkis. Staged in a sand-filled arena, it was an extremely boisterous production, with cast members flitting past on bikes and rickshaws. Filmed by the BBC, it was later shown on terrestrial television.

During this period he also made his worst movie to date: the Disney flick *A Kid In King Arthur's Court*. Billed with the appalling tagline JOUST DO IT, the plot revolved around an American teenager who is pulled into King Arthur's Court by Merlin. Midway through a baseball game, when an earthquake strikes and he suddenly wakes up in

Arthurian England wearing his 'Knights' team kit and a backpack. He is given a task to save Camelot. To do this he must overcome a villain known as Lord Belscoe, train to become a knight and rescue Princess Catherine, who has fallen in love with him. Above all, he has the task of restoring Arthur's shaken confidence.

Daniel played the character of Master Kane, a stable boy who longs to marry the King's beautiful daughter (played by Kate Winslet). Needless to say, years later when he was quizzed about the film, he wasn't particularly forthcoming. Asked by a journalist to name his biggest turkey, he squirmed in his seat before admitting, 'There's a thing called *A Kid In King Arthur's Court*. Fucking there you go, you bastard! I know you're going to print that and it's going to be like in a year's time, some journalist will go, "So, *A Kid In King Arthur's Court*."' As if to offer some justification for his poor judgement, Daniel quickly added, 'Kate Winslet's in it too!'

By his mid-20s he had clocked up a number of reputable performances. Despite this, the big-money pay cheques had failed to materialise, however. Although critically acclaimed, he still hovered in the shadows. For the most part, he was unperturbed by this. He was just happy to be acting. Although his marriage had failed, Daniel remained in close contact with his ex-wife and daughter. Financially he managed to keep the wolves at bay but he was growing increasingly tired of living on a shoestring. Thankfully, all this would change when he landed a part in a new TV drama. Little did he know it, but he was about to become a household name.

## CHAPTER 2

# OUR FRIENDS

*Our Friends In The North* (1996) told the story of four friends in the city of Newcastle, north-east England, over 31 years, from 1964 to 1995. Each episode was named after a different year and followed the characters' changing lives, careers and relationships against a backdrop of the political and social events in Britain during that period. Humorous and chilling in equal measure, it was a damning account of modern Britain.

The nine-part series went on to become hugely popular and was hailed as one of the most successful BBC television dramas of the 1990s. It was described by the *Daily Telegraph* as 'A production where all... worked to serve a writer's vision. We are not likely to look upon its like again.' What's more, in a poll of industry professionals conducted by the British Film Institute in 2000, it ranked

No. 25 in a list of the 100 'Greatest British Television Programmes' of the 20th century. Because the drama was based on real politicians and real political events, there was a certain degree of controversy surrounding it. The BBC waited several years to commission the series for fear of political implications.

When Daniel agreed to take on the role of Geordie (George) Peacock (a feckless sex club owner turned vagrant arsonist), he had little idea of the implications it would have for his career. 'When I got the role, I was in some ways incredibly successful,' he says. 'I'd done a year at The National Theatre and was doing bits of television. But there was something missing, and that was *Our Friends*... There are benchmarks in a career, and you do something like that and producers see it and go, "Oh, he can do it!" I'm very proud of *Our Friends*, and I always will be.'

Fortunately for him, Geordie Peacock was easily the most colourful of the cast. While his co-stars were embroiled in a serious pursuit of Labour politics, Geordie enjoyed a far more depraved lifestyle. Ditching a career as a dodgy pop star, he starts working for London porn baron Malcolm McDowell. From that point onwards he courts trouble at every turn. He sells drugs to police, dabbles with arson and lands himself in prison – only to escape and discover his old friends. The tabloids instantly lapped up this sexy reprobate.

It took Daniel several attempts to secure the role and he even had to pick up a Geordie accent. 'I got in the frame somehow!' he laughs. 'I had to go back five times; I had to learn to do a Geordie accent.' He would later credit his dialect coaches and several Newcastle pubs for the authenticity of his performance. But he would only take method acting to a certain point. 'I didn't hang out with homeless people though – it would have been patronising. Destitution is not a big step to make from the depressions we've all suffered. I don't like going to people and saying, "Hey, I'm an actor. Can I hang out with you?" If it was me, I'd say fuck off!'

Ironically, Daniel was verging on becoming homeless himself at the time when the offer of work landed on his doorstep. 'He was never actually homeless but he did spend the night on the odd park bench,' remembers a friend. 'I remember him having to plead with the BBC to give him his cheque for *Our Friends In The North*. When he paid it into his bank account, it just cleared his overdraft.'

From early on Daniel and fellow cast members realised they were part of something very special. 'Mark Strong [who played Tosker Cox] and I secretly would get drunk and say, "This could be quite good,"' admits Daniel. 'But we were very nervous about saying it. When you are starting out usually it's about ninety per cent disappointment, so you tend to harden yourself. It's a bullshit approach but it makes it easier to deal with the rejection you get three times a week if you go for interviews. To have the luck of it landing on my doorstep and also to be offered the sex, drugs and rock'n'roll part, with the confidence that I gained from doing that; to spend a year filming something like that and being given

responsibility of a large role, my learning curve was acute.'
'It was a peculiar production,' he continues. 'I don't think
you can measure anything else by it. When we started
doing it we realised we were doing something special. We
thought the critics would get hold of it and rip it to pieces,
especially the bits that were political. But every single
critic pushed how affecting the relationships were, and
that was the nicest result.' *Our Friends* was to become one
of the most talked about TV shows of the decade. 'It was
considered to be a proper worthy piece,' agrees Daniel.
'Everybody who watched it – and who liked it – said,
"That's what television's about."'

His own character proved to be particularly popular
with both the public and critics. 'I've had people burst into
tears over me!' he admits. 'And I've had to say, "Look,
Geordie's fine, he's OK, at the end he just walked off. He's
quite all right."' Even to this day fans continue to approach
him about the role. 'I still get people saying, "You're that
Geordie, aren't you?"' he says, laughing.

Most importantly, the experience gave him a renewed
vigour for his work. The role of Geordie underlined the
very reasons he had started acting in the first place. Here
was a meaty character with real depth. After several
disappointing productions, it was just the tonic he needed.
'It helped me start to enjoy myself again,' he says with a
smile. 'I showed it to a friend the other day and it stood up.
Gina [McKee], Mark [Strong] and Chris [Eccleston] were
fantastic. They all seem fabulously real. It was because we
spent time discovering things about each other. It was like

being taught all over again how to make a character and get it watchable. Like a year with a Russian theatre!'

Prior to filming *Our Friends*, he had had little contact with the press. But the success of the show required him to take part in a number of interviews. It was the beginning of a difficult relationship with the prying tabloids. Daniel had always considered himself to be an actor rather than a celebrity. Subsequently, he couldn't understand why so much fuss was necessary.

With no media training behind him, he learned the hard way how to deal with journalists. Pressured in an interview to come up with an interesting story, he blurted out an anecdote involving Malcolm McDowell and a Rolls-Royce. When Daniel picked up the paper a few weeks later, he read the headline, CRAIG WRITES OFF ROLLS-ROYCE. He was incensed: the story had been blown completely out of proportion. 'That was a lesson to learn about the press,' he conceded afterwards. 'I did a few interviews and I didn't feel I was very interesting. They tended to ask me if I had any good stories. So I said, "Well, I scraped the bottom of this Rolls-Royce." And then all of a sudden, I had driven it into a brick wall.'

*Our Friends In The North* clearly demonstrated that Daniel had the talent to be a major star and all of a sudden he began to receive bigger and better offers. 'It was simple, really. I couldn't get a lead in a television series because I didn't have a track record. But as soon as I did that, I was offered them.' Never having been an ambitious type, he admits it was just the push he needed to get his career off the ground. 'It was a kick in the rear end up the stairs.'

And it wasn't only the tempting job offers that started to flood in. Daniel was inundated with fan mail from adoring female admirers. His piercing blue eyes and brooding good looks fulfilled almost every woman's fantasy, or so it seemed. On the topic of Daniel, Stephen Fry would even declare, 'He is so good looking, his face is a piece of outstanding beauty.' One newspaper reported he was receiving up to 500 letters a week. 'Rubbish! Rubbish!' he protested at the claims. 'It didn't happen.' If he was shy of celebrity status, he was even more repelled by the idea of being tagged a sex symbol.

Eventually he had to relent. 'OK, I did this thing about eligible bachelors for a women's magazine, thinking it was just part of the press for *Our Friends*, but it turned out to be one of those things where you're getting into self-promotion – and that's why I'm careful about doing press now. And I get loads and loads of letters, which freaked me out completely. I wanted to write back to everybody and say, "I didn't mean it! I'm not eligible. At all!" I think you've got to be kind of sick to want knickers through the post.'

In fact, he found the whole episode extremely disconcerting. 'It drove me insane,' he says with a shudder. 'I made a decision then, "I can't be arsed," because it's a full-time occupation. I've got better things to do.' He never set out to court attention and certainly wouldn't be planning to hire a press agent in a hurry. 'My thing isn't about getting on the cover of this or that, it's about people I want to work with.'

Besides, there was always an inevitable backlash from the tabloids: 'You can be beefcake one week and Mr Potato Head the next!' (Daniel was referring to that revelation in the *Daily Mail* that his nickname at school had been Mr Potato Head). According to him it was utter rubbish. 'It was made up! What do you think!' he snarled sarcastically to one persistent journalist.

Now edging towards his 30s he considered himself too old to be a sex symbol. In his mind, it was a much younger man's game. 'I was lucky to become known at thirty; at least people will never say about me, "He was so beautiful when he was young." My big break was playing a drunk, so there's not a long way to fall. That's good...

'I didn't have a career when I was twenty-five, and that's when you should be a sex symbol.' He shrugged. 'When you can eat and drink as much as you want and still wake up in the morning and look fantastic. If I was ever set up as a sex symbol, there would be photos of me lying in the gutter with a kebab on my head.'

Most of the female population, however, would disagree. Daniel was becoming not only a respected actor, but also a fanciable pin-up. Women's magazines approached the actor for several interviews and he was even photographed by the model Helena Christiansen for *Elle* magazine's 18th-birthday issue. Speaking about the pictures, Daniel said, 'They were quite nice pictures, yes. But can I just say, I didn't get my cock out like Michael Stipe did.' Although flattered by so much attention, he still found it quite overwhelming. 'My female fan base frightens me. I just imagine there's this room somewhere called DANIEL'S FEMALE FAN BASE.'

Numerous critics would comment on his ability to transfix an audience with his stunning blue eyes. 'They're grey mostly,' he would say with a shrug, in a characteristically self-deprecating manner. 'Stick enough light on them, they're blue... They run in the family. Maybe they're getting bluer though, ha ha. Or maybe in ten years' time they're going to go buoomph! And just go out, and that'll be it! Old grey eyes is back.'

After *Our Friends In The North*, Daniel went on to star in several more TV productions. He appeared in an episode of *Tales From The Crypt* with Gayle Hunnicutt and Ute Lemper, and grabbed a headlining role in the police drama *Kiss And Tell*, in which he played an underachieving cop. Matt Kearney stakes his career on catching a man suspected of murdering his missing wife. With some persuasion his psychologist ex-girlfriend agrees to woo the subject in an attempt to elicit a confession from him. However, the plan backfires when Matt becomes extremely jealous. In the meantime, his wife, if still alive, must be found and treated for cancer.

A far less commercial project was the BBC production *Saint-Ex*, a biopic of Antoine de Saint-Exupery, the French author of *The Little Prince* and a daring pilot for the French postal service and air force during the Second World War. Daniel was cast as the lead's inspirational best friend Guillaumet, who survives a crash in the Andes, only to be lost at war. Heavyweight stars Miranda Richardson, Janet McTeer and Katrin Cartlidge also starred alongside him.

A much more light-hearted project came along in the form of ITV miniseries *The Fortunes And Misfortunes Of Moll Flanders*, an adaptation of Daniel Defoe's novel. Set in 17th-century England, the series was a brash antidote to the stream of popular Jane Austen period dramas that were currently flooding the market. Moll Flanders (played by Alex Kingston) is a street girl who attempts to secure a fortune by seducing men. She returns from a trip to Virginia posing as a lady in order to find a rich husband. Along the way, however, she falls in love with highwayman James 'Jemmy' Seagrave. Ironically, he is also posing as a wealthy suitor hoping to find a wife willing to restore his bankrupt estate. The pair found an instant attraction.

Literally a romp a minute, Daniel spent most of the series in a state of undress. Cast as swashbuckling highwayman Jemmy Seagrave, he was also Moll's main love interest. On ravishing actress Alex Kingston he laughed and said, 'Well, you have to really, in these situations, don't you?'

All jokes aside, the series did manage to raise several eyebrows and even Daniel was surprised by the number of sex scenes in the final edit. 'I watched the final version the other day and it shocked me. I kept thinking, "Not another sex scene!" There's at least four an episode and they're full-on bums in the air, or against the wall, or oops, Missus, there go my trousers,' he exclaimed. 'Obviously they've gone for the sex angle – it's a big kick against the Austens and all that stuff. I was a little worried it was going to turn out as *Carry On Moll Flanders*, but I'm really surprised by the end product. The last episode is so dark, it actually does get to you. I was in tears by the end... but then I'm just an emotional wreck,' he says, with a wry smile.

Understandably, ITV had to censor much of the material and the unedited cut of the series was only available on video. A tamer version of the series also proved a big hit in the USA. 'I think they just didn't linger on the arses going up and down as much as they did over here,' offered Daniel in explanation.

While plenty of actors would have balked at having to do so many nude scenes, Daniel was happy to oblige. He had no qualms about doing whatever the role required. 'Any embarrassment quickly passes,' he pointed out. 'All you see is maybe thirty seconds of a scene that took three hours to shoot, and after a while you forget the fact that you're walking around naked, or you try to. Well, I do.' Playfully, he added, 'Maybe I'm just an exhibitionist. Maybe that's my problem. I love getting my kit off!'

But if the truth be told, Daniel would rather keep his body under wraps. 'It is embarrassing and I get very nervous and uptight about it,' he confessed. 'I have to control all those sorts of feelings and control myself as well.' Even working with some of the world's most beautiful women did little to calm his nerves. Contrary to belief, romping in front of the camera was actually quite off-putting. 'It isn't very sexual because you're always thinking, Will this look good?' he pointed out. 'And the best sex is when you're not analysing it, when you're just doing it. I'm sure that with the right person, at the right time, you couldn't help but get turned on but that hasn't happened to me yet.

'It really is an old cliché about sex scenes,' he continued. 'There are lots of people in the room and they last for much longer than sex lasts – two or three hours. Maybe if you're into tantric you can go on for that long... But you'll be doing them and suddenly think, "What am I doing? For God's sake, this is ridiculous." And – "Who are you?"' he laughed, turning to an imaginary bed partner. 'I have always been a bit of a prude really. Someone once rather cruelly wrote all this stuff about Ewan McGregor talking about his dick. He's obviously very happy and proud of it. I wouldn't talk about my dick, but I don't mind taking my kit off. I wouldn't say it's empowering – in many ways it's the opposite.'

Once the cameras started to roll, Daniel always had his mind fixed firmly on the job in hand. But off screen he would happily entertain the thought of dating another actress. In 1997 he started work on a German–French production called *Obsession*. Directed by Peter Sehr, the storyline revolved around two men desperately in love with the same woman. Miriam (played by the German actress Heike Makatsch) already has a long-term lover, but when she meets John (Daniel Craig) in a Berlin train station, the three become involved in an intense love triangle. Miriam loves both men equally and struggles to decide which one she will ultimately choose.

Taking on the script was a brave move for Daniel. Arthouse cinema – and particularly foreign films –

notoriously gave little financial return. Although the film was nominated for three awards, it was only ever released in Germany, Canada, France and Denmark. But this was of little consequence to Daniel. He had never been motivated by commercial gain. He was far more interested in the creative value of a project. It was a trend that would continue throughout his career.

'I don't look at things that way,' he said, when asked about his pay packet. 'The script came along and it was a good script, and it meant Berlin for three months, then we went to France, then to Paris. I wasn't going to turn down an opportunity like that – plus it's quite a good movie.'

Even though *Obsession* would have limited impact on his professional career, it had dramatic implications for his personal life. While on set, he met and fell in love with Heike Makatsch, who had played his love interest in the film. Blessed with wispy blonde hair and entrancing blue eyes, she instantly caught Daniel's attention. Typically, he remained coy about the finer details and refused to pinpoint exactly when fantasy had become reality. 'It's just where actors meet,' he said with a nonchalant sigh.

Born in 1971, Heike is the daughter of a former German national ice-hockey player. Degree educated, she started out as a TV presenter working on several music-chart shows. Dubbed a 'girlie girl', she surprised critics by undertaking several credible movie roles. Although considered a huge star in Germany, her profile in the UK is limited. She is best known for her roles in *Late Night*

*Shopping, Resident Evil* and as Alan Rickman's secretary in *Love Actually*.

Once the filming of *Obsession* was completed, Heike agreed to move to London with Daniel. Considering his general distaste for the traditional acting profession, it was perhaps strange that he should choose to date yet another actress. But even though they were both employed in the same profession, he was never concerned that they would have a conflict of interests.

'Actors and actresses living together can be a nightmare,' he admitted. 'But we seem to have got it balanced perfectly, touch wood.' Besides, the fact that Heike came from a completely different milieu made things a lot easier. 'She's German, so we don't have much crossover. She's a very successful actress in Germany. She's very famous there. There's a great thing because she didn't come from a traditional [acting background], she didn't train or anything like that, so her outlook on acting is really straight and it's adult.'

The nature of their work did, however, limit the amount of time that the couple could spend together. Acting was far from a 9–5 career. 'I did one job when I had it written into my contract that she could come out and spend some time with me. I'm not normally into that game, you know, "I must have my family with me…" but it's bloody lonely,' Daniel confessed. 'Film sets are peculiar places and have caused a lot of break-ups; marriages go down the tubes, so you need to keep in touch.'

In spite of all the obstacles, he was happier than he had

been in a long time. 'I have to say that I am at a very happy stage of my life. Whether we are going to get married I don't know. I think probably we'll end up being together, I hope for a long time, so we'll probably have to get married eventually.'

For most of his career, his personal life would be shrouded in secrecy. Fiercely private, he refused to divulge any details of his private life to the press. 'Self promotion, for me, is like going to the dentist,' he once famously commented. As far as he was concerned, such information was irrelevant. He was an actor, not a celebrity. While he was more than happy to discuss the projects he was currently working on, that's where the questioning would end. 'I don't go along with this thing that it's part of the job. It's not the reason I got into this game.

'You watch the mess people get into when they invite people into their homes and say, "This is the stress I'm under at the moment because I'm breaking up with so-and-so, or my child is dying, or my mother is dying, and I'd like to share this grief with you, because it would be good for other people." It may seem a valid statement, but I can only see it damaging you. Later, people will say, "But you shared your grief with us when your cat died, what do you mean you won't talk to us now you've had an affair with so-and-so."'

Very quickly, he developed a reputation for being difficult with the press. Journalists would arrive at interviews, prepared to do battle with a man notorious for his monosyllabic responses. When he did speak, his conversation was peppered with expletives. It wasn't that he had nothing to say – if anything he was worried about saying too much. 'I don't do press, but I can talk for fucking hours!' he dangerously revealed. 'You sort of wind me up and I'll go… I have to be quite guarded. I like to talk and I like people; I'd probably be a tabloid journalist's dream. Get enough drinks down me and I'll tell all.'

Reluctantly, he would conduct interviews only when it was absolutely necessary. 'I know I have to do it,' he said, sighing. 'It is much easier than it was. I can bullshit better these days.' But he never presented journalists with a frosty reception. If anything, he appeared quite nervous and unsure of himself in interviews. One writer for *Marie Claire* magazine commented, 'He stutters when unclear about what to say, rubs his head when he's nervous and seems concerned about appearing pretentious.' It was slowly becoming apparent that Daniel wasn't quite the overbearing and aggressive monster he had been made out to be.

On another occasion, photographers at *Arena* magazine almost tagged Daniel a 'quintessential cock' when he created problems during a photo shoot. At his request, his publicist had called the *Arena* office requesting that staff members didn't pop down to watch him being photographed. Not wanting to come across as a 'pretentious wanker', he went to great lengths to set the record straight.

'It suddenly occurred to me that you lot might be sat at your office thinking I was being a total luvvie cock and going all fucking actor-wanky on you,' he told the magazine by way of an apology. 'It's just that I find the whole standing there posing thing fucking weird. Puffing my chest out and pouting makes me feel, well, like a monumental twat, really.'

Many of his peers thought he was mad. With his career in the ascendant, now would be the ideal time to establish a profile. But Daniel disagreed: he had never set out on a career path and he stubbornly refused to be bound by the rules of convention. He would continue to do as he pleased, regardless of the outcome. 'I have nothing against self-promotion at all,' he said with a shrug. 'People who do it well, I'm slightly in awe of. It's a full-time occupation. And it does actually help you get cast, I know. But whether it's for me… I can't help it. It just sort of makes me sick to the stomach, really.

'If you are on the front cover of *Vanity Fair*, it goes a long way with producers. I would be stupid not to think that is the case. It is just that I can't get excited by it; I can't get active about it. But I am happy about that, because I am working and doing stuff that I really want to do. Why change course? I hope to have worked long enough now to have a body of work that stands on its own. When I am cast in something, it is not because I am famous. It is because I can act.'

Instead he took a different approach to furthering his career. 'I don't go after producers. I sit there and hope they come to me. Nine times out of ten they say, "Well, bugger him then!" But the most important thing for me is that

I'm really enjoying my work at the moment. I'm having a good time and I want to maintain this feeling for as long as possible.'

'He's never taken the easy route,' laughs fellow actor Nick Reding, a close friend of Daniel's. 'The road less travelled is what interests him. It's part of his nature but its what makes him such a good actor as well.'

Given that Daniel saw himself as an outsider in the acting industry, it was hardly surprising that he chose to adopt an alternative career path. He loathed the pretentiousness that seemed to shroud thespian productions of a classical ilk. In these instances, he would happily proclaim his lack of education. He would rant that the RSC needed 'a good boot up the arse' and should be run more like a football team, attracting young people and keeping them interested. Deeply suspicious of the avant-garde, he shied away from normal acting circles. He would much rather hang out at his local pub than any celebrity haunt. He hated self-consciously arty types.

That said, he sheepishly admitted to hanging out at The Groucho Club, in the exclusive members' bar. 'Well, actually I do go there,' he confessed. 'But only because my mates are members.' But a working-class background helped the aspiring actor keep his feet firmly on the ground and even London life could do little to sway him. He moved to Shepherds Bush because it was 'down and dirty', but he confessed to missing the normality of life in northern England. 'A weight drops off you when you get past Watford,' he insisted. 'People say, "Morning," and when you go shopping up north, you don't have to spend £50 every time. A newspaper, Sellotape and some drawing pins doesn't cost a fiver.'

A true northern lad, Daniel counted 'everything' among his vices. 'Everything I can get my hands on,' he said with a smile. On screen he was often seen tugging on a cigar or making a roll-up. And he would always carry on once the cameras stopped rolling. 'It doesn't help!' he said, laughing as he referred to his typecasting as a smoker. 'I stop and start all the time. And when I have a beer I really want to smoke. If I don't, I drink three times as much and fall over.'

Casting agent Mary Selway credits his down-to-earth attitude for securing most of his roles. 'What he has on stage or screen is a very masculine sexuality,' she says. 'But also a huge sense of compassion – you could see it in drama school, but that role in *Our Friends* let him grow into himself, and trust what he had to offer that is so special.'

According to friends Daniel was one of the most honest and switched on actors at work in the industry. 'The thing about Daniel is he's one of the most evolved people I've ever met,' said acting pal Nick Reding. 'His compassion and his understanding of other people is always spot on. You say one tiny thing to him and he gets it immediately. He's one of the nicest people on the planet, without any question.' Director John Maybury (who would later work with Daniel on *Love Is The Devil* and *The Jacket*) agreed: 'He's strangely ego-less for an actor... and able to distance himself from the rigmarole and palaver of celebrity.'

'A lot of actors reach the stage when they think there

must be more to life than this,' Daniel pondered. 'I had that when I was thirty – I felt I should be somewhere, be achieving something real... Acting is a silly game, with a lot of wankers involved, but you have to hold onto yourself.'

He wasn't about to shun the entire acting profession, though. That would be naïve and bullish. After all, he still had a lot to learn. 'There are plenty of wankers in acting like there are everywhere,' he said with a sigh. 'But on the other hand, if you get invertedly snobbish about it, it's part of the dumbing-down process. You take any intellectualism out of it and I'm sorry but I need intellectualism. I need to be steered. I don't have a great education, so I rely on other people to give me information. I don't want to be held back because "that's all bollocks and doesn't have any bearing on what's hard and good about acting". It's a sort of self-education. You have to work at it.'

On numerous occasions, after launching into a tirade, he would stop and check himself. 'I'm not at all scathing, really,' he apologised. 'Because I love it. It's my life. Maybe it's too much of my life, but that's the way it is. I just love doing it.'

In contrast to his controlled conduct on screen, in real life he was extremely restless. Unable to sit still for too long, he has a reputation for being a fidget. He would constantly undercut himself with self-deprecating jibes. It was almost a defence mechanism. A psychologist might have pointed out that Daniel was having difficulty reconciling his middle-class airy-fairy profession with his solid working-class roots. So why had he taken up acting in the first place? 'Well, I do it because I find it fulfilling and because I believe it has a place in the artistic...' At this point he stumbles, as if lost for words. 'I do it because I like showing off!'

Over time he has come to understand the power of acting and how it really does have the power to affect people's emotions and cause them to question big ideas. 'If I'm honest, I agree with people I grew up with who say that poncing around on stage is stupid, but when it moves people... Look at *Titanic* – I hated it but it moved people in a way that politics doesn't any more. I walk onto set at 7.30am and think, "I don't want to do this, to pretend to be someone else. I want to be me. Isn't that good enough?" But when it's right, and you are communicating some-thing, then it is fantastic.'

For many years, he shared a difficult relationship with his profession, regarding it with a mixture of awe and defiant contempt. At times he would catch himself slipping into 'actor speak' – perhaps referring to a character as 'emotionally vulnerable' – and would instantly recoil in disgust. But in a world of cut-throat ambition and terminal vanity, his indifference to his art was wonderfully refreshing. His talent spoke for itself. As journalist Lesley White pointed out, 'He swears too much. He smokes and possibly drinks too much. His talent, however, is one that feeds off an abrasive relationship with the actorly life, rather than a cosy smooch with its trappings of success.'

# CHAPTER 3

# INTO THE TRENCHES

After *Our Friends In The North*, Daniel was inundated with job offers but, rather than jump at the first opportunity to make money, he plotted his career moves carefully. Boosting his bank balance was the least of his concerns. As far as he was concerned, his integrity was priceless. On top of all that, he was extremely wary of over-saturation. Turning his back on blockbusters, he gravitated towards arthouse movies.

'I'd like to be able just to earn money and stay comfortable,' he claimed. 'I mean, you could price yourself out of the market. And you can do too much, and you can be on the screen too much.'

Even though he had good intentions, he confessed it was a struggle to turn down lucrative job offers. After all, he was only human. 'Money is a pain in the arse – the more you get, the more you spend, the more you have to pay back. I should have a home. Instead I have a whacking great tax bill but I didn't want the responsibility of a house – it traps you. Then maybe there's a job that pays more than another one and you're accepting it for the wrong reasons.'

Rather than take on more TV roles, he had his sights set on the movie theatres. 'There were some tempting offers but it was like a niggle in my head. It wasn't so much "Television? Fuck that…" It was more, "I like that but I'd rather do films."' Surprisingly, he had few designs on becoming a Hollywood celebrity. 'Not that I want to be a film star,' he said, shrugging. 'But movie theatres are places of excitement as far as I'm concerned.'

What's more, the type of films that attracted him weren't the big-budget epics his agents might have hoped for. Instead he was drawn towards the small-scale independents; projects that challenged and stretched his abilities to maximum capacity. 'I love obsessiveness in movies. I love being twisted,' he said with a grin.

'If something comes along with a good script and it's shot with a torch and an Instamatic, and set in a bike shed, then I'll do it,' he joked, when asked his criteria for taking on a role. In all seriousness, however, he didn't have a strict set of guidelines, preferring to act on instinct. 'I'm bewildered,' he admitted. 'I don't know what it all means. I think it's all about "Could you show this to your mates?" I would like to think I could sit down with my mates and see something I've done and they'd say, "Yes, you've got away with that, that's OK," and if that happens, it's cool.'

In many ways he hoped his growing profile would help

raise capital for independent films. His objective was to serve an art form rather than be a slave to his own ego. 'Some of the films I've done have struggled to get money to finish them. If I can get a bit of a name, maybe that can help to raise the money. It's great to have a choice and, yes, I guess things are going quite well.'

To everyone's annoyance, he seemed content with his tag as 'The Actor Most Likely' or 'The Next Big Thing'. He was in no particular hurry to hit the big time. In 1997 Daniel would also star in TV drama *The Ice House*. Three lonely women – suspected of lesbianism and witchcraft – live together on a country estate. The discovery of a corpse on their grounds revives a police investigation into the disappearance of one of the women's husbands 10 years previously. Senior policeman Detective Geore Walsh (Corin Redgrave) is determined to convict the women. However, problems arise when his deputy Andy McLoughlin (Daniel Craig), whose own marriage is in trouble, falls in love with one of the women. Both his professional and personal loyalties are put to the ultimate test.

After briefly appearing in an episode of *The Hunger* (the Terence Stamp-presented series of erotic versions of *Tales From The Dark Side*), Daniel returned to the stage with a run in *Hurlyburly* at London's Old Vic for Peter Hall's company. Daniel and Rupert Graves played divorced casting agents with a penchant for drink, drugs and treating women badly. During one performance, a bomb scare interrupted the show, leaving the cast to perform the remaining 20 minutes on a green outside.

In 1998 he gave some of his best performances to date. By now he was shaping up to be a sought-after, serious actor, comfortable both on screen and stage. He briefly appeared alongside Cate Blanchett and Joseph Fiennes in *Elizabeth*, as a monk involved in the Babington Plot against the Queen. His moment of glory came when he smashed a rock into the head of one of Francis Walsingham's spies. He would later admit that this was a completely improvised scene.

Daniel's next big project was *Love Is The Devil: Study For A Portrait Of Francis Bacon*. John Maybury's biopic of the early 20th-century British painter was set in the 1960s and Daniel was cast as his lover, George Dyer. The couple meet when Francis (played by Derek Jacobi) catches George trying to break into his house. He invites the working-class thief, 30 years his junior, to share his bed. George accepts and a sordid affair begins between the pair. George dominates their sexual relationship but battles with bouts of depression and alcoholism. Not only this but he finds it increasingly difficult to deal with Francis' casual infidelities. As his problems intensify, Francis wonders how much more he can tolerate.

The film was a daring move for Daniel. Malcolm McDowell, his co-star in *Our Friends In The North*, was originally cast in the role of Francis Bacon but dropped out at the 11th hour. When Daniel first heard the news he felt he couldn't carry on with the project. Informed that Derek Jacobi was to step in, he panicked. 'I said, "But he's a Shakespearian… I don't know what that's all about." But it worked brilliantly.'

It was the first time that he had ever played a real-life character. Eager to give an accurate portrait, he set about researching George Dyer. However, he very quickly came up against a brick wall for barely any of his contemporaries could remember the tragic working-class man. 'Playing him there was no research to do because nobody knew him,' says Daniel, shrugging. 'Nobody in the Colony Room [Bacon's Soho drinking club] acknowledged his existence.'

The director John Maybury sympathised with the difficult task Daniel had ahead of him. 'The role of George Dyer was pretty thankless,' he admitted. 'It was the least well-written because so little is known about him apart from the John Deakins photographs.' Despite this, he had little doubt that Daniel could rise to the challenge. 'Daniel managed to invest him with a real depth that wasn't in my screenplay,' he enthused. 'He brings an incredible stillness and complexity to his roles. He reminds me of Steve McQueen.'

In the absence of any concrete resources, Daniel was to rely on invention. He based his character on the sadism that he assumed to be present in all relationships. 'George beat Francis up in private; Francis beat George up in public – it's not uncommon, but Francis took it to the limit and made his lover commit suicide. He felt guilty but the catharsis made him carry on. We always survive at the expense of others – I just took it to extremes.'

He was, however, careful not to over-intellectualise the process, being far more interested in the nitty-gritty of real life rather than grandiose ideas. 'I'm not a fan of Derek

Jarman or Peter Greenaway so I was worried about making an art film but John [Maybury] made a film about people and what goes on between them.'

His deep suspicion of the avant-garde almost stopped him from accepting the role of George Dyer. As it turned out, this was to be one of the roles of which he was most proud to date. Not only this but his off-screen antics left no one in any doubt about his straight-speaking, salt-of-the-earth credentials. 'He's often up all night drinking, only gets two hours sleep,' remarked his co-star Derek Jacobi.

The character of George Dyer wasn't a comfortable part to play. Daniel spent much of the time covered in lubricant and surgical sealant for the S&M-themed love scenes. There was also a memorable dream sequence that involved Daniel standing naked and splattered with blood as part of his lover's tortured vision. Although he had experience of filming sex scenes, *Love Is The Devil* involved none of the tender lovemaking he was accustomed to. Instead the sex was violent and often graphic. In one scene he and Derek Jacobi undress slowly and Jacobi bends over the bed while Daniel winds a belt around his fist. The camera closes in on them as Daniel picks up a cigarette and stubs it out on his lover's flesh.

Despite the controversial content, Daniel felt that the film suffered unfairly at the hand of censors. 'There was this one scene where I'm scrubbing my nails,' he explained, demonstrating a vigorous hand movement. 'We showed it in Berlin to some US distributors and they walked out because they thought I was fisting someone.

Hang on! When a taboo subject comes up, people's minds do go to the worst fucking scenario.'

His next role was as James Lynchehaun in the independent film *Love And Rage* (1998). Inspired partly by a true story and partly by the novel *The Playboy And The Yellow Lady* by James Carney (published 1986), the film was set in Ireland and dealt with the themes of romantic obsession and violence. Daniel's character James works at the estate of Agnes MacDonnell (played by Greta Scacchi), a wealthy women who values her own privacy. When he discovers that a local land agent is trying to cheat Agnes, he alerts her to the fact and they embark on a friendship that soon develops into romance. James starts to behave strangely, arriving at the estate dressed as a priest. But what starts out as erotic play-acting soon becomes something more sinister. Eventually he beats Agnes and leaves her to die in a fire before fleeing to America. Just like George Dyer, Daniel found the role of James fascinating to play. His commendable performance was further proof of his ability to understand and sympathise with the motivation of very dark and troubled individuals.

By 1999 he had established a reputable name for himself as a versatile actor, capable of portraying extremes of human emotion. Critics commented on his ability to shift between the hard and the vulnerable with relative ease. This was particularly evident in his portrayal of a soldier in novelist William Boyd's directorial debut *The Trench*, set two days before the 1916 bloodbath of the Somme. 'He plays the professional soldier, a hard-boiled sergeant commanding a platoon of young Kitchener volunteers,' explained Boyd. 'His sympathy is buried deep but gradually the man emerges from behind the uniform. Daniel's facility for that development was wonderful – he was definitely a mentor to the younger actors of how to interpret and analyse a role.'

Daniel had to confess, though, that he had never read a book by William Boyd prior to making the movie. Surrounded by actors aged between 16 and 25, he was the oldest member of the cast and he was instantly struck by their confidence. He himself had always been in awe of his co-stars. At the same age, he had been a jibbering wreck in front of the cameras.

Boyd wrote the screenplay and directed the film about the most disastrous offensive in the history of the British Army. In five months the Allies lost 600,000 soldiers. The film follows the emotional torment of a young platoon in the 48 hours leading up to the Battle of the Somme. The soldiers banter and bicker as they prepare to do war. Fears and tensions rise as it gradually dawns on the group that this is more than just a simple holding mission: they are about to make the first attack on German lines.

Although initially wary of the script, Daniel soon took to the project and gave one of his best performances to date. The subject matter was both difficult and controversial, and Daniel wondered whether he could do it justice. 'It is a gentle film… You know what's going to happen, every-one's going to die, but it works. I thought it might be boring but with all those young guys the energy is huge.'

He was cast as Telford Winter, a platoon sergeant who must maintain discipline and maintain high morale. 'I based him on the surrogate father figures you have in your youth,' he explained. 'The teacher who was like, "Come on boys, we can do it!" They were children and Winter had to treat them like children. It wasn't just about discipline, it was about stroking and saying, "It's going to be OK" – a balance between nice and hard.'

As a senior figure, Daniel's character also had to contend with the realities of war. 'When you're seventeen, you do what you are told. That's how armies are built,' he considered. 'Your only instinct is to kill and win, and it makes sense. But when you get older you think, "But what if I get killed?"'

He quickly found empathy with his working-class character, whose background might not have been too different to his own. 'I couldn't have played an officer,' he confessed, referring to the class difference. 'But films should be about everybody. The great thing is that everybody should talk to everybody.'

Impressed by his remarkable emotional control, Boyd went on to describe Daniel as 'One of our best actors... [there's an] incredible coiled latent energy which radiates from him.' He managed to imbue his character with a powerful blend of tenderness and violence. In a key scene he offers one of his men some of his wife's homemade jam. The soldier refuses and Daniel tries to persuade him otherwise by forcing the jar into his face. He stoops down, dejected, slowly spooning the jam into his mouth. The camera lingers on him, his face expressing a loss of home and happiness. 'Daniel has an amazing ability to express emotion of the most poignant kind as well as the most vehement kind,' said Boyd, in praise of the actor. 'Not all leading men have that – they can do the tough stuff but they can't always do both.'

In keeping with Daniel's previous choice of scripts, *The Trench* wasn't a typical war movie. William Boyd's script dealt with human relationships rather than high-octane action scenes. At the end of the film, when the soldiers are required to advance across the field towards German troops, they do so slowly and quietly. Their silence only intensifies the horror of the massacre. There are no graphic displays of violence – just dull thuds as the soldiers crumple to the floor.

'We had all seen *Saving Private Ryan*,' says Daniel, 'and there was no way we could recreate anything like that because we didn't have the money and that's not what the film's about. The Somme was an untrodden grass field. And it's a great analogy – these boys walking across virgin soil. It's a very gentle film.'

Preparing for the film was difficult. Not having been through a similar situation, it was hard for him to imagine the full extent of the hardships that the soldiers must have endured. To try and give his cast some idea of what conditions must have been like, William Boyd suggested they spend the night in a replica trench in Essex run by Khaki Chums, a group who recreate scenes from the First World War.

At the time Daniel was away filming *I Dreamed Of Africa* (2000) with Kim Basinger. 'I was spared the pleasure because I was working that night.' Judging by the reports he received afterwards, he was glad to have been out of the country! 'Everyone arrived in their uniform and the Khaki Chums started talking to them like they were real soldiers,' he explained. He went on to describe how the organisers would ask actors where they had come from. When they gave the response 'London' they were quickly corrected and asked, 'No, where were you last posted?'

He found the whole episode extremely amusing. 'The squaddies were stuck in this freezing trench all night with whiz-bombs going off, eating bully beef, the whole lot,' he laughed. But one actor found the experience far too overwhelming. Julian Rhind-Tutt, who played Officer Hart, jumped ship at the 11th hour. 'Halfway through the night, someone asked, "Where's Julian?"' Daniel remembered. 'Someone in uniform said, "I have a letter here from Hart." It said, "Dear Boys. Can't stick it. Gone back to Blighty." And he'd got a cab all the way back to London in full uniform with a Mars bar in his pocket and a gun by his side! It shows initiative. He would have done well in the trenches and survived.'

All joking aside, filming *The Trench* was a harrowing experience for everyone involved. 'Eight thousand dead in one day? It doesn't compute,' remarked Daniel, speaking about the horror of the Somme. 'It was Remembrance Sunday when we were shooting and we had a minute's silence on set.'

Fortunately, he was able to lighten up the situation by mucking about with his co-stars. 'Death scene are a piece of piss!' he said, laughing and enthusiastically detailing being shot in the back three times. 'Everyone's done them as a kid – "I'm dying! I'm dying!" It's just trying to make it not quite as corny as that.'

In marked contrast to *The Trench*, Daniel found himself in much warmer climes for *I Dreamed Of Africa*. The film revolved around an Italian socialite, Kuki (played by Kim Basinger), who makes a life-changing decision following a car crash. She accepts a marriage proposal from a man she barely knows and moves to Kenya to start a cattle ranch. There she faces a number of challenges, including raging storms, dangerous wildlife and murderous poachers. Her husband also displays an unpredictable streak and a thirst for danger.

A Hollywood epic, it was an unusual choice for the usually fussy actor. It was, in fact, Daniel's biggest picture to date. Many men would have leapt at the opportunity to work with sex siren Kim Basinger but he was unmoved. Instead he felt saddened by the amount of pressure Hollywood exerts on actors to look good. 'She has this porcelain skin and had to have someone carrying a parasol for her on location in Kenya,' he said of his famous co-star. 'You look at her in *9½ Weeks*, and imagine the pressure of the expectation that she will always look like that...' It was a world thankfully a million miles away from his own. He would rather embrace reality any day of the week.

*I Dreamed Of Africa* slots awkwardly into Daniel Craig's

resumé. Afterwards he claimed that he had simply been desperate for an injection of cash. In his defence, his role as a Kenyan gamekeeper was small and fleeting. 'I played a part in it which I could do standing on my head but it is a small part in a big film,' he insisted. 'I lurk around a lot, drive Jeeps and ride horses, and I shit myself every time I get on one. At another time in my career it would have been a lucky break but I was a bit cynical about it – it was just, "Don't fuck me about..."'

If he was honest with himself, he would much rather commit his energies to a worthwhile project and his philosophy has been quoted as such: 'You just think, "What's the point of doing that?" I'd rather do something that I really believe in here that only gets seen by ten people.'

Leaving behind his brief taste of Hollywood, Daniel moved on to scripts closer to his heart. Terence Gross's black comedy *Hotel Splendide* (2000) told the story of a health farm brought back to life with food and passion. The film was set on a remote and cold island accessible only by a once-a-month ferry. The original hotel is a dreary spa offering enema treatments and serving up seaweed and fish-based food. When the cantankerous owner dies, Kath – once the sous chef – receives an anonymous letter asking her to return. She is left with the responsibility of revamping the hotel.

As the character Ronald Blanche, brother to the owner, Daniel was expected to kill and skin eels. Understandably, this was a task he didn't particularly enjoy. 'It's the most horrendous job because eels don't die, they just keep slithering,' he explained with a shudder. But playing a chef allowed him to draw some comparisons between the culinary profession and his own. 'When chefs stop work they become normal people, but when they are working they are monstrous, just like actors... "I don't feel confident today so I'm going to be a complete and utter twat."' Although he was quick to point out that he didn't consider himself to be that sort of actor.

He made further forays into art house cinema with the low-budget project *Some Voices* (2000). In it he played Ray, a mentally impaired character released from care back into the life of his brother. After falling in love with Laura (played by Daniel's former *Hurlyburly* co-star Kelly MacDonald), Ray decides that he no longer needs to take medication. Consequently he begins to hallucinate and lose his mind.

Well received on the underground, the film was later dubbed the 'Anti-*Notting Hill*'. As part of the research process a psychotherapist offered to show him around the Maudsley psychiatric hospital, but Daniel refused, believing the exercise to be exploitative. Instead he sat down and spoke at length with the psychotherapist. He found new ways of understanding what schizophrenia must feel like and looked for commonalities between sane people and those diagnosed with the mental disorder.

Portraying the character of Ray with both authenticity and sensitivity posed a tricky challenge. But it wasn't only his acting abilities that were put to the test. He also had to stump up the confidence for some potentially embarrassing scenes. As part of the script, he was required to run naked down west London's Goldhawk Road. 'It was all down to my good friend Simon [Cellen Jones], who was the director.' He laughed. 'The scene was originally written as me running up and down Goldhawk Road, stripped to the waist and covered in tomato juice. But then I got drunk one night in Simon's room and said, "I know, I'll do it naked!" The key lesson to remember is: Don't get drunk with directors. I have to say my performance didn't gather much of a crowd.'

On an initial reading he didn't have a problem with the scene but, when it actually came to filming the scene, he suffered a bout of last-minute nerves. 'I drank three large brandies but they didn't even touch the sides!' he complained afterwards.

'I was slurping it back beforehand but no one gave me a second glance. Like a naked man running down the street happens every day in Shepherd's Bush!' he guffawed. 'Although, actually, it probably does.'

Although the directors had attempted to close off the road, their efforts were unsuccessful. Instead Daniel would have to dodge cars and buses as he sprinted frantically in nothing but his birthday suit. To make matters even worse, a group of policemen turned up unexpectedly. The crew members agreed they would have to inform the officers of what was about the take place. 'The assistant director went up and said, "Our guy's going to go naked now,"' recalls Daniel. 'The police said, "I cannot condone that but I'll go and get a cup of tea, shall I?" They could have arrested me for public exposure!'

In 2001 Daniel returned to TV screens as Guy Crouchback, the tortured hero of Evelyn Waugh's war trilogy *Sword Of Honour*. The story was concerned with an idealist who fights in the Second World War for reasons of chivalric honour, only to see the world overrun by cheats and liars. Ultimately he realises decency accounts for nothing in this new world.

It was the first time Daniel had played an upper-class character. 'I'd never really played posh before,' he joked, once filming was complete. 'I didn't know if I could do it justice; if I could bring a reality to this person without putting on a silly accent.' He was extremely conscious of sounding uncomfortably posh and didn't want to make his performance into a 'study of something'. But after reading around his subject, any fears he might have had were quickly allayed. 'Evelyn Waugh was very particular about his class system. That's what he lived for. The joke was that he was middle class himself, aspiring to be upper class. When I read that I thought, Well, that's quite cool, that's OK.'

He also had no intention of making Guy Crouchback a good guy. The absence of a tidy ending didn't seem to bother him. 'I don't care if there's no redemption,' he said, shrugging. 'That's not why I do something, to make him look good at the end.'

William Boyd, who had directed Daniel in *The Trench*, was responsible for adapting Waugh's trilogy into a screenplay. Daniel jumped at the opportunity to reunite with his old friend but he was reluctant to contribute to the British obsession with war. 'I wish we'd get over it,' he said, sighing. 'I really do. We do seem to fight it every night on television.'

Once again he delivered an impressive performance. With very few words he managed to encapsulate an Englishman's search for honour through joining a just war against the forces of evil. 'But there's no honour in war or death,' he concluded. Speaking about his character, he continued, 'His ideals are completely compromised, shattered by the end.'

In one scene Crouchback's wayward ex-wife (Megan Dodds) accuses him of trying to seduce her only because, in the eyes of the Church, she is the only woman with whom he can have conscience-free sex. Without uttering a word, Daniel delivered a wounded response simply by contracting his facial muscles.

Complimented for his powerful screen presence, he became uncharacteristically coy. 'God, I don't know really,' he said. 'I don't think about making something powerful. I'm just trying to get at the reality of it – if there is a reality.'

For a man without a game plan, Daniel Craig was making impressive headway as a serious actor. Audiences quickly warmed to his approachable working-class manner, while critics praised the diversity of his characterisation: one minute he was playing the rugged hard man and the next he became a vulnerable and emotional wreck. With every performance he was shaping up to be a big hope for British cinema. Although flattered, he preferred to eschew any particular career strategy in favour of simply picking roles that interested him. But even he wasn't infallible. Inevitably he would suffer blips in his career. As more and more lucrative offers landed on his doorstep, it became harder to put integrity before financial necessity. Eventually he would give in to his bank balance but it was an error of judgement that he would never forget.

# CHAPTER 4

# RAKING IN THE BIG BUCKS

Fame was something in his career that Daniel Craig had never bargained for so, when success came knocking at his door, he wasn't entirely sure how to handle it. The stubborn actor had always purposely steered clear of any grotesque self-promotion. Fiercely protective of his privacy, he would much rather have shielded himself beneath a cloak of anonymity. But with celebrity status foisted upon him, he had little option but to smile for the cameras and wear the uncomfortable tag of 'film star'.

Many industry professionals believed he had the potential to become an international movie star but a few wondered whether he would actually seize upon the opportunity. 'I really wonder if he would ever be prepared to make the choices that would take him there, the high-profile movies to put him in that category,' said casting agent Mary Selway.

Daniel was determined not to allow the success to go to his head. He had seen far too many actors confuse their priorities when dazzled by the bright lights of Hollywood. First and foremost he would always remain an actor: 'There is always the movie-star question but the more I get into the business, the more I realise that's not my priority. That whole Hollywood thing is a machine that has nothing to do with me.' As far as he was concerned, much of the fuss generated was no more than empty hype: 'There may be a buzz generated about you, but you can't start soaking that in because you'll get stuffed. Things change very quickly in this business. As soon as you start listening to that sort of shit, that way madness lies.'

Besides, he was reluctant to turn his back on British cinema. He remained steadfastly committed to projects that deserved to be made. 'People forget how many bad movies are also made in Hollywood,' he pointed out. 'It's completely different there. They have an industry where the studios invest their profits back into making more movies. We don't have that.' He also felt more comfortable with the British approach to filmmaking. Rather than sit passively on the sidelines, he preferred to offer directors his own input.

But he confessed the lure of Hollywood was difficult to resist – especially given the vast sums of money involved. In comparison to his contemporaries, Daniel remained relatively underpaid. At times he grew exasperated with the situation. Like he said, 'Money is a pain in the arse.'

For years Daniel's finances had been in disarray.

Organisation had never been his strong point. He had always shoved bills to the back of the kitchen drawer and bank statements were often left unopened for months. Recently he had been trying to introduce some order into his life but it wasn't easy for him. 'I try and get my head together when I'm not working,' he insisted. 'I don't use my time particularly well; I'm not organised. When I've got enough money I'll employ someone to look after me, which is a pretty pathetic, actory thing to say! Financially I'm hopeless, completely numerically dyslexic – that's another actor's whine. I'd quite fancy running clubs actually but I don't think it'll ever come about; it's a lot of organisation – and finance. I'd lose everything!'

After some persuasion, he hired an LA agent but he was sceptical as to whether anything would come of it. 'We said to each other, "Let's just see what happens,"' said Daniel. 'If I went over there and said, "I'm here!" they'd just say, "Well, who the fuck are you?" I'd be like, "Did you see *Our Friends In The North*? It was a nine-part series about the working classes and the T. Dan Smith affair…" It just doesn't work!'

Much to his surprise, offers of work came far more quickly than he had expected. He was invited to do a screen test for *Lara Croft: Tomb Raider* (2001), a high-octane blockbuster based on the popular computer game. Angelina Jolie was to star as the muscle-bound heroine who collects ancient artefacts from ruins around the world. The plot was based on a secret society called the Illuminati, who are searching for an ancient talisman which gives the possessor the ability to control time. It is Lara Croft's mission to stop them and subsequently save the world.

Daniel was cast as Lara's former lover Alex West, now a mercenary who has joined forces with the Iluminati. Angelina Jolie would later compliment the actor on his kissing technique, describing him as 'one of the best kissers'. But when the press asked Daniel what it was like to lock lips with the voluptuous siren, he gave them a characteristically dry response: 'Wet.'

For Daniel, this was a curious choice of role and one that he would ultimately regret. Usually he would agree on impulse to a role – the part had to feel right. 'The whole thing comes together – reading the script, meeting the director and thinking, "This is interesting because it's a bit weird,"' he explained. On this occasion, however, he ignored his better judgement and went on the advice of others. 'The thing is, you start getting, let's say, a bit more famous, and suddenly you get more scripts offered to you,' he claimed in his defence. 'So it all gets a bit confusing and I'm not very clever, you see.'

Daniel had been told that *Lara Croft* could be his big American break and he had no qualms about confessing his reluctance to be involved. 'I've lost count of the number of times people have said, "This is going to be good for you, Daniel." But I'm not going to bullshit about it – the reason I'm doing this film is to get a profile.'

In the past he had been repelled by action movies and, up until the very last minute, he wondered whether this was really the right move. 'I had mixed emotions because it was an action movie,' he says. 'And as an actor who asks himself, "What's the truth in this?" that can be a bit strange. I mean, fuck off – the truth of it is you just do it!'

His main criticism of the movie was that it did little to advance his acting skills. In fact, he joked that it was actually damaging to his career! 'I thought I'd got myself into something that I didn't understand. I didn't realise that I wouldn't be able to do my job as I saw it, and those films by their very nature stop you acting. You are going to do one line again and again, and the line will be something like, "Watch out!" I just don't think I can do it very well – I need to know more.'

A mammoth £80 million was invested in the video-game blockbuster. Most of it was spent on special effects and impressive set designs. Daniel recalled standing in an underground temple, surrounded by a 20-foot statue of a six-armed Vishnu-style God, dangling creepers and sword-wielding stone monkeys.

He soon became bored of standing around on set all day. It seemed to take an eternity to shoot one single scene. 'The big sets take ten minutes to reset every time you do a take,' he complained. 'You have to do them over and over and over again. You have to keep yourself sane.' He tried to amuse himself by joking around with his co-stars: 'There were times when you're doing a scene over and over again, and it's mind numbing! But you get each other through it and you try to have a laugh.'

Ultimately, *Tomb Raider* would turn out to be one of the

biggest regrets of Daniel's career. 'I didn't enjoy *Tomb Raider* at all!' he exclaims. 'I hated it – *hated* it! It just wasn't my cup of tea. It was a lesson. I did it to get a profile, and it didn't really... It didn't turn out like that.'

Lacking any commitment to the script, he couldn't summon up the motivation to do his job properly. He complained bitterly about the script. 'You're working on scenes that make no sense whatsoever. The script was all over the fucking place, waffling on about eight-foot fucking green monkeys (or some such bollocks), and I could just never get my head around what was supposed to be going on.' Given his credentials, the casting agents couldn't have got it more wrong. 'Sadly, I can't do that superhero bullshit. I can't do it,' he said, shaking his head. 'I felt like a bit of a spare prick at a wedding throughout. I probably looked like one too!'

Many critics would agree with him and the movie was universally panned. The actor sympathised with his leading lady. At least his smaller role ensured a damage limitation to his career: 'Angie had it worse. She was in every scene and had to take all the shit afterwards.' Unfortunately for Daniel, filming *Tomb Raider* also took a big chunk out of his schedule. 'It was four months!' he says, shuddering at the memory. 'It was boring as hell! But I went to Cambodia for two weeks and I tell you what, that saved my life. I will be back there again one day.'

While Daniel barely enjoyed the experience, his young daughter was in her element. She came out to visit Daniel on set and was overjoyed at the prospect of meeting bonafide Hollywood star Angelina Jolie. 'She also got her *Tomb Raider* bag that she takes to school,' says Daniel with a laugh. 'That part she loved!' But to his relief, his daughter wasn't a fan of the actual film: 'She saw straight through it and I was glad.'

On reflection, Daniel saw the project as a waste of his time. Rather than advance his career, it had done the exact opposite. 'It did slow things down a bit,' he admitted. His step-mum Shirley agreed: 'Dan's not motivated by money. To him it's a profession, a craft. I don't think he liked *Tomb Raider* as it was too commercial but it was a step up the ladder.'

More than anything, though, he had learned a valuable lesson. 'Personally I should never have said yes to the part,' he mused. 'That movie was so crap! But it was a lesson for me to see a film like that made. I've always felt like one of the problems is if you start a project and there's not a good script, or it's not in good shape, you are going to be battling against it. I don't believe you should be rewriting scenes as you're going along. I could just never get my head around what was supposed to be going on.'

Rather than dwell on the past, however, he decided to move on. There was nothing to be gained from regret and self-pity. 'I could kick myself for it but I don't,' he said in conclusion. 'I'm done bitching about it, really, because what's to bitch about? It was fine.'

To his relief, it wasn't long before his career was back on track. From now on he would revert to his tried and tested method of selecting film scripts. 'I just want to spice it up as much as possible because I don't want to lose interest. It's not a question of striking a balance, it's just job to job: what interests me, and where my head is at the time.'

Now in his early 30s, he had taken some time to reflect on the direction his career would take. 'A lot of actors reach the stage when they think there must be more to life,' he pondered. 'I had that when I was thirty – I felt I should be somewhere, be achieving something real... Acting is a silly game with a lot of wankers involved, but you have to hold onto yourself.'

Although he had a cynical head on his shoulders, he continued to behave like a man half his age. In the past he defiantly refused to carry a diary, deeming it to be an unnecessary sign of age. But buckling under the pressures of a professional career he agreed to start keeping a schedule. His 'diary' was nothing more than a blank notebook with a few scribbled notes, however. Fiercely resilient to the onset of age and responsibility, he was determined to continue his free-spirited lifestyle for as long as possible.

Fortunately for him, poor organisational skills didn't deter producers from offering him film scripts. Neither did his appearing in a big-budget flop. Although many critics were surprised by his involvement in *Tomb Raider*, no one doubted that he was capable of much, much more.

Daniel's next project in 2002 was proof that he could handle both a serious script and a Hollywood production. *The Road To Perdition* (2002) was Sam Mendes' eagerly anticipated follow-up to the acclaimed *American Beauty*

(1999). Set in Illinois during the Depression era, it was a *Godfather*-style saga about Irish mobsters. The main underlying themes were of family and loyalty. Tom Hanks and Paul Newman had already been cast in the film, so Daniel was instantly in good company.

The story centred round Michael Sullivan (Hanks), the adopted son and chief lieutenant of Irish mob patriarch John Rooney (Newman). Sullivan faces a crisis of conscience after his own son witnesses him committing a killing. After a confrontation with Rooney's menacing biological son Connor (Daniel Craig), Sullivan and his son are forced to take flight. Jude Law was to co-star as a hitman hired to kill Sullivan.

'Connor is the person who sets the story in motion,' said the director, Sam Mendes. 'I wanted a relative unknown to play him so the audience wouldn't know from the first moment that he was going to be a central player. I felt, if his character were to work, he would almost have to creep up on the audience.'

Daniel seemed an appropriate choice to play a menacing and unscrupulous killer. More importantly, he was invited to take the role at the request of Mendes himself! 'Danny is dark, brooding and hugely charismatic but there is a great vulnerability there,' Mendes revealed. 'I knew when I met him that he was the right man for the job.'

Although they moved in the same London industry circles, the pair barely knew each other. Daniel recalled they might have exchanged pleasantries at a couple of social events and even played cricket together but he doubted the director would remember. Their eventual meeting was much more dramatic, though: 'Seriously, this is one of those silly stories that may sound like I'm making it up for a good gag, but it's true.' While in pre-production in Chicago, Mendes returned to the UK to collect a few items of clothing. 'The story goes that he was watching television with Patrick Marber and *Sword Of Honour* was on,' explained Daniel. 'Apparently Marber said, "That's who you want for Connor." So Sam got me in the following day and basically told me I was doing this film.'

He was initially stunned and quite speechless but once Mendes had filled him in on the finer details he couldn't wait to sign on the dotted line. 'He told me the story and I thought, "Fucking great!"' enthuses Daniel. 'And when he said, "I've got Tom Hanks, and Paul Newman's playing your dad," I said, "Don't tell me any more because I can't cope with this."' It was the kind of job offer all aspiring actors dream about. 'Tom Hanks, Jennifer Jason Leigh, Jude Law, and I play Paul Newman's son!' he exclaimed. 'What did I say when I got the part? "Christ!" Actually, I didn't say that, I said something unprintable.'

A month later Sam Mendes flew him out to Chicago for the day. 'It was enough time for me to kind of forget about it,' admitted Daniel. The director invited him into his offices to do a reading of the script. Daniel flicked nervously through the pages. He cringes at the memory. Hand on chin, Mendes sat patiently listening to the actor. Blessed with a poker face, he gave nothing away. Daniel didn't dare look to gauge a reaction. Halfway through, however, Mendes suddenly stood up and yelled, 'Stop!'. Daniel wondered what he must have done wrong and for a moment there was silence. Mendes turned away distracted by a memo on his desk. With a casual wave of his arm, he gestured, 'Yeah, yeah – the job's yours.'

Daniel was in shock. On leaving Mendes' offices, he headed straight to the nearest bar and christened his new job offer with a drink. 'I went into a bar, asked for two beers and two bourbons,' he said, grinning. Slightly bemused, the girl behind the bar wondered where his other guests might be. Save for the delirious British actor, the place appeared to be empty. But she wasn't about to argue with him. Instead she poured the drinks and set them down on the bar, watching in amazement as he proceeded to knock them back, one after the other.

'You're happy, aren't you?' she enquired, raising an eyebrow. Daniel stared blankly at her. 'I couldn't say anything,' he recalled. He could hardly blurt out, 'Yeah, I've just been offered a job where I play Paul Newman's son.' At best she'd have thought he was lying, at worst she'd consider him mad. 'I'd have been chucked out,' he chuckled.

Eager to move forward with the project, Mendes invited Daniel to an introductory dinner with his fellow cast members at a plush restaurant in Chicago. Sandwiched between Paul Newman, Tom Hanks and Jennifer Jason Leigh, he was suddenly struck by the incredulity of the situation. He played nervously with his dinner napkin and then proceeded to do what any respecting Englishman would do – drink.

'I just had to stop myself drinking really heavily,' he said with a laugh. 'I was sort of controlling my beer intake.' Recalling the dinner, he cringes with embarrassment. 'I was such an arsehole!' he confessed. 'All through dinner I was shitting it, so I just sat there giggling, fiddling with my watch, thinking to myself, "You fucking dick, sort it out!" But the more I thought that, the more dickish I became – I couldn't help it.'

One particular incident sticks in his mind. Overwhelmed at the prospect of being in Paul Newman's company, he lost the ability to hold a serious conversation. 'At one point Newman started talking about some racing team he was involved in and asked me what I thought. All I could think to say was, "I like cars, they're really cool." I mean, what a fucking idiot! It wasn't funny at all.'

As the table fell silent, all eyes were on him. Realising how ridiculous he must have sounded, he wanted to dive under the table and make his escape. Already he could feel his cheeks burning crimson. Other guests at the table shared his embarrassment but thankfully they were also amused rather than repelled. 'You should have seen Hanks – he nearly choked on his salad, he was laughing so fucking much!'

Unfortunately, Daniel didn't learn his lesson and he went on to make an even greater fool of himself when he engaged in conversation with his hero on set. 'The first time I worked with Paul Newman was scary,' he shuddered. 'I can remember watching *Cool Hand Luke*, *Hud* and *The Hustler* as a kid, so meeting him was nervewracking – you're talking about some of the greatest movies and acting there is.'

The 1967 cult movie *Cool Hand Luke* saw Newman cast as an unbreakable hard man who has been sent to a prison camp. In one famous scene he gorges on boiled eggs. Daniel couldn't resist asking whether he'd actually eaten them all. 'I *did*!' he winced, holding his head in his hands. 'He didn't eat one – didn't eat one egg. Each one was popped in and popped out again.' Trying to make light of the situation, he facetiously continued, 'Well, how come your belly was so fat? Did you drink beer or something?' He was met with a silent response.

Daniel was ashamed of himself for even bringing the subject up. Acutely self-conscious, he felt like an irritating and pathetic fan. Surely Paul Newman must have answered that very same question a thousand times. 'I mean, he's seventy-six now and doesn't want all this crap.' Being polite, Newman moved onto other topics of conversation. 'He tried to talk to me about cars. I have a car – I just don't drive it at two hundred and fifty miles per hour. It's not really my deal.'

After some time, though, the pair managed to find common ground. 'He's chilled,' said Daniel with a mischievous smile. 'He tells dirty jokes all the time – and I just had to match him with dirty jokes. That was our dialogue.'

Although initially intimidated by such a great screen presence, Daniel soon regained composure. He repeatedly told himself that it was important to be professional and to treat this like any other job. 'Of course, on the first day your sphincter's going a little bit – that's the only way to put it. But then you do have to get over it; you have to get on with it. You can't be thinking of those ephemeral things. Ultimately, the job is the thing.'

Daniel relished the opportunity of working alongside one of the industry's greatest actors and he was determined to pick up plenty of tips. 'Paul Newman was something to behold,' he praised. 'I watched him work. I could relate to his fears. He was worried about getting it right.' Daniel had only words of admiration for the man. 'What a wonderful, fantastic place to be: seventy-six years old and still acting,' he said in awe. 'He was still as interested and excited about doing it. If I get to fifty and I'm still as excited, I'll be happy.'

Working with Tom Hanks also gave him an insight into the absurdity of celebrity. 'Tom Hanks is like royalty in America,' he said, shaking his head. 'People stay out all night with their babies waiting for him to drive by. But it's nice to see that these people right at the top can just get on with the job and enjoy getting on with it. I've seen less-huge stars making such a fuss about doing things. That was confirmation for me that you don't have to behave like an arsehole to be noticed.'

If he was honest with himself, he had never counted Tom Hanks among his acting heroes. The American film icon belonged to that 'other' category of actors from which he tried so desperately hard to distance himself. But after working with the man, he had to confess that even Hollywood stars could be talented actors as well. 'I have to say, I've never been a huge Tom Hanks fan but I watched him and what he's done in this [film] and I just go, "This is superb."'

According to Daniel, most of the credit lay with the film's talented director. 'Sam Mendes has made him do something that he's never… I mean, maybe he could have gone further. But Sam Mendes has made Tom Hanks. And that in itself is quite exciting because you have to remember how big this man is.'

Very quickly, Daniel forgot his initial inhibitions and settled into working with the star-studded cast. They soon formed a close bond and shared plenty of jokes on set. Daniel watched with part amusement and part admiration, as his co-star Tom Hanks cultivated a double chin for his role by eating out at various Chicago restaurants. He would spend most of his time filming on location in Chicago. But after the first thrill of it all had subsided, homesickness soon crept in. He was longing to return home to London, to 'having a beer with my mates, being with my girlfriend, watching The Lions in Australia… I've been in Chicago for four months,' he complained. 'It's driving me nuts! I feel like I've emigrated. I went home last week because I had a break in the schedule and I didn't want to come back again.'

Focusing on the job in hand, he managed to quell any urges to return home and, once filming was complete, he breathed a sigh of relief. Overall, he was pleased with the final cut. However, he did have one objection: he wished his death scene could have been more dramatic. 'I wanted my killer to come in with a Tommy gun!' he said, grinning like a schoolboy. 'But Sam [Mendes] wanted a Jean-Paul Marat [French revolutionary stabbed in the bath] death so I got that.'

The little boy in Daniel always came out whenever shooting scenes were filmed. 'We were doing some squib shots,' he recalled, describing the small explosion that makes on-screen gunfire realistic, 'and this guy said, "God, you're really good at this!" I said, "This is why I became an actor."' He laughed.

The conversation sparked a vivid memory from his childhood. While on holiday he and a friend were playing on the beach. Closing his eyes he could picture the shimmering sea in the distance, the sun beating down on his back. Daniel ran to the top of a sand dune and instructed his friend to remain below. His friend then took aim with an imaginary gun and fired at him. Clenching a hand to his chest, Daniel collapsed to his knees, edging forward slightly before falling head first into the burning sand. As his body crumpled he let out an almighty groan. It was impressive performance. Anyone in the near vicinity might have mistakenly raised an alarm. Whenever he was required to film a shooting scene, Daniel would always reference that particular childhood memory. 'Right, now let's do that with a shotgun,' he would joke to his co-stars.

When *Road To Perdition* was finally released, however, the response was mixed. The *Independent* criticised the film for being 'a vaingloriously overblown gangster flick that seems incapable of articulating its own simple plot.' Fortunately for Daniel, though, his performance was singled out as the movie's saving grace. His poise and energy were demonstrated in one particular scene where, after offering a casual apology for allowing his bloodlust to get the better of him, he cowers under the impact of Paul Newman's anger.

After the New York première, whispers of an Oscar nomination started to circulate. The British press proudly declared that Daniel Craig had made it in America. Refusing to believe the hype, the man in question remained sceptical. 'I'm like, "Hey great! But what does that mean? I've no idea!"' He paused, before adding sarcastically, 'It means the marketing department at Dreamworks are spending a lot of money telling the press that there's an Oscar buzz. You know, there probably is. Once it starts, it doesn't matter where it came from.'

Despite his reservations, Hollywood agents were keen to sign up the actor for future projects, clearly aware of his great potential. But burned by his experience with *Tomb Raider*, Daniel refused to be blinded by promises of fame and flashing dollar signs. 'In the past I've turned things down that, financially, would have been very nice. I know what I'm like with money, and I also know what I'm like with boredom. And I know that being on a long film would just bring out the worst in me. I don't want to do work that's about getting a house in Portugal. Money's obviously an issue and it's nice to have it, but I've tried to go for the jobs which are the most interesting available.'

While some advised him to seize on the opportunity, he preferred to take everything in his own stride. Confident in his ability, he would welcome success when he was good and ready. 'I think the film is great, I think I get away with it. Good directors will watch something like that and they'll clock it and put it in their bank. But it just doesn't happen immediately. There's that thing in America that I should go and hustle my arse and ride this wave but I've just never done that and don't see why I should start now. Ten years' time I could be going, "I was in *The Road To Perdition*, you know" – "Oh, fuck off!" As for striking while the iron's hot, I'll strike when it's slightly warm.'

As far as he was concerned, he'd heard it all before. For as long as he could remember, he'd been the next big thing. 'I've had people saying "This could be a big one for you" since school plays! What? Eh?' Personally he preferred to keep things in perspective. There was more to life than winning an Academy Award. More than just an actor, he was a human being with many ambitions to fulfil: 'You know, if you've got kids, there are bigger things in life. It's important to be enthusiastic and excited about what you do for a living, but ultimately there are other things.'

# CHAPTER 5

# HONING HIS ART

Although enjoyable, Daniel's brief flirtation with Hollywood fame had left him hankering for a sobering dose of reality. Returning to his old theatre stomping ground in 2002, he landed back down to earth with a part in Stephen Daldry's adaptation of Carol Churchill's play, *A Number*. Concerned with the themes of genetics and family, the hotly anticipated production was staged at The Royal Court in London. A two-hander, the play also starred Michael Gambon, who Daniel described as a joy to work with.

Prior to the opening night, all members of the cast were under strict instructions to keep details of the plot under wraps. Excited about the script, Daniel found it extremely difficult to keep quiet. He tried to discreetly explain the plot to journalists. 'It nails a few things about how we feel about our relationships and our place in relationships,' he hinted. 'We just have to keep it a secret. When people come to the theatre on the first night they won't really know what to expect. I'm not sure if *I* know what to expect.'

Michael Gambon remained equally coy about the finer details. 'It's a very difficult play,' he revealed. 'It's very difficult to rehearse because, like all great writing, the play gives you so many choices and so much subtext, so we're constantly talking about it.' Although unwilling to disclose any further details about the project, Gambon was more than happy to shower praise on his co-star. 'I've never worked with such a young actor so smoothly,' he enthused. 'He's so intelligent and sharp and clever. And I'm not saying that he's just perfect – he can do anything. We rehearse for hours and hours on end and we try to reach conclusions... and he's got it all off pat. He can sum it all up. I'm an old carthorse really; a bit lazy so it's very nice to have Daniel around.'

Daniel himself admitted that he was nervous about returning to the immediacy of a theatre production. 'I'm so scared, I can't tell you!' he confided in friends. He'd been cast in yet another emotionally demanding role. 'Oh, I'm incredibly sensitive,' he mocked. Ultimately, though, he didn't believe he was alone: emotional awareness was a prerequisite of his job: 'I think all actors are to a degree. Some actors show it by being a complete nightmare. You know it's a pain. It's not nice on the first day of filming, getting up in front of forty strangers and making a fool of yourself. It does make you feel incredibly vulnerable.

You're basically going to yourself, "OK, I'm gonna do this for the next two and a half months."'

By now he had been tagged as an actor capable of portraying emotional characters but he couldn't understand what all the fuss was about. As far as he was concerned, those were the easy parts to play. 'People say, "Ah, you do these big emotional scenes. Was it hard?" I'm like, "No, they're the easy ones." It's when you have to pick up a glass and talk to somebody, that's the hard stuff – the quiet stuff.' Herein lay the core of Daniel's approach to acting. 'The only deal about acting is to make it real. It's clichéd but it's the truth. Do you believe it? And if you believe it, then it's probably right.'

Several more small film projects followed suit. Daniel made a brief appearance in *Ten Minutes Older: The Cello* (2002), a collection of short films where eight directors, including Jean Luc Godard and Antonio Bertolucci, were given ten minutes to express a vision of time. Daniel appeared in Michael Radford's segment, *Addicted To The Stars*, playing a spaceman that returns to earth after 80 years, having aged just 10 minutes.

Returning to more small-screen war dramas, his next project was *Copenhagen* (2002), a television adaptation of Michael Frayn's acclaimed play about quantum physics, set against the backdrop of Nazi Germany. It was a complicated topic, but Daniel joked that after a few drinks he could explain the theory to anyone! Next came the film short *Occasional, Strong* (2002) about a man who signs up as a driver for a group of criminals on a dangerous mission.

On the way to the job the man hears the lottery numbers and realises he has the winning ticket in his possession. However, the job goes badly wrong and the ticket is collected as litter by a street cleaner. The gang leader then chases the cleaner in a bid to retrieve the winning ticket.

Although all these small projects were worthy, very soon Daniel was hankering after a meatier role in which to sink his teeth. He found himself irresistibly drawn to confrontational roles. His next project, *The Mother* (2003), would certainly turn out to be a challenge. Adapted from a novel by Hanif Kureshi, it was the story of a 65-year-old woman who embarks on a passionate affair with a man half her age. May meets Darren when he is contracted to build a solarium for her son. Darren is in an unhappy marriage with an autistic son, and responds to her advances. Unfortunately, he's already having an affair with her daughter, who's been expecting him to leave his wife. Inevitably the trio find themselves embroiled in a web of lies fuelled by insatiable lust. Daniel would play Darren, the two-timing decorator, opposite Anne Reid as the grandmother May. Hailing from Manchester, Anne's CV to date included minor roles in *Coronation Street* and Victoria Wood's *Dinnerladies*.

Hanif Kureshi's films were noted for the sexually explicit nature of their content. In his previous movie *Intimacy (2001)*, there were graphic sex scenes involving stars Mark Rylance and Kerry Fox. Thankfully, the sex scenes featured in *The Mother* were relatively toned down, although Daniel admitted simulating sex with an older woman was daunting. 'I had problems with it,' he confessed. 'But that was one of the reasons why I wanted to do the job, because I *shouldn't* have problems with it, if you see what I mean.'

On a first run-through of the script he sat down with director Roger Mitchell and aired his reservations. 'I read *The Mother* and I was nervous about doing sex scenes with somebody who was in their sixties. But I had coffee with Roger and he was like, "Yeah, that's the fucking point.'

The film questioned several uncomfortable social taboos and Daniel felt inclined to face them head on rather than pass the project over for something less demanding. 'When an older man gets together with a much younger woman, his friends slap him on the back and say well done. But look at the flak Joan Collins gets. People make fun of it – I've done it myself; I'd be telling a lie if I said I hadn't. But what is actually wrong with it? Actually, it's nobody's business.'

Accepting everyone has a right to sexual urges was central to the film's plot. Making love was not a reserve of the young and beautiful. 'I think one of the whole points of the movie is that we have to deal with the fact that old people like to fuck and if you don't think that's true, you're living in a fool's paradise. Because healthcare's better, people live longer, so there are all these people in their seventies who want to have sex. I mean, I'm going to want to have sex right until the very end, thank you very much!'

But he would be the first to admit that he was treading on dangerous ground. 'It's a tricky subject but actually it's a *great* subject. It does happen...' And what did people expect? 'It's written by Hanif Kureshi,' he exclaimed. 'It's not lightweight.'

Even Kureshi knew full well *The Mother* would never be a box-office smash. 'I can't imagine hip young kids queuing at the Odeon to see a film about an old girl,' he said, smiling laconically. 'I don't really care. I didn't write it because I thought it would make me a rich man. I wrote it because I was interested in it. The idea of an older woman having sex does not go down well with people. It's shocking. Our mothers aren't supposed to be sexual; their bodies belong to us.'

Even though he had prepared himself mentally, when the time came to eventually film the sex scenes Daniel was struck by an attack of nerves. He was relieved to discover they would be shot tastefully, leaving most details to the audience's imagination. However, when the finished film was finally released in theatres, several critics alluded to an anal sex scene. Daniel was aghast. 'So many men have said that to me,' he said, shaking his head in disbelief. 'It's so sick! What is that? Is it like, "Oh, while I'm here…"

'I for one am not interested in seeing people screw on screen,' he defiantly stated. 'If I want to watch that, there are videos you can buy. As far as I'm concerned, it turns the actors into performing monkeys. So when you watch it, all you can see is erect penises or wet vaginas and I can't see how that will ever help a storyline. I'm quite anti it. Maybe I'm being prudish, but we all know we screw and fuck, and the act itself is fantastic and beautiful, and sometimes I like watching it, but there's no story to it.'

Besides, if he felt uncomfortable, his co-star Anne must have been suffering even greater anxiety. Daniel was an extremely good-looking actor with a notable female following. She was already mentally prepared for a barrage of cruel remarks from the tabloids. 'It was nervewracking for her and she handled it brilliantly,' said Daniel, with sympathy. Surprisingly, filming the sex scenes went extremely smoothly. 'Everyone asks how the love scenes went and, actually, they were very easy.' But the real question remained: would Daniel allow his mother to watch the film? 'I'd let my mum go and see it with her mates!' he joked. 'Y'know, that's my boy!'

Filming *The Mother* raised a number of important questions for Daniel. When did art become pornography? It was a controversial topic. 'Wouldn't pornography be great if it didn't exploit?' he pondered. 'But we know it exploits and that people are hurt and damaged by it, and don't ever recover, so it always has a tinge of badness. How do you explain to your partner what you've been doing at work all day? I didn't get into this game to hurt other people.'

As he had pointed out in the past, there was nothing sexual about acting out scenes of lovemaking on screen. 'The sex is taken out of it very, very quickly,' he revealed. 'You're on a cold and windy set with somebody who you know, and it takes ages so you sit there with a cup of tea, smoking a cigarette and talking about the weather, and it just becomes banal. On the whole, sex scenes are pretty boring!'

But *The Mother* wasn't purely a vehicle for taboo sexual relations. It also dealt with several other difficult topics.

'It's also about the fact [that] families don't talk to each other and weird things happen,' he pointed out. Remarkably, he'd also managed to unearth a comical sub-plot. 'I think *The Mother* is funny – darkly funny and that really appeals to me. If you can combine that with popular film-making, it *is* funny, not because it is meant to be but because of the situations people get themselves into.'

Although a small-scale film, *The Mother* added yet another credible string to his already well-strung bow. It was nominated for a BAFTA, while Anne Reid won an ALFS award in the London Critics Circle Film Awards 2004. Daniel's next project, *Sylvia* (2003), gave the actor an even greater opportunity to demonstrate his acting worth. As a child he had been a big fan of Ted Hughes so it seemed appropriate he should play the role of the great poet in a biopic of his troubled wife. Gwyneth Paltrow was cast in the lead role of Sylvia Plath.

The main plot focused on the tumultuous relationship of the two poets, who met at a Cambridge dance in 1956 when Sylvia bit Ted's cheek and drew blood. Four months later they were married. Their marriage was dominated both by Ted's ambition and his success. As he gains critical acclaim, as well as a string of female admirers, his wife is left watching from the shadows. Finding herself at a loss of creative inspiration, Sylvia senses Ted's infidelity. While she can suppress her professional envy, sexual jealousy is another matter. Are Ted's affairs the result of Sylvia's insecurities, or does his cheating feed her depression? Eventually he leaves her for their mutual friend Assia (the wife of the poet David Wevill). It's only after their separation that Sylvia feels able to write the brilliant poetry that sealed her fame. She would write over 40 of the 'Ariel' poems, argued to be her best work.

Bizarrely, the film omits any reference to the fact that six years later Assia took her own life and that of her daughter by Hughes. 'I don't know why they wouldn't put it in,' said Daniel, bewildered. 'It's a heavy fucking deal! I mean, I don't know how you drive somebody to commit suicide with their child. Maybe this is a romantic idea, but maybe he still loved Sylvia.'

In 1963, aged 31, Sylvia Plath also committed suicide. At the time she was living in Fitzroy Road, London, with her two children: Frieda, aged two, and eight-month-old Nicholas. Her novel *The Bell Jar* (written under the pseudonym Victoria Lucas in 1963) had received lukewarm reviews and she was suffering a bout of depression. On the advice of her doctor, she took up residence with a friend and ranted about her husband's infidelities. Claiming to be capable, she eventually returned home. Aside from a brief conversation with her neighbour, it was the last time that she would be seen alive. She laid out bread and milk for her children, opened their window during one of the coldest winters on record, sealed their bedroom door and put her head in the gas oven. Since childhood she had had a history of mental illness and depression. As recounted in *The Bell Jar*, she was treated by Electro-convulsive therapy. Already she had attempted suicide on two separate occasions; at the age of twenty she took an overdose of sleeping pills and, after a temporary separation with Ted, she ran her car off the road in a deserted airfield.

The BBC-financed film was in development for several years, with working titles flicking between *Ted And Sylvia*, *The Beekeeper's Daughter* and *Bitter Fame*. Gwyneth Paltrow seemed an obvious choice for the quietly contemplative character of Sylvia. Daniel, however, was up against competition from Russell Crowe and Colin Firth for the lead role. Although a little shorter than Hughes, he seemed an obvious choice, blending both 'intellectualism and incipient savagery', according to the *Independent on Sunday*. His craggy features and startling blue eyes portrayed a character teetering on the edge of genius and emotional cruelty. 'He is perfect for Ted Hughes,' praised Michael Gambon. 'All he'll have to do is dye the hair.'

As with all his characters, Daniel went to great lengths to portray Ted Hughes. 'I've been reading him for as long as I can remember,' he boasted enthusiastically. 'He's always been a big part of my life. My dad's a big Ted Hughes and Seamus Heaney fan, and my mother bought me poetry books when I was a kid and they rub off.'

As a young boy he'd heard the poet give a reading in the girls' grammar school down the road from him in Liverpool. Unfortunately, he was extremely under-whelmed when the great wordsmith recited his words in a monotonous and largely disinterested tone. 'I mean, bless him, he didn't read poetry particularly well,' said Daniel sympathetically. 'It was just this monotone crap.' To demonstrate, he quoted several poems in a low and gloomy northern accent. 'This is called "Crow". Crow sits in... duh duh duh... Blood and otters... Birth and death... thank you very much.'

Although uninspiring at the time, the memory of Ted's recital would prove vital in shaping his vocal delivery. 'If you listen to it,' he pointed out, 'his accent does not exist. Nowhere on earth does that accent exist – it's absolutely peculiar to Ted Hughes. He came down from Yorkshire and went to Cambridge and, of course, he got rid of it. What he did was he flattened it out. It's his interpretation of what a posh accent should sound like, but not too posh because he's from the north. It's bizarre and heartbreaking – feeling that you have to mask it and not mask it.'

Over the years, Daniel's own accent had been significantly diluted so that barely a trace of his Liverpudlian roots remained. '*Exactly!*' he cried. 'What has happened to it? It's gone.' He joked that he had toned down the northern inflections in a bid to secure better roles for himself: 'When I left drama school it was Merchant Ivory or nothing.' Ironically, he failed to land any such roles and, in fact, he purposely avoided them. 'I think they figured out that I was common as muck.'

Both Ted Hughes and Daniel Craig hailed from a similar class background. While Ted's father was a carpenter, Daniel was the son of a merchant seaman. 'I can relate to the male thing of not being able to look to others for help or "talk about yourself",' admitted Daniel. 'The UK is not an island of therapy – Jung and Freud passed us by.'

Although he already had the right facial expressions for Ted Hughes, he had to adapt his dress code to fit in with the dapper poet. 'Yes, thin black ties and big dark overcoats. If you look at photographs, he's always posing – there's an Elvis thing going on. You can see the ego scowling like James Dean.'

His most difficult task was to portray Ted Hughes with a degree of humanity. Vilified by feminists worldwide for driving Sylvia Plath to her death, Daniel had more than enough convincing to do. 'There's quite a bit of pressure riding on it,' he admitted. 'And also just the whole shit that goes with it – you know, the hatred directed at Ted Hughes. People are still scrawling "pig" on his grave.' He instantly felt a sense of empathy with the demonised poet. 'I've read Ted Hughes for as long as I can remember,' he claimed. 'Sylvia's a different matter. The whole *Bell Jar* thing is hard feminist stuff.' But he understood the film was primarily about Sylvia, and he wasn't about to try and steal the show. 'We had a common goal. With this film it wasn't about being even handed. The film is called *Sylvia* for a reason: it's *her* story. In that sense, we weren't exploring Ted. I did that in my head. But it's about her illness, outlook, how she coped with life and being a foreigner. None of us disagreed on this. It would have been easy to make a film about a couple having problems but I'm not sure how interesting that is.'

As far as he was concerned, the situation wasn't that black and white and he went to great lengths to understand his character's motivation. Eventually he developed a certain degree of sympathy for Ted. 'Ultimately, within a relationship there's an unknown, which is just about those two people.' It would be easy to read Sylvia as the victim, but he preferred to steer clear of taking sides. 'You know, when you have friends that split up, the worst thing you can do is get involved.'

In a relationship with an actress himself, he understood the pressures of a creative relationship. 'I relate to how tough it is for two artists – be it poets or actors – to have a relationship. There's pressure if both parties do the same thing. Ambition can corrode. Ted and Sylvia set themselves apart. Their only ambition was to write and to be in the right place to write. Ted could be anywhere – in a room full of screaming kids. Sylvia had a real problem if the feeling wasn't really right.

'Any relationship has to be about two people sharing problems, and the compromises they have to make to make their relationship and careers work. It's not always a happy medium but it has to be done. That's at the crux of this relationship but also at the crux of every relationship, and add that to the pressures of fame, and the lack of success on Sylvia's part, and you can see why problems arose. Him having affairs is all too easy an excuse.'

To cast Ted Hughes as a villain would be to ignore the intricate and fascinating complexities of his character. 'I think he probably was a shit but then I think he was probably lots of things,' remarked Daniel diplomatically. 'There are so many people who've met Ted and they all have a different story to tell. I read a lot and talked to as many people as I could. In the end you have to make up your character because you can only take on so much. There is this idea that if you write poetry or act you get all this emotional stuff out, and I don't know if that's true or if that was ever possible for Hughes. He seems to have always thought he could handle everything on his own.'

The research process proved to be emotionally taxing. 'That's what doing this part has made me realise and probably why I won't be in a hurry to play another real figure again. I feel very strongly that it was an incredibly complex situation and all you can do is open a huge can of worms. You go, "How do you make sense of that?" Actually, that's a relationship and that's something you can't portray on film.'

Deep down he suspected the couple were very much in love. There was a fine line between love and hate, and unfortunately in Ted and Sylvia's case the relationship tipped the balance. Set with the challenge of playing a real-life character, he embarked on a period of meticulous research. His primary source was Elisabeth Sigmund, a close friend of Sylvia's and the dedicatee of *The Bell Jar*. After Sylvia's death she had taken over the couple's cottage in Devon. 'She was very close to both of them,' revealed Daniel. 'The first question I asked her was, "Look, I've read the books and I'm very close to him in my mind and my heart. I just need to know: were they in love? I really need to know."' Smiling, she gave Daniel all the answers he needed: 'You couldn't put a cigarette paper between them when they were in love.'

'That meant so much to me,' admitted Daniel. 'I genuinely believe that, even if he did have affairs, it was part of a relationship – he wasn't a serial polygamist. He was in love with Sylvia, and he was always in love with Sylvia. They were an amazing couple. They must have been something else to be with.'

He refused to pass judgement on Ted's actions. 'Yes, they loved each other; yes, it was an awful situation; yes, she was sick; yes, he was incredibly attractive and he was becoming famous and he was open to all these temptations; so yes, anything is possible. But I'm not going to judge the man because of that. And I don't know whether any of us can. Because in the same situation, who knows?'

Fortunately, Daniel shared a dramatic on-screen chemistry with his co-star Gwyneth Paltrow. 'It was intense but also fun, because you have to break and laugh,' he said of filming. 'We were doing stuff that you had to get away from and break – there was a lot of pain going on. But I think that is why I became an actor. I wanted to explore those sorts of things. Gwyneth is a dream to work with, an intelligent actress. She loves what she's doing... and I love what I'm doing. We just hopefully sparked a bit.'

As soon as filming finished, the directors hurriedly made a brief trailer for the cast from the rushes. It was obviously apparent *Sylvia* was to be no picnic in the park. 'It looks like it's going to be a sad movie,' confirmed Daniel. 'But what can you do about that?' During the shoot Gwyneth Paltrow lost her father, which gave her portrayal of the troubled poet an even greater sadness.

'It was very, very hard for me to get through the day,' she recalls. 'I was under a cloud most of the time. But it was an amazing experience, because I think I was so torn up with grief. In a way I felt this bravery and this lust to do the role as honestly as I could, and be as raw and open as possible. To let go of any image I had of myself playing the role, and be as true to it as I could.'

Daniel praised Gwyneth for her strength and determination. 'That brings a reality into it,' he pondered. 'It was very upsetting. I don't think the filming process itself was upsetting – it was just too big a deal. I don't know how she coped really. She did brilliantly. And her mum was there – Blythe Danner. She plays Plath's mother in the movie.'

Sylvia's suicide scene proved to be particularly harrowing. 'I wasn't there, but I heard it was horrendous,' Daniel shuddered. 'The kids who were playing our kids wouldn't go back on set afterwards – it freaked them out. We tried our best not to let the material affect them but they're probably in therapy now and will pummel my knees if they see me in the street!'

He was extremely happy with the end result and, regardless of what critics might say, he'd done the best job possible. 'I'm sure if it gets on *Newsnight Review* they can pick holes in it until the cows come home,' he said, sighing. 'But I know where it lies in my heart and I'm secure about that.' But once again critics praised him for his performance and the usual round of Oscar suggestions were heard. Unfortunately, though, not everyone was quite so supportive of the project. Sylvia's eldest daughter vehemently objected to the film, condemning it in a poem called 'Suicide Doll'. 'Her prerogative,' shrugged Daniel. 'Absolutely. I wouldn't even question her right to feel angry and I do care. But I am also interested in telling stories.'

By now he had established himself as an actor capable of undertaking both arthouse and commercial movies. Even in the role of supporting actor, his star quality dazzled critics. He had also demonstrated an ability to tackle tricky subject matters with sensitivity and grace. With every new project his reputation was growing. It seemed Daniel's philosophy of waiting patiently for the right roles was starting to pay off.

CHAPTER 6

# BEST OF BRITISH

Towards the end of the 1990s, British cinema became a hot topic of conversation in the film world. Historically overlooked by Hollywood, British movies were finally gaining the recognition they deserved. International filmgoers were particularly interested in titles dealing with uniquely British subjects. The actor Hugh Grant was singled out for praise. His turns in *Four Weddings And A Funeral* (1994) and *Notting Hill* (1999) were lapped up by the American public; they couldn't get enough of this polite but befuddled English gentleman.

At the same time another strain of British cinema was emerging: the gangster flick. Guy Ritchie's *Lock Stock And Two Smokin' Barrels* (1998) and *Snatch* (2000) sparked a new genre of filmmaking. People were fascinated by the uniquely British 'wideboys' of London's East End. As a working-class hero adept at playing troubled and menacing characters, Daniel became a casting agent's dream. When Matthew Vaughn (producer of *Lock, Stock*) made his directorial debut with *Layer Cake* (2004), he felt compelled to cast Daniel in the lead role.

Written in a similar vein to Guy Ritchie's films, *Layer Cake* was a British mafia movie based on a novel by JJ Connolly (2000). A successful cocaine dealer (Daniel's character, who is never referred to by name in the film and appears only as XXXX on the credits) is planning an early retirement from the business, but before leaving he must complete his toughest assignment yet. He is instructed to find Charlotte Ryder, a rich socialite and daughter of a powerful construction worker who happens to be best friends with the mafia boss.

It's not an easy task – slowly he discovers that the rules of the modern underworld have changed drastically. There are no 'code' and 'families' with people willing to double-cross him at every turn. On top of this, he must deal with an international drug ring, a brutal sect of neo-Nazis and a love interest called Tammy (played by Sienna Miller). The title of the movie referred to the layers anyone in business goes through in rising to the top. Most importantly of all, our lead must avoid being drawn back into the 'cake mix'.

Cast in the lead role (his first to date), Daniel would effectively carry the film. Matthew Vaughn acknowledged this was a difficult task and, although he sympathised with the actor, he knew there wasn't a better man for the job. 'It's a hard character to play as an actor,' he admitted. 'The whole point about XXXX is that he's a poker player. It doesn't matter what's going on around him, you never know what he's thinking, which means you've got to be a very good actor, a very subtle actor to play him.'

JJ Connolly, who adapted the novel for a screenplay, was equally pleased about Daniel's involvement. 'Casting the untitled central character was always going to be hard. A lot of very good actors really wanted it but when Daniel Craig was suggested it was a done-deal. We wanted to get as far away as possible from jolly-ups and banter, guys trying to look too cool throughout the movie. We needed an actor who was prepared to go to the depths of emotion without anchors – not wanting to remain too cool for school.'

When first approached about the project by Matthew Vaughn, Daniel was admittedly sceptical. Perpetually seeking new challenges, he had no desire to take part in a remake verbatim but Vaughn reassured him that this wouldn't be the case. For his part, he had also been nervous about his first meeting with Daniel. 'When I first met Daniel, I thought, "Oh Christ, is he going to be a real luvvie thespian?" But after ten minutes I discovered that we're both Harry Potter fans and that our idea of a good evening is being left alone with a PlayStation.'

Having found common ground, Daniel himself quickly warmed to the director. 'We clicked early on,' he explained. 'We share a lot of our favourite films, especially from the late 1960s and early 1970s that came out of the UK, but also out of the US. Sort of the classic crime films.'

That common interest sparked a conversation about the direction *Layer Cake* should take. Between them, they decided that, as Daniel said, 'This movie had to look as cinematic as possible, and it had to have a grand scale and make London look as cinematic as possible.' It also needed to 'steer away from being "tricksy". Not using the camera as another character but the camera just tells the story.'

By the end of their conversation Daniel was suitably convinced. *Layer Cake* would be far from a replica of *Lock, Stock*. He made a distinction between the two films, describing one as a crime film and the other as a gangster flick. 'I think gangster movies involve the behaviour of gangsters and how despicable they are, or how they control people,' he pondered. 'This is much more a movie which has a strong story line based upon the rise and the fall of characters with a crime setting. Hopefully, it's more sophisticated than your average gangster movie. I believe it is. You have to think more. There [are] very complicated plot twists, which will all work out, but you have to sort of sit and concentrate if you want to follow the movie. Which, as far as I'm concerned, that's more the type of movie that I enjoy watching.'

Most importantly, he believed the crew had a strong script on their hands. 'If you don't have a script that is ready to go on the first day of shooting, you are fucked,' he said, shaking his head. 'If you are trying to rewrite the film while you are shooting it, in my experience it just doesn't fucking work and it ruins the movie because no one has a fucking idea of what to do. You have to have a script sitting there that you are ready to shoot. You can change things but there is this myth about improvisation that it is a spontaneous thing where you can do anything as long as you know your character. You can only improvise if you have a good script because the story has to be there. That is what I look for – when I am giving a script and people say, "Oh, we are going to do this and this," I get nervous and ask, "Well, when are you going to do this?" There have been times when I have been rewriting scenes on the day of shooting and I am not a fucking writer!'

He found Vaughn's intentions admirable. 'I was really intrigued that Matthew was making this step. He was very clear that he didn't want to make another *Lock, Stock* or *Snatch*,' said Daniel. 'He wanted to do a big British movie using London as a big character.' He also had a good feeling about the project. Already, there was a lot of serendipity involved. The day it was suggested Vaughn should read JJ Connolly's book *Layer Cake* he found himself sitting opposite the author on the train. Daniel smiled when Matthew retold him the story. After all, the unconventional actor had based his entire career on serendipity.

'Things have a way of fitting together,' he mused. 'There is a serendipity about everything. You ignore the signs at your peril, and those situations make you make the right choices. I had no problem getting involved with this film and throwing myself into it – which Matthew allowed me to do.'

Daniel even applied the theory to the world at large. While in LA he watched the film *What The $! Do We Know?*

(2004), a docu-drama about quantum physics and how our thoughts can shape our destiny. He explained the concept: 'These scientists sit around in the film and say our reality can be changed by every thought. We have a major influence on what happens around us. In Washington, DC, they got four hundred people to come in and meditate on the idea of lowering the crime rate. The people who ended up paying for it were the Washington police force. They did it nine times because the crime rate fell by twenty-five per cent. There was another study, in Japan, about how talking to water angrily changes the molecular level of it. I am absolutely certain that we shape our own destinies and we have to take care of it.'

Once again, he reiterated that he had never actively sought out work: it had come to him. 'I met Roger Mitchell, Stephen Daldry and Sam Mendes all because of the work I've done,' he said proudly. 'And that's the way I'd like it to continue. Certainly, you have to be careful you don't do anything where you blow it for yourself. You have to take care.'

By now he had a nose for good scripts. 'A lot of it's instinct but I read scripts and, as I read, I want to know that something's going to change me and affect me, and make me do something that I haven't necessarily done before. It genuinely has never really been about the money. I've earned a living, which for an actor to say is usually quite rare. I've had a lot of luck, and I've made some mistakes in my time, but I really believe you've got to keep yourself as busy and as interested as possible in what you do because then you can maintain it.'

It wasn't that Daniel had anything against accepting

more lucrative projects, he just didn't want it to eclipse all other considerations. 'I think as soon as you do decide to take [big] money, that's fine, but you've got to get your priorities right. If it stops you doing other things, then you have to think very carefully about which way you need to go.' Reluctant to rush into making any hasty decisions, he preferred to choose his projects carefully and wisely. 'I just give it as much thought as I can. And it takes me a long time to decide whether I want to do something or not. If I do need to make a decision very quickly, I just apply the same rule, namely, will it change me?'

Of course, he wasn't infallible. While the mere mention of films such as *Tomb Raider* and *A Kid In King Arthur's Court* made him cringe, at the time they had been necessary evils. 'I've done a lot of work to earn money because I've had to, because I need to pay the rent, and I need to do those things,' he pleaded in his defence. 'So they're not mistakes. It's just sometimes I wish they'd disappear. I've been lucky enough that, with some success, I've been able to have more choices.'

Although he had been apprehensive about taking on the role in *Layer Cake*, it was a decision he felt destined to make. 'It's unnerving to be the lead in *Layer Cake* because I really want to do it well. But when I got the script I felt it was time. I can't quite put my finger on when it happened, but one day I woke up and realised that I could do this. It's such a liberating feeling to be on set and feel like you actually fucking *deserve* to be there!'

In the past he had turned down gangster films for being

too gratuitously violent but *Layer Cake* was different. Here was a script that didn't rely on violence to engage an audience. 'I'd been offered gangster films and none of them appealed to me,' he shrugged. 'Scripts with huge amounts of violence in them, with supposedly scary people in them, but whom I don't find scary. But what was different about the movie was its intelligent through-line. I think it's very close to the truth; it's what successful drug dealers are like. They don't drive around in flashy cars, they don't show off – they behave quietly.'

In the film, his character abhors guns but still has to use one. 'If you want to talk about the politics of guns, I'm totally opposed to gun ownership, anything that's for shooting people,' he said, with vehement disgust. 'However, there's something enticing about them. I'm a bloke, and the smell of gun oil turns me on.'

As a reference point, Daniel and Mathew Vaughn looked to Quentin Tarantino's *Reservoir Dogs* (1992). 'The violence in *Reservoir Dogs* is really not nice,' said Daniel. 'It really affects me emotionally. In this film, the violence is extreme, but it's emotionally connected. When someone gets shot in this movie, I hope people go, "Ooh! That's not good."'

Indeed, when the film was eventually released it was championed as an anti-gangster movie. This was largely down to Daniel's input in the script. 'Daniel was quite clear that he didn't want to make guns and violence look cool,' said Matthew Vaughn. 'Even when we did the beating-up scene, he was very involved in making sure it looked horrible, not fun.'

Rather than relying on his fists, Daniel conveyed power in a different way. 'What he doesn't do on screen is as important as what he does,' said Vaughn. 'Brave actors are the people who look like they're doing nothing, and then you cut it all together and there's a hell of a performance.' Michael Gambon, who was also cast in the film as gangland boss Eddie Temple, seconded that view. He fondly referred to Daniel as 'a subtle, intelligent, knowing, wise bastard'.

One of the biggest – and most bizarre – challenges facing Daniel was the fact that his character didn't actually have a name! 'The point about it is that he's someone who doesn't have an identity,' he explained. 'He doesn't have an identity for a very good reason, because he doesn't want to sort of allow too much of himself to be known. So it kind of just played into the character.' As a joke he would refer to his character as 'Cynthia' on set. Others came up with 'Four X' or 'Quadruple X'. 'I was talking to someone today who called him "Deleted" – and that's probably the best name for him,' he concluded.

Without any background on which to base his character, Daniel relied on the script for clues as to how he should play the part. 'You need a good script and that's what we had. Most of the character and most of his traits are on the page. And then I just wanted to instill this sort of sense of mystery about him and make sure that we're not... You know you can't get too close to him. But actually what I liked, what really attracted me to the movie, is that you get closer to him because of, to put it bluntly, the shit he gets into!

'We meet him when he is getting out of the drug business. He's had this plan to get out for years and the only reason he is squirreling away his money is because he wants to do one deal then leave. I think it's all planned in his head but that's the flaw in his character. He has it planned but then messes it up worse than he ever could've imagined. He tries to assassinate the man who is stalking him and kill his boss Jimmy Price because he thinks he can keep it under control.

'But fuck it, he's a coke dealer! By its nature it's a world of criminals and you're going to come unstuck at some stage. And that is the moral: if you're in there, you're in. For God's sake, don't pity him!

'I approached the character in the same way I approach everything really. I was interested in making him someone who was not faceless but someone that could just mix anywhere, could get on anywhere because I felt that was important for his character to be able to mix in every circle and consequently in every layer of the cake.'

Although not strictly a Method actor, Daniel would often apply the same techniques. 'Method actors suggest that you do sense memory exercises every time you do a scene. I use every method I can. Whatever works, I'll use.' Sense memory exercises enable an actor to recall sensory impressions by concentrating on the stimuli associated with them. One website on the subject cites an example of an actor being asked to recreate a scene from the North Pole in a studio. Rather than shiver and pretend to be cold, he would imagine how the cold affects him and relives that experience.

Daniel's background work on the character consisted of making him absolutely neutral. 'He would walk into a hotel, walk into the lobby, meet people, talk to people, walk out and no one would notice he was there,' he explained. He relied on facial expressions to convey a message. 'It's the beauty of the human face – an audience fills it in. Good cinema lets the audience guess all the way through.'

That wasn't to say that Daniel didn't do his homework. Prior to filming, he sat down and read through the script. Keen to mould his character into an unassuming type rather than an obvious gangster, he refrained from making any research into real-life drug dealers. 'All I wanted to do was make a character that you would pass on the streets and not notice,' he said. 'I think that's closer to reality than having someone drive past in a car with spinning wheels and having someone wear gold chains and things. I think that these people are, as I say, businessman and they like to keep a low profile.'

He found another useful resource in the form of JJ Connolly, author of the original novel. 'Although he says he hasn't had contact with that world, he seems to know an awful lot about it!' he said, laughing. 'He was very good for stories and he was very insightful as far as me asking, "Do you think this is a good behaviour at this particular moment?" and that sort of thing. He always had very good advice for me.'

He was fascinated by the whole 'Layer Cake' concept. Mulling over the script, he considered the role drug dealers play in our society. 'There is a moral tale to this and that's if you lie down with dogs, you wake up with fleas. The overlying sort of thing is that we are kidding ourselves if we don't think of the drug business as a legitimate business. It's what funds governments and it's too much money to ignore. The whole point of the 'Layer Cake' is that you have the bottom of it with Duke, who is in it for the cash and the cars, and then you have the top, which is Michael Gambon's character, who never even touches drugs in any way, shape or form. It's just another commodity that makes him a lot of money. That is fascinating.'

More than ever before, Daniel found a fantastic support network among the cast and crew of *Layer Cake*. He praised Vaughn for his directorial debut. 'Matthew planned the movie incredibly well. He storyboarded the movie shot for shot and we basically did that. We shot the script and we shot his ideas. And he had a very, very, very clear vision about what he wanted to do, which, thankfully, I agreed with. He employed a great [director of photography] in Ben Davis so visually that was all very clear as far as how he wanted to make London look, and how he wanted to make the movie look. I mean, I can't say enough about it really. He did it brilliantly.'

Not content with simply acting in front of the camera, he involved himself in several other aspects of the film-making process. He had no qualms about approaching Vaughn with suggestions as to how things might be done better. For the most part, these were gladly received. 'I'm thinking about everything all the time,' joked Daniel. 'You have to, that's part of the job; you can't not think about it.

For me it's very important because of the whole process. The whole creative process is about making movies and making movies is part technical, part artistic, part emotion, part communication. You have to have an eye on all of these things when you're making them.'

Unlike many of his fellow actors, he refused to sit back and watch from the sidelines. He wholeheartedly threw himself into the project. 'If you're in a job and it's not working in the right way, it's part of your job to make it work in the right way,' he explained. 'It would worry me, getting to a stage where you just do job after job after job; you tend to get jaded and you tend to get lazy. Because some jobs take an effort, and I don't mean effort as in acting, they take effort in management, in encouraging people to do better.'

As far as he was concerned, the choice was simple. 'You can either lay back and say, "Well, I'm an actor – I turn up to do my job and go away – or I can get involved," which means you have to go shout, or you're going to have to sit down and have meetings. And I believe that's part of your job, but that's exhausting!' But the chances of him ever moving into a directorial role were unlikely. 'I'd rather stick needles in my eyes!' he exclaimed. But despite this, he did joke that he should have been given an executive producer's credit on *Layer Cake*.

Although *Layer Cake* was not an action movie per se, it did involve a number of stunt scenes. In many instances, Daniel refused a double, preferring to tackle the daredevil activities on his own. 'I had to hang off a forty-storey building – one of the new blocks in Canary Wharf,' he recalled. 'I felt like David Blaine. I was expecting to get pelted with eggs, and a burger van to park underneath next to a bloke playing bongos.' Unfortunately, however, he never had an opportunity to drive the Audi featured in the film. 'I was able to take it out for a bit and I almost totalled it because it's terribly fast.'

While he enjoyed every aspect of filming ('the whole thing was a ride'), he was continually quizzed by journalists about one scene in particular – his steamy sexual liaison with Sienna Miller. The beautiful young actress, who would later date the actor Jude Law, was just starting out in her career. Although new to the game, she had already been hailed a sex symbol.

In interviews, Sienna joked about how great it was to work with an actor as sexy as Daniel Craig. 'Aghhh! You can only imagine what it was like! I loved being flung on to the bed. It wasn't difficult – I could think of worse people to be flung on beds by!' She winked mischievously. 'He's really rugged. He's beautiful but not a novice. He's a real man, isn't he? Great eyes. Ol' blue eyes!' But the seasoned actor played down the love scenes, saying, 'I don't think you can ever really make yourself comfortable when you're doing a sex scene where there are ten people in the room you don't know that well. They're not exactly… sexy.'

But he couldn't deny that Sienna Miller was a beautiful woman. Asked to compare her with his former screen-siren co-star Angelina Jolie, he joked, 'I couldn't put a cigarette paper between them but I would like to.

Someone has to do it.' Although the two both ruled out any off-screen attraction, they did become close friends during the course of filming. Making her film debut, Miller was extremely nervous when she arrived on set. 'It was a real boy's set!' she would later recall. 'There was a lot of yelling and shouting on set. I felt like the honorary girl!' Sensing her unease, Daniel did his best to make the young actress feel at home.

Spending most of her time in Agent Provocateur underwear, Sienna described her character Tammy as 'a complete slut... Part of me was nervous about playing someone who was that obviously sexual and tarty, but once we got on set all of those worries disappeared because it was such a laugh.' She gushed about the kindness Daniel had shown her. On a number of occasions he stayed late to help her through scenes, including a 'hideously embarrassing' dancing scene. It was a beginning of a friendship that would last for some years.

She may have been the token girl in *Layer Cake*, but Sienna Miller wasn't the only beautiful woman to grace the set with her presence. Matthew Vaughn also happened to be married to the supermodel Claudia Schiffer. Daniel recalled the day she came on set to say hello. He had to admit that she was even more striking in the flesh than in her modelling campaigns. He gave Matthew a knowing pat on the back – he was certainly a lucky man!

When it came to filming the final scene of *Layer Cake*, Vaughn decided to play a trick on the distributors Sony. 'We kidded Sony,' said Daniel, laughing. 'They thought we were shooting a different ending than we shot.' Originally the idea was to shoot Daniel and Sienna driving off into the sunset but Matthew Vaughn had other plans. In his preferred version, our anti-hero XXXX would be shot dead. 'We shot that [the final] scene and then Matthew cut it together and showed it to them, and they went up the fucking wall!' recalled Daniel, chuckling to himself. 'But it tested really positively. You know, the fact is he gets shot by Sid, by someone who was personally affected by him, was cut up by this man stealing his girlfriend.'

Given the hype surrounding the film, Daniel seemed destined to finally smash the American market. Although he had a respectable foothold in Hollywood, he was yet to make the leap into international stardom. Now all that seemed likely to change. Once again he refused to be drawn into speculation. This was an all-too familiar story. 'Who knows?' he said. 'I don't really know how that will work out. It's not my cause in life to be filthy rich. Being comfortable is enough. If money comes along I will take it. I just want good scripts that try to make you think. I've been offered lots of money in the past but I just know that I would abuse it and get drunk.'

Little did he know it, but he was about to become a household name. Unfortunately, it was for all the wrong reasons...

## CHAPTER 7

# LOVE COMPLICATIONS

Although Daniel had cultivated quite a healthy professional profile, he was fiercely protective of his private life. While many were familiar with Daniel Craig on screen, after-hours he remained something of an enigma. While he was happy to discuss movie roles in public, anything else seemed completely irrelevant. As far as he was concerned, he was not in the acting business to be a celebrity and had no interest in airing his dirty laundry in public.

Over the course of his career, he had seen many high-profile relationships collapse under the strain of public interference and he was determined his own relationship would not suffer a similar fate. By dating another actress in the industry, he placed himself in the direct line of fire from the press. The only way for him to deal with the situation was to remain silent. He would very rarely discuss his girlfriend Heike Makatsch in public and the pair tended to steer clear of celebrity events, instead preferring to entertain guests at their north London home.

For seven years the couple had enjoyed a relatively stress-free relationship. When Heike first arrived in London, she was barely recognised in the street. Known only as 'Daniel Craig's other half', she emerged from her boyfriend's shadow by appearing in the 2003 cult Brit flick *Love Actually*. Set five weeks before Christmas, the romantic comedy followed the lives of eight different characters who were all falling in and out of love. At certain points the separate storylines would converge, creating even greater complications.

Heike was cast in the role of Mia, a secretary who falls for her married manager Harry (Alan Rickman). Suffering a mid-life crisis, he welcomes her advances and even buys her an expensive necklace. His wife Karen (Emma Thompson) stumbles upon the necklace in his coat pocket and assumes it's a gift for her. On Christmas day, when the presents are given out, Karen opens a box she assumes is the necklace but is disappointed to discover it's a Joni Mitchell CD (one of her favourite singers). She breaks down in private but somehow manages to quickly compose herself and accompanies Harry to their children's nativity play. Afterwards she confronts him and he admits that he's been a fool. At the end of the film the pair agree to give their marriage a second shot.

Even though it wasn't exactly the kind of script Daniel

would have chosen for himself, he commended Heike for her performance. 'There are some brilliant actors in it, doing some lovely turns. I cannot criticise the movie and anyone who does is just wasting their time. Critics spend an hour and a half writing column inches of vitriol about that movie. What's the point? Get what it's about and go and write about something important!' Unfortunately, many critics weren't quite so sympathetic to the film's intentions. Despite the knocks, the director, Richard Curtis, remained upbeat. 'I'd rather make a film that most of the audience liked and some critics didn't, than a film that critics loved and nobody wanted to watch,' he shrugged.

Daniel accompanied Heike to the première of the movie in London's Leicester Square on 16 November. She had always been supportive of his career and so it was good for him to be able to return the favour. However, he couldn't lie. When journalists asked for his real thoughts on the film, he had to confess he wasn't a fan! He struggled to remain diplomatic, choosing his words carefully. 'It's whatever it is. And I knew it was always going to be that. Richard [Curtis] has done something that I admire him for doing. But I've seen it twice now and at the end of it I have to go, "Oh fuck off!"'

In public he would say very little about Heike, other than that they 'were happy' and 'may likely end up together'. Adept at keeping a low profile, they managed to dodge snooping photographers. On one rare occasion they were seen canoodling in an airport lounge, where Heike appeared to be consoling Daniel. Since childhood he had always detested flying. Cradling his head close to her chest, Heike appeared to be whispering words of reassurance in his ear. It was a touching image and testimony to the strength of their relationship.

Unfortunately, though, the relationship had to come to an end. After seven enjoyable years together they agreed to split and go their separate ways. For Daniel, it was an especially difficult time. Ending a relationship was never easy at the best of times but thrust under the intolerable glare of tabloid gossipmongers it seemed unbearable.

Desperately seeking distraction, he found some solace in his next major project, an adaptation of the Ian McEwan novel *Enduring Love*. While enjoying a romantic picnic in the countryside, a young couple (university lecturer Joe and sculptor Claire) witness an alarming accident involving a hot-air balloon. When the pilot catches his leg in the anchor rope, the only passenger – a boy – is too frightened to jump down. Several men come to the rescue (including Joe) and attempt to pull the balloon to safety.

Suddenly a gust of wind takes a hold and the rescuers are airborne. While Joe drops safely to the ground, another man isn't quite so lucky. He drifts skyward and eventually falls to his death. The incident has terrible psychological repercussions for Joe. He sets out to retrieve the dead man's body, only to discover he has remarkably survived. Jed (the survivor) feels instantly drawn towards Joe, believing they have a connection. This develops into a dangerous infatuation that risks ruining Joe's life.

The project presented Daniel with yet another

challenging script. He would star alongside Rhys Ifans and Samantha Morton. Daniel and the director Roger Mitchell had already worked together on the controversial film *The Mother*. 'Roger is probably the best British film director there is and I say that unreservedly!' praised Daniel. Although after a moment's consideration, he quickly backtracked. 'Actually, I can't say that, because I've got mates who are directors and they're the best as well.'

But he was glad to be reunited with the director. 'Well, there are two things. There's Roger and the appeal of working with him is that it's terribly rewarding. He employs you because he trusts in your talent. He knows that you have ability and what he does is he manipulates it and sort of empowers you. The other thing is they are challenging roles. Also, we wouldn't start working unless the script was right – that's the most important thing with Roger. And the script was absolutely bang on. I don't know, I can't say enough about him. If we could start a film tomorrow, I would love it.'

Mitchell initially approached him about the project while filming *The Mother*. 'It was very simple,' recalled Daniel. 'We were a week from finishing shooting on *The Mother* and Roger came up to me and asked if I had read the novel. I said I had and that it was a great book, and he said, "Don't read it again. We're writing the script as we speak – are you in?" and I said yes. I wanted to work with him again straightaway and there was never an argument about it. I knew the story, and when Rhys Ifans and Samantha Morton got involved, I knew that, no matter how it turned out, it would be a good thing to do. That is the kind of security that you have – that you know you will get something out of it.'

Mitchell explained the plot to Daniel and the role that his character would play. 'What happens to this man is that he's sitting in this field and it's like the Garden of Eden in a way and everything's fine. He's going to propose; he thinks he wants to. He thinks he's in love with this woman and he thinks the world makes sense; he's quite a rational person. And then this accident happens, which has no meaning at all. It has no meaning partly because the boy survives, partly because the man who is killed is so tangentially involved with the accident. Joe feels, well, if this man's death has no meaning, and it clearly has no meaning, then why does anything else have meaning? What prevents us from being just bacteria?'

The film sparked debate on a number of philosophical issues. Daniel's character Joe starts to question existence and wonders if there is any spiritual meaning or purpose to life or love. 'He begins to believe that love is simply a biological imperative to fuck and reproduce before we die. It's all about whether love is enduring, or whether you have to endure love.' Ironically, Joe is surrounded by examples of enduring love from Claire and, oddly, Jed.

Daniel had his own thoughts on the subject. 'It's true that we're microbes that share genes with everything – like this horrible carnation on the table or the slug outside – that we're all part of one bio-organism. But who set that in motion, whether there's a God, and why there's love – I don't know. Anything is possible. I'm happy to cling onto the fact that there's something else.'

But did he still believe in true love? That was the question on every adoring female fan's lips. 'I think there's a great possibility love is just impulse. That doesn't mean it's meaningless but we're just organisms who share genes with the slug outside. It's depressing once you get into it.'

Rhys Ifans was cast opposite Daniel in the role of Jed. The Welsh-born actor had already enjoyed roles in *Notting Hill* and *The Shipping News* (2001). Although never properly acquainted, he and Daniel had both been students at The Guildhall. 'Rhys was in the third year when I was in the first,' explained Daniel. 'Over the years we bumped into each other, but we'd never been cast together.'

Very soon, however, the two actors would get to know each other more intimately than they could ever have imagined! At one point in the script their characters were required to kiss. Daniel was unfazed. After filming the graphic homosexual sex scene in *Love Is The Devil* this seemed like a breeze! Nevertheless, both actors avoided discussing the scene until the day of filming.

'We shot it towards the end of the movie. We'd been taking the piss out of each other relentlessly. We were going, "Three days to go. Two days to go..." But it was all over in a flash, thank goodness,' said Daniel.

As the cameras rolled the two actors moved in for their kiss. Daniel had to confess that he felt slightly odd embracing a friend but, like a true professional, he instantly switched into character. 'Rhys was wearing these cracked plastic teeth so it was bizarre when we did it. But it was fine. We filmed it at the end and by the time we got there we were into the groove of things,' he explained.

As soon as the director called 'Cut!' however, the pair pulled away instantly. 'Ugh! Mouthwash, please!' spat Daniel in jest. 'He put his tongue in!' squealed Rhys. The entire crew collapsed into fits of laughter. 'Of course I didn't,' insisted Daniel afterwards. 'It was just a kiss, nothing more. Honest!' Far from embarrassing, the entire scene was hilarious.

In the film, Rhys's character Jed stalks Joe. Thankfully, Daniel was unable to draw on real-life experience for the scenes. Asked if he'd ever been stalked, he replied, 'I don't think so… They're very good if they are there. But I do know people that have stalkers and it's not nice.' As research for the part he spoke to several of these friends and asked how they'd dealt with the problem. 'Court injunctions, bodyguards, the lot – depending on the stalker,' he said, in summary of his findings. 'Some stalkers are quite benign but finding someone in your garden at three o'clock in the morning with a meat cleaver and a hard-on can't be much fun.'

Given that their characters were so emotionally involved, it was hardly surprising that the two men forged a strong friendship bond. Daniel learned a lot from the comical actor – particularly about not taking yourself too seriously. 'When Rhys was asked what he took with him to every set, he said, "My sense of humour." And he's absolutely right because you can lose the bigger picture so easily,' said Daniel. 'Because making a film, basically, is a collective sense of panic controlled, because who knows where the money's going to go? Who knows who's going to be spending the money? I love film sets which are like borderline hysteria, because then sparks fly.'

Off screen Daniel and Rhys would regularly socialise together. They shared the same sense of humour and enjoyed a drink or two! Rhys introduced Daniel to a number of new friends, including the supermodel Kate Moss. Despite her fame, Moss was an extremely down-to-earth person. Just like Daniel, she would much rather spend a night out in the local pub than at an exclusive celebrity haunt.

She had recently split from her journalist boyfriend Jefferson Hack, the father of her daughter Lila-Grace. In the past she had been linked to a number of high-profile men and for several years she dated Hollywood actor Johnny Depp. Quite often, though, she found herself at the centre of controversy. Her party-loving behaviour had landed the superwaif model a reputation for being a hellraiser. Discovered at the age of 14 in JFK Airport by Storm Model Management, she ushered in an era of 'heroin chic' in the fashion world.

Her split with Jefferson Hack led to speculation that she might be on the lookout for a new lover. Any man who passed through her sphere of influence was instantly tagged a potential suitor by the press. No sooner had she and Daniel exchanged phone numbers, the tabloids were declaring the pair an item.

For press-shy Daniel it was a shock to the system. He

had never experienced tabloid intrusion on such an intense level. Photographers would lie in wait outside his house and follow him across town. He couldn't even take a trip to the supermarket without having it documented in the paper the following day. He described the experience as an 'eye opener'.

'But only in the sense that everything I'd been led to believe about the press was true. It's like having the Secret Service on your back. You can be in the middle of nowhere and the mobile will go and it's so-and-so from whatever paper. They were at my mum's house in ten minutes... Of course, self-promotion is part of the job but, unless I'm talking about a piece of work that I've done, I don't see the point.'

Kate and Daniel were spotted together on several occasions. They were rumoured to have taken a romantic minibreak to New York together. Photographers descended on restaurants, forcing the startled couple to flee through kitchen back doors. In a separate incident, gossipmongers claimed to have seen the couple kissing backstage at an Alexander McQueen fashion show.

There was even suggestion that Kate's ex-boyfriend was still on the scene and that the three stars were embroiled in a complicated love triangle. After months of arguing, Jefferson Hack had moved out of her house in March 2004. He still lived close by and the pair vowed to remain friends for the sake of their daughter. They were reportedly seen enjoying dinner at The Ivy and were allegedly planning a family holiday to Mustique in the

West Indies. However, one tabloid suggested that he had accepted Kate's relationship with Daniel. They allegedly quoted his mother as saying, 'We're not angry about Daniel – certainly not!'

Although Daniel was shocked by the degree of press interest in his relationship with Kate Moss, he wasn't wholly surprised. 'Look, I'm not stupid, I read *Heat*! It happens all the time. So when it happened to me it wasn't a surprise. But it was incredibly disturbing. I can't imagine anyone enjoying it and, if they do, I find that quite peculiar.'

Soon mild irritation turned to anger and he vowed to stamp out the rumours once and for all by declaring that he and Kate were nothing more than close friends. 'We're mates – end of story!' he fumed. 'All I did was walk out of a restaurant with somebody and it made the news. If half the things they wrote about Kate and I had actually happened, it would have been an interesting story, but they didn't. It was all a load of shit!'

Matters came to a head when one journalist called him directly on his mobile. He was extremely guarded about giving out his number and couldn't imagine how it could have been leaked to the press. 'I mean, where the fuck did they get my telephone number from?' he asked incredulously. 'The government would struggle to get my fucking mobile number, but the press got it!'

He grew tired of being asked the same question in interviews. 'What's going on with Kate?' journalists would sheepishly enquire. During an interview with men's glossy *Arena*, he waited for the inevitable question. When the topic was finally broached he felt a sense of relief. 'Thank fuck for that!' he joked. 'Look, I knew you'd ask – I mean, she's gorgeous, she's one of *Arena*'s favourite girls, so naturally you were going to ask – and I really didn't want to talk about all this crap. But as we are, let's get this straight: me and Kate are just mates. Always have been. If there was anything to tell, I would but there isn't. She's gorgeous, for crying out loud! If something had happened, would I really be sat here trying to deny it? What, am I mad?'

He claimed any tales of romance were complete fabrication created by tabloids in desperate need of a headline story: 'The story was blatantly untrue, one of those bullshit ones drummed up by the tabs when they were having a slow day because, oh, I don't know, because Jennifer Lopez hadn't worn a new frock for a while, or someone from the soaps hadn't got pissed and whipped their tits out!'

Despite his protests to the contrary, there did seem to be an element of truth in the rumours. After four months, though, the affair came to an end. Daniel would only ever speak about the liaison in ambiguous terms. He left the public guessing as to whether his relationship with Kate was of a platonic or romantic nature. Either way, even association with the supermodel had massive implications on his private life.

It was a difficult period of his life. He felt particularly sensitive towards his ex-girlfriend Heike, who was still struggling to deal with their break-up. The last thing she wanted to do was open a newspaper and read about Daniel's latest squeeze. 'I don't regret it at all,' he said of his 'friendship' with Kate. 'I regret that what happened had to do with a messy part of my life. To get publicity like that is unfair on the people in your life.'

However, he did take some valuable lessons from the experience. He realised that, although difficult, it was possible to keep his private life from public view. 'I've learned from it. I used to think the press was a necessary evil and now I don't think it is. I think it's something you choose. It was a relief, in a way, to be able to say, "Oh, that's how it works!"'

The press were a 'pain in the arse' but he refused to let them rule his life. Dusting himself down, he prepared to carry on with his life as normal. 'I could get paranoid about it, but fuck that! That's not how I want to live my life,' he sighed. 'My personal life is totally my personal life and I'll cling to that as aggressively as I can. And, touch wood, with the thing with Kate or whatever, I think I've maintained a little of that and, if I can keep maintaining it, I will.'

Less noble actors might have capitalised on the 'Kate-gate' affair to boost their own career, but Daniel refused point blank. 'I'd never talk about a previous relationship even if it wasn't somebody famous and so I think the same rule has to be applied. The only reason I'd ever talk about that would be for my own advantage and that's really bad news. That's as low as you can go, as far as I'm concerned.'

Although he sympathised with celebrity couples whose

relationships had been torn apart by the tabloids, he concluded that the ones who courted the attention only had themselves to blame. 'If you're in a relationship with somebody – and we've all seen the relationship where they start battling it out in the press, God forbid that should ever happen – then you have to keep your counsel; you *have* to. For your family, for your friends, for your children, whatever, because only they should know what the truth is. Then they'll feel secure about themselves and if someone says to them, "He said this and blah blah," they'll be able to say, "I know the truth, you don't." That's the only way I can see it. That's the story. That's the way it goes.'

By battening down the hatches, he had survived the press storm and emerged unscathed. Rather than lose his temper with journalists, he greeted them with indifference. After all, the gossipmongers would soon find something else to talk about. But Daniel hadn't escaped the public glare just yet: he was about to make headline news once again and this time it would be for far more favourable reasons.

# CHAPTER 8

# LADIES' MAN

At some point or another, every small boy dreams of being James Bond. Having entertained several generations of film viewers, Ian Fleming's fictional spy hero had become a national institution. The 20 Bond movies made by EON Productions since 1962 make up the second highest-grossing film franchise since *Star Wars*. In the UK the series accounted for three of the five most-watched television movies.

Ironically, one novel the company hadn't yet filmed was *Casino Royale* – Fleming's first novel. An introduction to the character of Bond, the story describes how the spy gets his double-0 number and licence to kill. The Americanised adaptation was shown on TV in 1954 (with our hero referred to as 'Jimmy Bond') and a later version starring David Niven as Bond appeared in 1967.

'When they decided to make the film series they obviously wanted to start with the first one,' explained Barbara Broccoli, who inherited the Bond franchise from her father Albert 'Cubby' Broccoli. 'But the rights weren't available so they started with *Dr No*.' Both the film versions that followed bore little resemblance to the original novel.

'It was done as well as a spoof – I think that's the only way you could describe it,' she continued. 'Cubby wanted to make the real story but he just accepted that it probably wasn't going to happen. I like to think that I'm doing it for him.'

As Bond's 50th anniversary drew closer EON were keen to film the tale that had started it all. Unfortunately, one obstacle stood in their way: Sony Pictures Entertainment retained the film rights and had even commissioned their own version and a rival series. Legal wrangling ensued, with a final settlement reached in 1999. Sony agreed to hand over the rights to Bond in exchange for certain rights to *Spider-Man* (2002). The only problem that remained was who would be cast in the lead role?

In October 2004 ripples of excitement spread throughout Hollywood when it was announced that 53-year-old Pierce Brosnan, the current Bond, would not be reprising his role. After four outings in the part, it would be difficult for him to play the young agent embarking on his first mission. 'It's absolutely over,' confirmed the actor. Now the search was on for a younger, 21st-century 007.

EON considered a number of eligible candidates but it

was a lengthy and difficult process. Inevitably, not everyone would be pleased with the final choice. Bond fans were notoriously fanatical and set in their ways. The director Martin Campbell, also responsible for 1995's *GoldenEye*, was all too familiar with the problem. Back then Pierce Brosnan had been the new boy on the block, replacing Timothy Dalton.

It was a tough period for Bond. In a post-feminist, post-Cold War society, audiences were beginning to question the character's relevancy. Campbell was given the task of bringing Bond back into the 21st century, but he quickly realised that it would be difficult to tamper with tradition. Fans were fond of Bond and his old-school mannerisms. 'I was in New York with *GoldenEye*,' he recalled, 'and I was invited to one of those fan conventions. I was naïve enough to think those people didn't take this kind of thing seriously. And I went on stage and I was amazed at the questions... They *hammered* me!'

Criticisms thrown at the director included his choice of Brosnan, the exchange of Bond's trademark Aston Martin for a BMW and that Bernard Lee would be dropped from the character of M in favour of a woman!

Although, over time, fans had warmed to Judi Dench, they were still fiercely protective of Bond. Campbell and his team knew they would have to tread carefully. The tabloids were rife with rumours as to who might be the next candidate. Along with Colin Farrell, Ewan McGregor and Australian actors Eric Bana and Hugh Jackman, Daniel Craig found his name on the shortlist.

Daniel was shocked to hear the news. Never in his wildest dreams had he imagined portraying the character. 'It's kind of, wow! But it's never been one of my ambitions,' he admitted. 'You can't really have ambitions to do something that only five people have done... Someone said there have been more men on the moon than have played 007!'

Hailing from a working-class background with a comprehensive school education, Daniel hardly fitted the privileged mould sketched out by Ian Fleming. His craggy complexion and blond hair also seemed a million miles from the archetypal 007. By all accounts, he was the wild card.

Once the rumours were out, Daniel knew there was no point in denying that he was a contender. 'I've spoken to Barbara Broccoli [daughter of the original Bond producer Cubby Broccoli] because I know her,' he admitted. Overnight he became A-list celebrity fodder. At the time he was doing promotional work for *Layer Cake*, but at every press junket all anyone wanted to know was whether he would be donning a tuxedo and bow tie in the near future. 'It's like the time I went to do a press talk on *Layer Cake*. Everyone was given the brief not to ask me about Bond. And everyone asked me about Bond – and that's cool,' he said.

That remained to be seen. If he was honest, he wasn't sure whether he really wanted the role. It would be a life-changing career move and one that should be treated with trepidation. 'I don't know, I really don't,' he sighed, when asked about his ambitions. 'Yes, it's film to film for me. But I would still have to apply the same rule: if you go for something that is incredibly exposing, is that going to be detrimental to what your ambitions as an actor are? That is the only criterion.'

Most importantly he could never lose sight of his overriding ambition 'to continue testing myself but also trying to find what I do as political as possible. I think every piece of cinema is a political message… I'm looking for something that changes. I mean, as far as I'm concerned, every piece of art or whatever you do should have some sort of political import. By political, I mean the wider meaning of politics. Something that has something to say and hopefully engages a little debate when you walk out of the cinema.'

He also had several problems with the actual script and the current characterisation of James Bond. 'Well, the emotional level is not there and that's important for me. I'd want that to change but I don't know how ready they'd be to change that,' he mused. 'I don't know how much of a fight that would be. You'd have to flip the whole thing on its head. I think they want to do that seriously but it's a big machine and it makes a lot of money. So why would you change something that makes a lot of money?'

But the production company continued deliberating their choice of actor. As the weeks turned to months, sceptics wondered whether it was, in fact, a deliberate ploy to drum up interest in the flagging franchise. More than likely Pierce Brosnan's agents were hard at work negotiating a more favourable deal. Growing tired of the indecision, journalists grilled Daniel for answers.

'Well, I can't go into details but I just think they're in a huge sort of transition period. They need to do something and, if I was being honest, I'd love to play him but I'm just not sure it's possible. The problem is, it's always looking back. It has to because it was brilliant when it started, and it slowly got worse and worse. I think Pierce Brosnan did a fantastic job when he came in, but that was ten years ago. And the world is a much more cynical place now. And spies are fucking nasty cunts, and I feel that's the way they have to go.'

Despite his criticisms, Daniel sympathised with the scriptwriters. They were faced with an incredibly difficult task. 'I don't know how you do that. I don't know how you make it so you fear for that man's life... Because why worry? It's James Bond! He's Superman, for fuck's sake!'

Fame was another consideration. Even as a middling celebrity, Daniel had struggled to protect his privacy. Were he to be named the next James Bond, there would be no hope of conducting his personal life behind closed doors. Was he really ready for that level of fame? Perhaps it would be better to hang back in the shadows and be content with low-budget arthouse movies.

'I don't want to be a celebrity because that sucks,' he stated. 'It's just madness. But how do you quantify fame? I'm not into self-promotion; my front room is nobody's business. If you invite someone into your front room, you can't be surprised when there are suddenly people outside your windows with cameras.'

Having made several high-profile films, his treasured

*Above left*: A school photograph of Daniel Craig from 1979, when he was attending Hoylake School in the Wirral.

*Above right and below*: Aged 15 appearing in the Heswall Woolgatherers Amateur Dramatic Society production of Alan Bleasdale's *No More Sitting on the Old School Bench*.

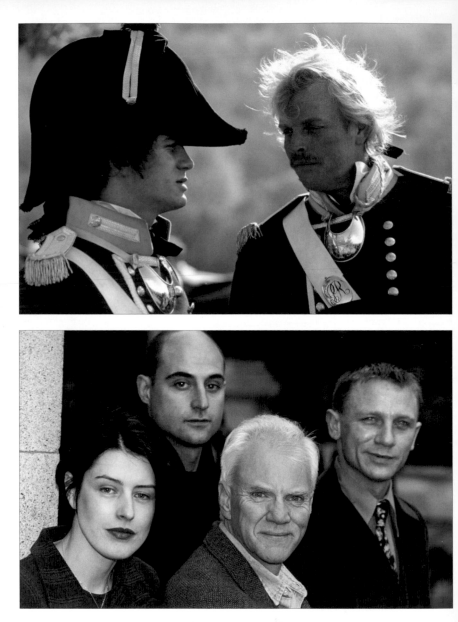

*Above*: In 1993, Daniel appeared in the major TV drama *Sharpe's Eagle* with Gavan O'Herlihy. He played a belligerent officer determined to insult and undermine the hero Sharpe, played by Sean Bean.

*Below*: The hugely popular BBC television drama *Our Friends In The North* demonstrated Daniel's excellent acting talents. He's pictured here with cast members Gina McKee, Mark Strong and Malcolm McDowell.

*Left*: A still from the Hollywood blockbuster *Road to Perdition*. Daniel played Paul Newman's character's biological son, Connor Rooney.

*Right*: Having read the works of poet Ted Hughes all his life it seemed only right that Daniel would play him in the film *Sylvia*, with Gwyneth Paltrow as the leading lady.

*Left*: Daniel landed the lead role in Matthew Vaughn's directorial debut *Layer Cake*. He's pictured here in the famous steamy bedroom scene with Sienna Miller.

*Above*: A scene from the 21st James Bond movie, *Casino Royale*. Mads Mikkelsen is far right.

*Below left*: In the classic James Bond tuxedo.

*Below right*: With the Bond girls Eva Green *(left)* and Caterina Murino *(right)*.

*Above*: Demonstrating his versatility, Daniel undertook a variety of roles after Bond. *Main picture*: Starring in *Infamous*, a film about the writer Truman Capote and his 1966 novel, *In Cold Blood*. (Left to right) Toby Jones, Daniel Craig, Lee Pace and Peter Bogdonavich.

*Inset*: Portraying convicted murderer Perry Smith, who embarked on a relationship with Capote.

*Below*: A still from *The Golden Compass*, a film based on the first instalment in Philip Pullman's *His Dark Materials* trilogy.

*Above left*: An action-packed scene from *Quantum of Solace*.

*Above right*: With co-star Rooney Mara at the premiere of *The Girl with the Dragon Tattoo*.

*Below*: Daniel with his *Cowboys and Aliens* co-stars Olivia Wilde and Harrison Ford.

*Above*: Javier Bardem played one of the greatest Bond villains of all time when he appeared alongside Daniel in *Skyfall*.

*Below*: Although Daniel would appear in *Sceptre* in 2015, this was to be Judi Dench's final appearance as M, leading to some of the most emotional scenes ever witnessed in a Bond film.

*Above left*: Daniel Craig is now happily married to Rachel Weisz, after starring alongside her in *Dream House* in 2011.

*Above right*: An uncomfortably chilly photocall alongside Lea Seydoux and Dave Bautista for *Spectre*.

*Below left*: Monica Bellucci plays the oldest Bond girl ever – her casting led to Weisz describing Daniel as 'lucky'.

*Below right*: Always aware that acting isn't the most important thing in the world, Daniel has tried to put his fame to good use and was appointed by Ban Ki-moon as an Anti-Mine Advocate for the UN.

anonymity was already waning. 'It's getting a bit battered,' he sighed. 'All I know is that I've tried to protect my privacy as long as possible and I will continue to do so because it's got fuck all to do with anybody. I mean, this hasn't. This is what I do and is part of what I do for a living, but the rest of it is nobody's business! The same as nobody's private life is anyone's business, even if you are in the public eye. There should be a clearly defined line and I don't think it's brain surgery to try and figure that out. It's fairly simple. There's privacy and then there's public life. If you choose to be in the public life, maybe you open yourself up to all sorts of rubbish. But if you don't, I think that should be respected.'

From experience, he knew full well just how persistent the press could be. 'I've had various members of the press knocking on my family's door at various hours of the morning. I hate to say but my father has lots of guns...' For the most part, though, he did his best to avoid the typical paparazzi haunts. 'If you go to these restaurants here, you'll get your photograph taken, but I don't like these restaurants. If I get caught, it's unusual. On the whole, I don't think people are that interested in just me, so I don't get bothered that much.'

He was also concerned that a big-budget Hollywood blockbuster would alienate the small-time independent film directors who had offered him so many great roles in the past. 'I'd like to be able to be in both big and small movies and I wonder that, if I do Bond, whether or not directors would employ me, which would be a big shame.'

Despite his reservations, the lure of playing James Bond was too difficult to resist. When pressed on the issue, he had to admit that he would probably consider the role seriously. 'You'd be stupid to not think about it. If something were to happen with it, I would certainly think about it.... I played James Bond in the playground. Every fucking kid I know played James Bond! And if it was the right deal, yes, I would.'

As speculation continued he mulled over his options. However, a chance meeting with Pierce Brosnan in February 2005 provided some clear direction when the pair were guests at the BAFTA Awards ceremony. 'He was on the same table as me,' recalled Daniel. 'I thought, I have to talk to him. I would feel like a dick if I didn't.' He took the opportunity to ask the former Bond's advice. 'It's a possibility – what do you think?' he asked. Smiling, Brosnan took his hand and replied, 'Go for it! It's a ride.'

For the most part shrouded in secrecy, casting for the Bond movie was like nothing Daniel had ever experienced before. All the candidates were required to read the scene from *From Russia With Love*, where Bond steps out of the bathroom armed with a towel around his waist and a Walther PPK, only to find a beautiful stranger on his bed. Every would-be James Bond – including Sean Connery and Roger Moore – had tested that very same scene. 'It's a tradition, apparently,' Daniel explained. 'Why? I've never got it out of Barbara yet.' The director Martin joked that it was partly down to the fact that the new film script was rarely ready at that early stage in the game.

As far as Daniel was concerned, his screen test was a disaster. Walking out of the audition studio, he felt extremely dissatisfied with his performance. 'Oh God,' he groaned, when asked. 'If she [Barbara] hasn't destroyed that piece of film yet, I hope she will. It's *awful*! I don't want anybody to ever see it. My eyes were just swimming.'

At least he could console himself with the fact that he hadn't been asked to recite the 'famous five words' usually associated with Bond. 'If I'd had to say that line on the first day, I think I probably would have crumbled!' he shuddered.

The audition completed, he tried to block the whole thing out of his mind. Given the amount of press interest, however, this was almost impossible. Every day he would open the paper to read another speculative story about his involvement in the project.

'I'm not tired of it,' he said with a laugh in response to the daily drip-feed of rumours. 'Look, it's a high-class problem to have. But there's an awful lot of smoke and very little fire at the moment – there's a lot of names in the pot and I happen to be one of them. And you know, I've said to people that I'd be very silly not to give it very careful consideration. But we're not that far down the line yet. They've got a lot of working out to do; what they want to do. And if the call comes, obviously we'll think about it very carefully. But it's… You know, the British press… I love them but they've decided that they wanted to call it and they've called it.'

Although he didn't wish to raise any false hopes, Daniel

knew how pivotal the 007 role could be to his career. Up until then all his roles had been relatively small fry. 'I'm potentially worth a lot of money,' he admitted. 'But I've got to go and make something that's worth a lot of money. I'm just not known in the States. Well, I'm known, but not in an "Oh my God, it's him!" way.' For years he had been touted as 'the next big thing', a label that always amused him. 'I read my press and I see "Daniel Craig – *Layer Cake* breakthrough movie" and I think, "I'm thirty-fucking-eight!"' he exclaimed.

Over time he had not only matured as an actor but his outlook on the whole industry had also changed. 'I'm sort of in a bizarre situation,' he mused. Finding himself halfway through being a serious actor and a box-office film star. 'When I was young I had ideas about wanting to be a star, but then as I got older I went, "No, fuck that! I want to be an actor," and I wanted to be serious. And now, suddenly I'm thirty-eight and I'm being looked at as someone who could be very successful. And I'm like, "Fuck, how did that happen?" It's a bizarre kind of way that it's come around because it didn't really shoot off for me in the beginning.'

Confident in his abilities, he knew that he was in a strong position. 'I have a situation which is easily enviable,' he admitted. 'And I would like it to be more enviable; not in the sense of being more successful but in the sense of getting it right – not to make people jealous but that they might say, "Oh, that's one way of doing it."'

Enjoying the ride so far, he was in no hurry to move on.

He waited patiently as EON continued to deliberate over their choice of actor. He'd waited this long for a major breakthrough and a few months more would do him no harm. Besides, there were plenty of new and interesting projects to be getting on with.

Later in 2004 he made a brief appearance in *Sorstalanság* (2005), a historical drama adapted from Nobel Prize winner Imre Kertesz's masterpiece about a young Hungarian Jew caught up in the Second World War and then The Holocaust. Filmed in sepia, black and white and colour, shades changed to fit the mood of the film. Daniel starred as an American GI who liberates the camp at Buchenwald, where 14-year-old Gyorgy has been imprisoned. A touching film, it won several awards.

His next major project saw him reunited with the director John Maybury (*Love Is The Devil*) in *The Jacket* (2005). Jack Starks, a military soldier posted in Iraq, is shot in the head and presumed dead. But when he blinks his eyes open in a morgue a doctor is called. Suffering amnesia, he is discharged from the army. A year later he is hitchhiking from Vermont when he helps a drunken woman and her daughter to fix their car. They offer him a lift but when stopped by the police the driver shoots an officer dead. Jack is also shot in the head and incriminated by the killer. He is taken to court and sentenced to a mental institution for criminals. Dr Thomas Becker begins to experiment on Jack, dressing him in a jacket and locking him in a drawer for corpses in a morgue. Jack travels into the future, where he meets Jackie Price (Keira Knightly) and falls in love. He is convinced that the only way to escape the institution is through the jacket.

'John's a very, very good friend of mine,' explained Daniel, who was cast in the role of Rudy Mackenzie. 'If he has something, he always lets me look at it. With *The Jacket*, Adrien [Brody] was cast in the lead, and Keira [Knightly] was cast, and he said there's this part, and I'm like, "John, I'm there!"' His portrayal of the sad, delusional schizophrenic was extremely moving. It was proof, once again, that the actor was capable of handling emotionally complex roles. 'It was a week's filming in Glasgow and I was quite happy to go out there and shoot it for him [John]. And who wouldn't want to play a mental patient in a hospital? It's fun!

'I play the only speaking-part mad person! There were lots of dribblers in there too, you'll notice. I think he's less mad than he makes out to be. I think he's sick and troubled, and he's been tortured. He's been put through the mill so I think his rambling is more about keeping people at a distance than him being genuinely mad.'

It wasn't the first time that he had portrayed a schizophrenic character. In preparation for *Some Voices* (2000) he had undertaken research into mental health. 'I did use a lot of what I'd done on *Some Voices*,' he admitted. 'I'd spoken to a lot of people, a lot of healthcare professionals, about mental health. The scary thing is when you start looking into mental health... we walk a thin line. What we do is try and make sense of our world and lives. And if there is a chemical imbalance in the brain or you're suffering from abuse as a child, if you do not deal with it, the thin line we walk on called sanity is very easy to fall off. We've all had dark moments – it's just that someone who is mentally ill tends to fall off quite a long way. It's terrifying. You look at schizophrenia and you go, "Well, I've got five of the six symptoms!" It's not too far from everybody's reality anyway.'

The two men had struck up a relationship of mutual admiration while working together on *Love Is The Devil*. 'He's truly individual as a filmmaker, I think. He's also a very close friend and that all goes along with it. I trust his taste. With this film, he's taken this very strange script, which has been around for a while and people said would be unmakable, and has made it into something that – beyond being visually beautiful – is entertaining and scary. You can't define it. And that's what John Maybury is all about. He doesn't make it easy for an audience but you come away thinking, Well, I haven't seen anything like that before.'

He was especially fond of Maybury's approach to cinematography. 'John's visual style is so individual. If you watch it, and see it again, his artwork is all over the walls. There are little clues everywhere about things that are going on within the movie. John works with a team that he works with all the time, and he's very particular about that.'

As part of the role he was required to dye his hair black. 'John's visual image was Jack Kerouac. It was something he'd wanted and we'd agreed on, and it would be nice to go with that. He does have a habit of always wanting to dye my hair dark in films.'

Unfortunately, *The Jacket* did little for Daniel's profile in the States. Billed as a horror movie, it failed to attract the right audiences. 'Which is a shame,' Daniel sighed. In his opinion, the film reached into far greater thematic depths. 'I think what John has very successfully done with it is to take this very convoluted plot and bring out the essential element of the story. It's a story about redemption. It's about someone who's trying to figure out their life, trying to find the point where it went wrong, then trying to fix it... I think it's a reflection of American society. This man who had major problems has fought for his country... Actually, it's a reflection of Western society much more than American society. It's not deeply political but, if you start to pick at it, you would find there are major political references in there.

'What I hope is that it'll have some legs and that people will see it. Once it gets on DVD people will watch it for what it is. It's not a horror film. It's a psychological thriller and it's also a bit of a fairy story, to tell you the truth.'

Filming *The Jacket* wasn't just a creatively rewarding experience for Daniel. It also introduced him to new love Satsuki Mitchell, who was executive producer for the movie. Employed by the 2929 production company, her past credits included *Criminal* and *Godsend* (2004). Impressively, Daniel managed to keep his relationship with the American dark-haired beauty under wraps. Their first public appearance together would be almost a year later.

Sources close to the couple reported their relationship was going well. 'Daniel always needs a committed woman in his life back home but he likes to enjoy his freedom,' said one anonymous friend. 'Satsuki understands that a man like Daniel will never agree to be on a ball and chain. She lets him get on with it and come back to her later when he's ready.'

Unfortunately, though, their fledgling relationship would be put to the test when reports in the tabloids surfaced that Daniel was having an affair with his former *Layer Cake* co-star Sienna Miller. For the past few years she had enjoyed a high-profile relationship with the actor Jude Law. The pair had met while filming *Alfie* in 2004. Hailed as the luckiest woman alive, Sienna had been plunged into the spotlight. Finding fame for all the wrong reasons, she struggled to establish herself as a credible actress in her own right. Unfortunately, she could never quite wrestle free from her associations with Law.

Prior to dating Sienna, Jude Law was married to actress and fashion designer Sadie Frost. Although passionate, their relationship had been tumultuous and their much-publicised divorce was headline news. Moving in the same social circles, Daniel had become close friends with Jude and Sienna. They were spotted buying groceries together in Primrose Hill and would often drink together in the same pubs.

Since filming *Layer Cake*, Sienna had developed a close bond with Daniel. He offered her both professional and personal advice, and she would often turn to him in times of need. One such occasion arose when it transpired that Jude had been cheating on her with 25-year-old nanny Daisy Wright. Daisy had been employed by Jude and his ex-wife Sadie to take care of their three young children. An extremely affable character, she fitted effortlessly into the household. When Jude was sent to New Orleans to film his new movie *All The King's Men* (2006), it their suggested that Daisy should accompany him.

According to newspaper reports published much later, Sienna and Jude had been experiencing problems in their relationship. Jude felt that Sienna was devoting too much time to her social life at the expense of her newfound family. Hitting an all-time low, he turned to Daisy for support. One thing led to another and the pair ended up in bed together. This affair continued for several months until they were eventually rumbled by Jude's ex-wife Sadie and Daisy was fired.

The ease with which Jude erased Daisy from his life left her heartbroken and angry. When journalists approached the nanny several days later, they found her in a vulnerable position. Not wishing to be miss-quoted, she sold her story to the press under the direction of PR guru Max Clifford. Overnight the anonymous nanny became a household name. When Sienna sat down to breakfast the following morning, she opened the papers to find a blow-by-blow account of the affair. She immediately broke off her engagement to Jude, declaring him a liar and a cheat.

At the time she was appearing in *As You Like It* in London's West End. Although work served as a distraction, unfortunately it also gave the press ample opportunity to pinpoint the young star's every move. Eventually Sienna agreed to forgive Jude and give their relationship a second shot, but she still felt extremely hurt. Not wishing to see her upset, close pals rallied round for support. One of those friends happened to be Daniel Craig.

Wishing to console Sienna, he invited her out to dinner at The Ivy. During the course of the evening he cracked jokes in an attempt to bring a smile to his sad friend's face. After a few drinks, the pair agreed to go on to the Elysium nightclub, not wanting the night to end quite yet. Aware of prying eyes, they left the restaurant through separate exits. Daniel was then spotted dropping Sienna back at her mum's house at 7am the following morning. Rumours of a romance started to spread.

Sienna lashed out at reports, claiming they were insensitive to her situation. By now she was sick and tired of intruding journalists. 'We did a film together three years ago and have been great friends ever since,' she fumed in exasperation. 'And apparently you're not allowed to have male friends!'

But her efforts were to no avail. The tabloids persisted with their story and, days later, claimed to have amassed evidence to suggest Sienna had been enjoying a two-week fling with Daniel behind Jude's back. 'Jude is incandescent with rage,' a source told the *News of the World*. 'He thinks Sienna's a hypocrite for giving him such a hard time over his affair when she'd been carrying on with Daniel. They vowed a pact of fidelity after Daisy's affair but she's broken it. To make matters worse, Daniel is one of Jude's oldest pals and he feels utterly betrayed.' Angered by reports, Jude threw Sienna out of their £4 million house and once again the relationship was off.

Allegedly Jude phoned Daniel in a fit of fury and 'gave him both barrels'. The *Daily Mail* reported, 'Jude is devastated and depressed; he is not in a good state right now. Sienna's friendship with Daniel has always made Jude nervous but he cannot believe that she has done this to him – especially as she always goes on about the importance of monogamy.

'A friend told Jude about the fling last week and when he confronted Sienna she admitted it was true. He is just so low, and feels as though he has bent over backwards trying to win her trust and this is how she has repaid him. Ever since he confessed to his affair with Daisy, he has done everything he can to make it up to Sienna. But since they got back together, she has treated him so badly – going out all the time and not telling him where she's been going. Now this...'

Another report even suggested that Daniel and Sienna had been romantically involved as far back as the filming of *Layer Cake*. 'Sienna and Daniel became exceptionally close during the filming of *Layer Cake*. When Jude and Sienna subsequently got together, Daniel and Sienna's relationship deteriorated badly, to the extent that they stopped speaking,' a source told the *Mail*.

'Sienna only recently confessed just how close she and Daniel once were – much to Jude's upset. Then, after she and Jude split up, she arranged to meet Daniel and even cooked him an amazingly romantic Thai meal complete with an exotic Thai massage. When Jude found out about the meal, he was livid – because Sienna had done exactly the same thing for him only weeks earlier. Sienna is not at all contrite about her affair with Daniel and isn't upset about the split. She even told Jude, "You and I are one of a kind," because she believes neither of them is capable of fidelity.'

Sienna herself refuted the claims as being nonsense. Wishing to stay out of the affair, Daniel kept a low profile. The situation was an unpleasant reminder of the press furore surrounding his supposed relationship with Kate Moss. Both Daniel and a spokesperson for Sienna claimed the newspaper reports were false. 'Sienna and Daniel Craig are very good friends and have been for a while... It's all just too ridiculous for words,' said a close friend. 'There is nothing going on between me and Daniel,' reiterated Sienna. When asked about the alleged affair in interviews years later, Daniel would merely respond, 'Oh fuck off!'

In the meantime, he had more pressing issues to deal with. After turning down a lucrative role in the TV adaptation of *Biggles*, he started work on *Archangel* (2005). Set in communist Russia, Daniel played an academic in search of Stalin's notebook, allegedly snatched from the dictator's deathbed by the head of the NKVD.

After a short break, he embarked on another epic project, Steven Spielberg's *Munich* (2005). A political drama, the film was based on a true story about 11 Israeli athletes who were taken hostage and murdered by a terrorist group called Black September during the 1972 Olympic games. In retaliation the Israeli government recruited a group of Mossad agents to track down and execute those responsible for the attack.

Starring alongside Eric Bana, Daniel was cast in the supporting role as Steve, a South African Jew recruited to the squad. Initially hungry for revenge, over time he begins to question the moral justification of their actions. 'It's about how vengeance doesn't fucking work,' summarised Daniel. 'Blood breeds blood.'

Now considered a serious actor of fine pedigree, he received a personal invitation from Steven Spielberg to star in the film. 'I got the call to go and see him in Paris. And I did,' he recalled. Stunned, he couldn't quite believe what was happening. Instructed to board the next Eurostar to Paris, he was given no further information. He began to question whether the project itself was, in fact, a piece of high-class espionage. 'I didn't fucking believe it because they were being so secretive. I thought it was a fucking joke! I thought I'd get there and they'd say, "It's fucking Stefan Spielberg, mate – porn producer."'

When he arrived, he was taken straight to Spielberg's office. Once the director himself had explained the project and sworn Daniel to secrecy, he turned to the actor and offered him the part. 'He basically said, "I'd like you to do this. I'd like you to get involved."' Daniel didn't know what to say. He had at least expected to audition for the role first. 'I went prepared. I had like four or five pages of a script – that was about it. I expected to go in and read, but I just went in and we had a chat.'

Later he admitted that he had been nervous about the encounter with one of Hollywood's biggest directors. But as it turned out, he had nothing to worry about. The story instantly appealed and he knew he had to be involved. On leaving Spielberg's office, he headed straight for the nearest bar and celebrated with a few beers. By now this had become something of a tradition.

When *Munich* was finally released in the US in December 2005, it caused a great deal of controversy. Even though it was set in 1972, the themes of revenge, terrorism, religious warfare and unrest in the Middle East were very applicable to the current political climate.

'The movie is about revenge and you get to see how revenge works and how it's completely cyclical,' explained Daniel in defence of the film. 'You can compare it to the Northern Ireland conflict or take it back to Oliver Cromwell if you really want to. The only way to end a crisis like this is to start talking, and not just on a civilian level, but at the highest level possible and, until that happens, there will be continual violence. I believe that human beings really do want to live in peace. Steven has described this movie as a "Prayer for Peace" and I think that's a lovely expression. It's a prayer, not for reconciliation but for dialogue. Reconciliation is too hard a concept – too many people have been hurt.'

Prior to filming, he knew *Munich* was likely to cause a great deal of controversy. The script dealt with extremely sensitive matters but he was no stranger to films of a complex nature and enjoyed tackling subjects other actors might shun away from. 'When we were shooting the Beirut scene we had young Palistinian actors and young Israeli actors and, at the end of the day, we all went out for a drink together,' he recalled. 'It was actually very moving because the guys said, "We would never get to meet usually." Despite being geographically very close, they were world's apart. Even on a small, but poignant level, I thought, "There's something the movie's done before we've even finished it." I'm just proud to be part of it. As an actor it's part of the job to do things that tackle the difficult questions.'

*Munich* certainly challenged his mettle as an actor – both on a high brow and more basic levels. Reading through the script he was horrified to discover he would actually have to sing! 'There was something in an early script that had mentioned me singing. It was actually a Beatles track, but it was going to cost an arm and a leg to get cleared. One of the producers came up and said, "What about 'Papa Was A Rolling Stone?'" and I had one of those moments where I was like, "Er, I don't remember how it goes." We had fifteen minutes of mumbling along, trying to remember the lyrics – I don't think I will be pursuing a singing career just yet!'

Ultimately, though, he was pleased with his efforts in the film. 'This is my opinion, and I have to say this, as it's obviously a very touchy subject, but I was bowled over by it. I think that any movie that raises a debate is a good thing. I think it's a film that needs a second look as a lot happens in it. I've only seen it once and I feel I need to see it again. The trouble is, when I go and see a movie which I'm in for the first time, I have a tendency to watch myself, which you can't help but do, but it can distract you from the story.'

It had been an eventful few months for Daniel, both professionally and personally. Having starred in *Munich*, he was now considered to be a major player in an exclusive circle of serious Hollywood actors. Although the new boy on the block, he was rapidly making progress. But one of his biggest learning curves had been in dealing with the press. By now he knew how to deal with the difficult tabloids. Much to their irritation, he refused to rise to cruel jibes and instead took greater satisfaction from simply smiling and walking away. It was a media training that was about to come in very useful for him. Very soon every aspect of his life would be under a microscopic glare. Although it had been on the cards for several months, he was about to be officially named the sixth James Bond.

## CHAPTER 9

# A BLOND BOND?

Ending almost a year of speculation, it was announced in October 2005 that Daniel Craig would be the sixth incarnation of James Bond. Ironically, it wasn't the production company EON who declared the news – but Daniel's mum!

Speculation was already rife that Daniel would be named the new Bond. Although it was not yet public knowledge, he had actually been offered the part several weeks previously. It was just a matter of time before the announcement would be made. However, one bright spark at the *Liverpool Daily Post* decided it was their duty to make national headline news and break the story first. With a bit of investigative work they managed to track down Olivia (Carol) Craig's home telephone number. Taking a chance, they tapped in the digits.

'Hello?' said Olivia, picking up the phone.

'Hi. Sorry to disturb you but we're calling about your son Daniel. Isn't it fantastic news?'

Caught off guard, Olivia wasn't sure how to react. 'Erm, yes, it is,' she replied.

She could have sworn the official announcement was not for another week or so! Perhaps they had brought the date forward.

'Obviously we are thrilled to bits,' she went on to say. 'It has come at a very good time in his career. He has worked extremely hard all his life and this would be his biggest populist role. I think he could bring something very interesting to the part. It will be life changing.'

By this point the paper had all the confirmation necessary to run a news story. Realising almost immediately that she'd been caught out, Olivia dropped the receiver in stunned silence. She was mortified. Daniel had told her about the role in strictest confidence. Even MI5 would have had trouble coaxing it out of her and now some young upstart on the local paper had managed to break her vow of confidence with a single phone call.

Slamming down the receiver, she instantly picked it up again and dialled her son. As she explained what had happened, she was trembling. However, she needn't have worried for Daniel knew only too well how crafty and underhand the press could be. In fact, he was far angrier that the newspaper had managed to put his mother in such a compromising position. 'The press fucked her!' he fumed. 'She was mortified. She'd known I'd had the role for three weeks and had been silent. And then these cunts...' He broke off, sensing his temper was escalating out of control. 'Sorry, I shouldn't go down that road! Really, it doesn't matter. What a great story! There's no better copy than that. But she got into a real state about it. It's a very old trick, but they did it.'

In light of the circumstances, EON prepared an official announcement for the press. The press conference took place on 14 October in London aboard the *HMS President* on the River Thames. It was an overcast day. Daniel made a dramatic entrance in a speedboat, accompanied by officers from the Royal Navy, to the sound of the James Bond theme music. Disembarking, he turned to the officers and said, 'I'd like to thank the Royal Marines for bringing me in like that, and scaring the shit out of me!'

To an audience of gathered journalists, Producer Michael G. Wilson revealed that 200 candidates had been considered in a search that lasted a year and a half. Director Martin Campbell promised the new Bond movie would be 'tougher, grittier and more realistic'. But he went on to reassure hardcore fans that key elements of the Bond character would remain intact.

'It's not a question of redefining, it's a matter of going somewhere they haven't before,' said Daniel. 'We want to do it the right way. It's going to take an approach we haven't taken before,' added Wilson. 'I love all the suits and bow ties, all of that. [In *Casino Royale*] you'll learn the ingredients of the Martini, perhaps how he gets the Aston Martin...'

He went on to reveal details of the exotic locations where filming would take place. 'We're filming in Pinewood in part, Prague in part, [the] Bahamas in part and down in Italy in part. It's very much a location-driven film.' When quizzed about the budget, director Martin Campbell said, 'The budget will probably be north of a hundred million dollars.' Michael Wilson added, 'We have plenty of action in this film. We'll be lucky to keep it within the budget of the last film [*Die Another Day* – 2002].' Throughout the room there were audible gasps as members of the gathered press attempted to digest the information.

Asked whether he was intimidated about following on from the previous five actors, Daniel said, 'I've got a big pair of shoes to step in from Pierce. I've just got to step up to the plate and deal with it.' But he knew this was a great opportunity. 'It hasn't sunk in yet. It's a responsibility but it's also a huge adventure so I want to get as much out of it as I can. It's a huge challenge and life is all about challenges. It's one of the big ones as an actor. He's an iconic figure in movie history and these things don't come along very often.'

Both Barbara Broccoli and Michael Wilson were confident in their choice of actor. They described Daniel as 'the definitive actor of his generation'. From very early on, they knew he would be perfect for the role. 'When we audition for the role of Bond, we ask actors to do the scene in *From Russia With Love*, where Bond meets Tatiana Romanova for the first time,' explained Barbara. 'The scene has everything you want to know about the potential Bond: drama, romance and action.'

Even though Daniel's own recollections of the audition were quite different, Barbara felt his performance was exemplary. 'He passed with flying colours,' she beamed. 'As soon as we met him, Daniel was the obvious choice for Bond. He is charismatic, versatile and sexy. The role is a big challenge but he has proven to us that he is an incredible Bond.'

Daniel was filming *The Invasion* (2007) with Nicole Kidman on location in Maryland when he received the phone call that would change his life for ever. It happened to be his day off and he was in the local grocery store picking up supplies. Glancing down at the screen on his mobile phone, he noticed a UK number: 'Hello, Daniel.' Immediately he recognised Barbara Broccoli's voice and his heart skipped a beat. He knew exactly the news that was coming. 'It's over to you, kiddo!' she exclaimed.

Struggling to contain his whoops of joy, he rushed out of the grocery shop and headed for the nearest liquor store, where he reached for a bottle of Grey Goose vodka. 'Just that, please,' he said to the shopkeeper, handing over several dollar bills. 'Celebrating something, are we?' said the proprietor with a raised eyebrow. 'Something like that,' Daniel grinned.

'I had a confidence about getting the role but that's because of the people around me who made me feel good about it. I was in Baltimore when I took the call. My first reaction was, I need a drink.

'Apart from getting blindingly drunk, which was my first

step [with Vodka Martinis], it really sank in a couple of days later when we did the press launch in London,' he went on. 'After that, I just thought, "OK, let's make the best Bond movie we can. Let's go on with the show."'

In actual fact, he had been offered the role several months previously but, lacking any faith in the script, he had turned it down. At first he thought the production team were playing a joke on him. 'I got approached by Barbara and Michael. They brought me into EON and I was laughing my tits off, saying, "You're having a laugh, aren't you?"'

Barbara Broccoli invited him for a meeting at the EON offices in Piccadilly, London. Daniel had spent all morning calmly preparing for the meeting. He had a good idea they were about to offer him the part, but he had several niggling reservations about it. 'There was no script to speak of, which to me [was] the most crucial element,' he later explained. While other actors would have jumped at the chance merely to add the James Bond name to their CV, he felt he had to treat this just like any other job. 'I couldn't actually consider this. In a fantasy, yes, but not in reality.

'We sat around the table and discussed things,' said Daniel. 'I told them Bond needed to change. Even if it fails, you have to turn it around.' But any fears he might have had about offending the franchise holders quickly evaporated. They eagerly took his comments on board. In the past he had proved his talents extended beyond acting and he was more than capable, if necessary, of getting his hands dirty behind the scenes.

Although some would argue that he was mad not to jump at the opportunity, Daniel was savvy enough to realise that the James Bond brand could do his career just as much harm as good. 'Potentially you cheapen your brand if you do this,' he argued. 'Some people I talked to were against it. They said, "You may lose the chance to do the stuff you want to do."'

In fact, it took almost 18 months for him to commit to the role. 'Barbara Broccoli and Michael Wilson approached me a long time ago, but I said I need to see the script.' In response EON produced a script written by Oscar-winning screenwriter Paul Haggis. Had Daniel been unhappy with the final version he would have walked away quietly without a second thought but, after an initial run-through, he had to confess that he was quite impressed.

'I genuinely wanted to hate it. I wanted to just read something that was lightweight, unemotional, unengaging and just a Bond movie. Then great, they'll go and make that, and the Bond thing moves on without me. But I read it, then read it again two more times immediately. I loved it – it was exactly what it should have been. It engaged me, it made me laugh; it did all the things you want. So then I thought, "I've got to throw myself into this," and I started asking people what they thought.' Now he was faced with a difficult decision, for he hadn't anticipated the role of James Bond being one of his ambitions. What had started out as an unlikely flight of fancy was now a very viable consideration.

'I was doing back-to-back work, the kind of work I want to do... But this is one of those opportunities you'd be crazy not to consider... Once I read it, I said to myself, "I have to have a go at this because if I don't do it, I'll regret it. I screen-tested while Barbara did a lot of winking at me, saying, "It's OK," so I had a little more confidence.'

Any fears of being dropped from the arthouse cinema circuit were also put to rest when Daniel approached several directors and asked for their advice. They laughed, telling him he had nothing to worry about. He was one of their most valued actors. Of course they would continue to offer him roles. 'I asked everybody!' he joked. 'Passers-by, the lot! "Hello, mate, can I talk to you about James Bond?" "Will you fuck off? Lunatic!" I asked Steven Spielberg. I said, "Would you employ me again if I did Bond?" He said, "Of course I fucking would!" Well, not quite with that accent – or that profanity. But he's a huge Bond fan. I asked everybody. It divided my friends a bit. Some of them said, "You're gonna fuck yourself here."'

But content that his career was in safe hands, Daniel signed up to a three-film deal, reportedly for a mammoth £8 million. 'Seems like a lifetime!' he sighed. 'But that is standard.'

At least he could rest assured he would be financially secure for the next few months. 'Most actors can't dream of that,' he acknowledged. He also reasoned that his raised profile could even help independent films. 'And if there is a movie being made and it lacks friends and my name is attached – then it might get made.' But he conceded Bond was unlikely to be an Oscar-winning role. 'No, I don't think you can get an Oscar for Bond!'

But wealth and fame weren't to be scorned at. 'I think you'd have to be stupid not to consider something like that if it came along,' he said of the role. 'If you're not in the game for doing something like that, then what *are* you in the game for? I mean, at a certain point, if an opportunity doesn't arise to be famous, wealthy and successful and whatever, then why are you doing it? It's a really big thing to think about. Because I'm sure by doing something like that, you lose out on an awful lot of other things. And if you gain things, it'll be a bigger fence around your house. There would definitely be a downside to it.'

Daniel's friends and family were thrilled at the news. His daughter Ella was especially excited. She couldn't wait to boast to friends about her father's new role. 'Ella's proud of me being James Bond. I think she's comfortable with it. I try to communicate all the time about it. I'm very happy with the film but I want to protect her.'

In fact, his only fear was that his fame might put Ella in the spotlight. He desperately tried to shield his family from any press intrusion. 'I don't bring her up in conversations much because the more I talk about her, the more the press have a right to take those photographs.'

Ella idolised her father and also had designs on becoming an actress. Daniel claimed to have no qualms about her following in his footsteps. After all, there were worse professions in the world! He simply hoped that he could offer her some good advice.

As the news of his appointment spread, old acquaintances appeared to give their opinion. One school friend, Anthony Lewis, told the *Sun* newspaper, 'Daniel was the least likely Bond as a kid. We were really young when we started going to the cinema to see things like *One Of Our Dinosaurs Is Missing* and Disney's *Robin Hood*. In those days Roger Moore was Bond and *Live And Let Die* was the big movie. It's almost unbelievable that he will be in the next Bond movie.'

His former drama teacher, Hilary Green, wasn't wholly shocked by his success. 'I'm not surprised he's done so well. James Bond is not the way I would have expected his career to go – I thought he would have been more of a serious stage actor. But I think he'll do extremely well as Bond. He has this ability to convey this menacing quality as well as a humorous side.'

Almost from the very start, Barbara Broccoli and Michael Wilson were convinced that Daniel was the right man to play Bond. No matter what they had to do, they were determined to cast him in the role. 'Barbara had no doubts,' confirmed Wilson. 'We live here; we are familiar with the actors here. I saw Daniel in *Our Friends In The North*; I saw him in *Elizabeth*, just walking down the hallway. I thought, "My God. He does have extraordinary presence – just look at the body of work." He can be a character actor but he can also be a leading man, and a star. It's a pretty unique thing. He seemed the obvious choice.'

Barbara Broccoli agreed. 'The idea of doing Bond's first mission, where he gets his double-0 status just wouldn't work with someone established. We were aware that Daniel is probably the most distinguished and versatile actor of his generation, but after meeting him it was clear that he would recreate Bond in a way that would be individual to him.'

As Martin Campbell would later point out, it was as if the script had been written specifically for Daniel. 'I wasn't prepared for how Daniel would play the role,' the director confessed. 'He's an actor who can do nothing but character, and it's a story that gives him the opportunity to do that. It's unlike any of the Bond stories – it's edgy and emotional.'

A memo from EON that was later leaked to the press revealed that Daniel had been head and shoulders above his rivals – in some cases quite literally! The memo revealed that Eric Bana (who played the Incredible Hulk, and Hector in *Troy*) was 'not handsome enough'; Hugh Jackman, who played Wolverine in the *X-Men* movies was 'too fey'; Colin Farrell 'too sleazy'; and Ewan McGregor 'too short'. The memo also went on to suggest that, although Barbara Broccoli was keen on Daniel, Michael Wilson was 'cool to him'. His preferred choice had been Hugh Jackman. But after some persuasion, Michael had to agree that Daniel was the best man for the job. 'The thing about James Bond is that each actor who has filled the role has brought his own style and imprint. With Daniel as our new Bond, I am thrilled to be returning to shepherd the new 007 in the Bond adventure.'

Daniel claimed to have no prior knowledge of the other candidates being considered for the role. 'I don't know who Barbara and Michael saw,' he protested. 'I wasn't interested. They asked me if I wanted to know. I said, "I don't give a shit!"' In a typically humble manner, Daniel refused to believe this was a one-man race. 'I'm sure they considered everybody. Barbara says she didn't but she could sell snow to the Eskimos! They do the sweep – that's their job. They're constantly on the lookout and they're probably on the lookout as we speak.' Despite Barbara's words of praise, the modest actor refused to be complacent. 'One always has to have one eye over your shoulder. I don't know what the truth is, but I know it's not because I'm two inches taller than Ewan. We're about the same height!'

When pressed to reveal details of his actual height, Daniel gave the flippant response, 'In heels or out? Five to six feet.' Such questions were quite ridiculous but he was by now growing accustomed to having to answer them. 'I'd like to think tall enough, but I'll never be tall enough in some people's eyes.'

Although in terms of ability he seemed to be the obvious choice, lookswise he didn't exactly fit the James Bond bill. In contrast to the 'full head of black hair' described by Ian Fleming, Daniel was the first blond 007. At just 6 feet tall, he was also the shortest actor to have ever played James Bond. 'It would go Sean Connery, George Lazenby, Roger Moore, Timothy Dalton, Pierce Brosnan... Daniel Craig? I wouldn't want to have to carry the rap for destroying such an amazing sequence,' he joked.

Daniel wasn't as suave as Roger Moore or indeed as bewitching as Sean Connery. In fact, he had more in common with one of Bond's rugged enemies! But Martin Campbell was confident that he could make the character his own.

'I think that Daniel is not the traditional pretty boy, handsome Pierce Brosnan-type,' he explained. 'He looks different to the stereotype of Bond but he's good looking in a tough, rugged way. He's more weighty than Pierce and, to be honest, he fitted the *Casino Royale* Bond much better than the other actors we saw. I mean, the image we have of Bond is false – it's almost entirely created by the movies. If you read the books, there's no humour. The guy smokes and drinks – he has doubts about himself. And Daniel can do that. Sean Connery had that presence on the screen of someone who could definitely take care of himself. Daniel has that too.'

Unfortunately, not everyone shared EON's faith in the actor. Although there had been grumblings in the past (Sean Connery was derided as a former coffin-polisher from Scotland), the criticisms levied against Daniel were unparalleled in the history of Bond. Never before had there been so much controversy over the casting of 007. For the most part, Daniel wasn't surprised. Bond fans were extremely protective of the brand. But the cruel jibes directed at him were beyond anything he could ever have anticipated.

'Bond means a lot to people, it really does. But some of the stuff that's been said is as close to a playground taunt as you're going to get. "You've got big ears!" Fucking hell! But ask anyone who's been bullied – they know it hurts.

It's not right. There's a part of me that would love to turn around and shove it up their arse!'

Daniel's physical appearance immediately came under fire. Many argued that he simply wasn't good looking enough to carry off the suave role of James Bond. His craggy and rugged complexion was ridiculed by certain tabloids who called him 'Mr Potato Head' or 'putridly ugly'. 'What can I say?' said Daniel, laughing. '"He's too ugly?" Well, my mother still loves me!'

His hair colour also turned out to be a major bone of contention, for his blond locks hardly fitted the bill of the dark-haired 007 that the fans had become accustomed to. Several anti-Daniel Craig websites cropped up, including craigisnotbond.com. One site even urged visitors to campaign against his appointment, showing doctored photographs of Daniel alongside so-called lookalikes. These included the Russian premier Vladimir Putin, Kramer from Seinfeld and Gollum from *Lord Of The Rings*. It was rumoured Daniel might even have to dye his hair brunette for greater authenticity. A spokesman for EON commented, 'There has been no decision made on his hair yet. He will undergo hair and make-up tests in January.'

But Daniel wasn't the first Bond to present filmmakers with a follicle challenge. Sean Connery was forced to wear a toupé to cover his bald patch while filming *Goldfinger* (1964) and Roger Moore required several different haircuts before the director was satisfied with his look, eventually thickening his hair for his final role, aged 58. Both Timothy Dalton and Pierce Brosnan also required hairpieces to restore their hairlines as they aged in their roles. However, Barbara Broccoli and Michael Wilson insisted that, regardless of his hairstyling, Daniel Craig would bring a 'contemporary edge to the role'.

But hair colour wasn't the only problem. Some reports even suggested Daniel lacked sufficient machismo to fulfil the role. 'There was a piece in the paper that said, BOND USES WET WIPES! he fumed. 'What should I use? Sandpaper? Yes, I use grooming products. They are given to me.' But the truth of the matter was that he didn't see why he should have to defend his actions. Raising an eyebrow, he smiled sarcastically. 'Occasionally I have a bit of a regime, then get bored with all that three-step T-zone bollocks!'

Another report jeered at him for wearing a life jacket on the speedboat that took him to his first press conference, and claimed he suffered from seasickness. 'You know, normally I wouldn't answer these questions,' fumed an exasperated Daniel. 'But fuck it! Every sailor I have ever known has got seasick on occasion!' When journalists approached him with the accusation, he simply responded, 'You haven't got a fucking clue! No, I didn't get queasy on a boat!'

One story claimed, falsely, that he couldn't drive a manual car. 'I can drive a manual car!' he fumed. 'I flogged the arse out of an Aston Martin DBS around Jeremy Clarkson's very own *Top Gear* track just recently.' He had no idea where the story could have originated. 'Completely fucking made up! I don't have a car at the moment, but the last car I had was an automatic. Sorry! Most posh cars *are* automatic! I think someone leaked it that I drove an automatic car, that immediately gets changed to, "Ha ha, you can't change gear."'

The reports grew ever more ridiculous – one suggested he had a fear of guns, while another story claimed he was frightened of water. Fed up with the lies, several of Daniel's colleagues leapt to his defence. 'I hate how people have been attacking Daniel Craig,' exclaimed his co-star Dame Judi Dench, cast as M in *Casino Royale*. 'It's despicable and it disgusts me. He is a fine actor and can bring something new and edgy to the role. His critics will be proved wrong.' Roger Moore, who played 007 in seven movies, pleaded with the critics to give Daniel a chance. 'He's a helluva good actor! No one has seen the film yet, so why attack him?'

Even his former lover Marina Pepper, who sold her story to *Closer* magazine, leapt to Daniel's defence. 'He'll be a huge hit as 007. He has so much charisma. He's a fantastic actor and is one of the sexiest men I've ever met. He'd be so hurt by people saying he's not good enough to play Bond. He's found the role of his dreams that will make him the star he always wanted to be. He may not have been the ideal boyfriend, but he'll definitely make an ideal Bond.'

Putting on a brave face, Daniel tried to ignore the cruel remarks. But it was impossible to remain completely indifferent. 'It was difficult. I was affected by the criticism – of course I was! At first I had this horrible kind of sado-masochistic fascination and the feeling that I had to read it all. A lot of it was name-calling and playground stuff but it was hard not to take it in on some level.'

What bothered him most was that people had hardly

given him a chance. 'I work very hard at what I do and I think that sometimes I actually do a halfway decent job at it. And usually when I'm in a movie, I go to the première and the following day there are good reviews and bad reviews, and I take them as they come. But this time I was being criticised by people who hadn't even *seen* my work. I was being attacked before I had done the work!' he exclaimed. 'My response was, "See the movie and then you can have the right to criticise."'

His immediate reaction was to lash out at the press but from past experience he knew it was better to remain calm. Losing his cool would only load them up with more ammunition. 'Believe me, I would love to answer this shit! I do read reviews. I have been on the websites; I *had* to! There is too much temptation. You write your emails and then you think, "Let's have a little look" – I had a very dark two or three days [when] I was very despondent. But I realised I was peeing into the wind. There was no way I could get into a tit-for-tat argument with people who said things like, "But you're… you're blond!" I really don't know how to answer that, except to say, "Well, yes, I am. And by the way, if you look at the Roger Moore films, you'll see he was pretty light-haired too." Fuck off, I've got more important things to think about! I vowed to work twice as hard to get it right.'

Essentially he had no option but to prove his critics wrong. 'I had two choices, either buckle under it, or knuckle down. Hopefully, the latter has happened. I just went, "OK, let's get on with it." The only way I can do that is to get this right. Believe me, no one cares about this more than I do. And at the end of the day, I've given a hundred per cent on this, I've given everything I could. And I'll present it and if people don't like it, stuff 'em! I'm not being rude, I'm just saying that I've given it my best shot.

'I only know how to do my job one way. I don't think that you can please all of the people all of the time. If I was doing my patter, I would say, "Don't worry, there is enough in here to entertain every Bond fan." And that is true. But these people think I'm gonna fuck with it in a way that is going to destroy it.'

Daniel had no intention of tampering with the Bond franchise. He understood the power of the brand. As he saw it, his responsibility was to remain faithful to the script and to portray the character as faithfully as possible. His ego was firmly in check. In the grand scheme of things, 007 was far greater than Daniel Craig. 'This is bigger than me,' he said, smirking. 'Nobody cares about this film more than I do. I know James Bond is incredibly important to a lot of fans. I want to make it clear that he is incredibly important to me as well. It's a particularly British movie we're doing here. It's British talent producing something special. It's going to give Bond fans – and believe me, I'm careful about that because I know what it means to them – it's going to give them what they want.'

# CHAPTER 10

# OO7 SHAPES UP

Published in 1954, *Casino Royale* was widely regarded as the best thing Ian Fleming ever wrote. Introducing the character of James Bond, it was written in the same year as John F. Kennedy (an admirer of Fleming's work) came to power, and it coincided with Hugh Hefner's launch of *Playboy* magazine. The latter appeared to shape Bond's worldly, hedonistic philosophy.

The Cold War thriller documented a battle of wits between a licensed-to-kill British agent and gambling addict, Monsieur le Chiffre, a bagman for the Soviet terror organisation Smersh. Unlike the slapstick, high-octane Bond movies of later years, *Casino Royale* was much darker and more serious. The film's torture scenes were particularly graphic.

The book featured a scene in a casino, where Bond

attempts to outplay the enemy at the gambling table. Allegedly the account was inspired by a real-life wartime experience. Ian Fleming was travelling through Lisbon when he stopped by at a casino. Nazi agents were on the premises and Fleming had the idea of clearing them out as a strike against Hitler's funds. Unfortunately, though, he himself was cleared out instead. His official biographer, Andrew Lycett, cast doubt on this account, however, suggesting that Fleming merely played against Portuguese businessmen.

Preparing a script for *Casino Royale* posed EON with a number of problems. Should they remain faithful to the book, or opt for a Bond movie in a similar vein to those already made? To cast Bond as a dark, brooding and amoral character would be at odds with the image cherished by so many fans. It was a brave move but EON felt they had no other choice but to represent the character portrayed by Fleming.

'Cubby always said when you're stuck, just go back to Fleming – go back to the essence,' stressed Barbara Broccoli. 'So instead of continuing on the path we were on, where the films were becoming more fanciful and effects-bound, we went back to the beginning.'

Both Barbara Broccoli and Martin Campbell were extremely committed to the project and felt a sense of responsibility to preserve the 007 heritage. 'We are the keepers of the flame,' Barbara grinned. 'We are preserving the whole history, the legacy. We are completely controlling and interfering. Everybody hates us – we are complete nightmares! Our dad used to say, "Don't let someone screw it up. It's OK if you do that, but not someone else."'

She and her step-brother Martin had inherited the Bond franchise from their father Albert Cubby Broccoli. At the age of 22 Barbara had begun work as an assistant director on *Octopussy* (1983). By 1983 she had worked her way up to become the producer of the Pierce Brosnan films. During the 1980s Martin Wilson co-wrote five Bond movies and played several minor roles in the films, including a soldier in *Goldfinger* (1964), a man in a casino and a Greek Orthodox priest.

One of the major issues surrounding Bond was relevancy. Were his attitudes outmoded? Did the world have any need or even interest in a secret agent equipped with high-tech gadgetry and a bewitching smile? 'People were saying that, with the Berlin Wall coming down, there was no more Cold War and Bond was not relevant any more,' shrugged Barbara. 'We said that he was *more* relevant. The world is ready for Bond – and even more so now! Look at the world situation and it's more serious than it was before.

'We just got to the point where the last film had taken the fantasy aspect to the limit,' she continued. 'Given the world situation, we felt we needed to do something more realistic and more serious, and this was the obvious thing for us to do. And we couldn't have an actor who had played the role before playing the first mission. Brosnan was a wonderful Bond but it wasn't about him, it was about making a decision to change the direction of the series.'

Martin Wilson agreed and called for a less frivolous approach. 'We wanted to change the style from fantasy to something a bit more gritty,' he explained. 'The only thing we have to be careful of is that the last four films have been suitable for children.' 'This film isn't,' admitted Barbara. 'Ten years old, eleven maybe... But it's too tough for kids, because we wanted to remain pretty much faithful to the book. That's the biggest challenge – preparing people for the fact that it's darker. There's still a lot of action and a lot of fun in it, but it's not really a kiddie ride.'

Moving away from the tried-and-tested Bond formula was a bold decision. The last of Pierce Brosnan's four films, *Die Another Day* (2002), took $456 million at the box office, more than any other 007 movie. But everyone involved in the project felt it was time for Bond to move on. EON weren't just hiring a new actor, they were adopting a whole new approach.

'*GoldenEye* was very much a traditional Bond,' explained Martin Campbell. 'There was a new actor but the story was very much along the normal Bond lines with all the usual scenarios, whereas this is much more down to earth. So no more exploding control rooms, no more unbelievable action sequences.'

'There are very few gadgets,' Daniel added. 'The Aston Martin DBS in this is a gadget, I suppose, and we kick the shit out of that. It's not gadget-less but there are fewer. It needed to change. You know, the last one took tons of money but, as Barbara and Michael said, "How long can we go on like this?" How long could you go on with that "man taking over the world" scenario? They just repeat themselves.'

He seconded the opinion that they shouldn't step over the same ground. 'All that was important to me was that we weren't going to get into a repeat of what had been done before,' he sighed. 'Not for any reasons of criticism but otherwise what's the point? If you are gonna start it all over again, then there's got to be a real sea change. But that doesn't mean this isn't a Bond movie. I mean, that's the criticism I've been getting on the net. It seems to me that people just think – well, they think I'm fucking ugly, but I'll have to live with that – they think it's gonna be fucked up. That's as far away from what's been done as you can possibly get. What's been done is very, very different, but it is religiously a Bond movie… It's *Casino fucking Royale*, for Christ's sake! It's the defining Ian Fleming book.'

In preparation for the role, Daniel studied his character at great length. It was his intention to create 'a darker, harder character – more what Fleming envisaged'. Ultimately, he was drawn to the movie because of the script's emotional complexity and the way his character evolves. 'We start right at the beginning of Bond's career when he has a lot of rough edges. He's a loner and he doesn't like to get involved with people. We wanted to base the story as much in reality as possible within the bounds of the franchise. As the story goes on, however, Bond becomes more refined.'

In preparation for the part he had gathered together

every Bond movie ever made and watched them back to back. 'I've got the box set and I went through them all religiously – I *had* to; not so that I can answer a question at a press conference but for tips. Some of those are great movies and any film-maker would be lying if they said they didn't copy off people, because you have to.

'I just wanted to go through them all. There was stuff that Sean did and Roger [Moore] did, and all of them did that were their little keys and you go, "Oh, that's cute, the way they did that..." It's not something to do consciously, but just to have a mental note of.'

He knew there was much to learn from his predecessors and he recognised the contributions they had all individually made to the character of Bond. 'Sean Connery set and defined the character,' he explained. 'He did something extraordinary with that role. He was bad, sexy, animalistic and stylish, and it is because of him [that] I am here today. I wanted Sean Connery's approval and he sent me messages of support, which meant a lot to me.'

Now it was Daniel's turn to shine and make his own additions to the Bond legacy. Although he was ready to take tips, he was also careful not to appropriate another actor's style. His Bond had to be very unique and individual, a 21st-century incarnation of the character. 'I watched every single Bond movie three or four times – then threw all that away once I started doing the role. I pushed all that behind me because I didn't want to do it unless I could take it in another direction and move forward. There's no point in making this movie unless it's different. It'd be a waste of time unless we took Bond to a place he's never been before.'

He purchased his own copy of *Casino Royale* and read it cover to cover. The Bond depicted by Ian Fleming seemed a million miles away from the tongue-in-cheek secret agents portrayed by Sean Connery and Roger Moore. He knew that he had a difficult task ahead of him. 'Believe me, I know the book and my first thought was, "How do we do this?" There's always been an unpleasant side to Bond. Sean Connery used to smack women around the face in films. Some of that is still in there; I think it has to be... There has to be a certain amount of cruelty. Certain things he does should be questionable. I think you should go, "Fuck, that's not nice!" After all, he was an assassin.

'All I was interested in was finding out why Bond is like that. It's not that you can forgive him, but at least you go, "Oh, OK. I see why he behaves like that." It seems to be morally corrupt; there's a reason for it because ultimately he's getting paid to kill people.'

He knew some people might find the new, hard-drinking, 70-cigarettes-a-day Bond difficult to accept, but the rugged and ruthless Bond of *Casino Royale* appealed to him. He was determined to slip under the skin of the character and discover his motivation. 'Bond always goes after the bad guys and there is no doubt in this movie that these are bad men but it is questionable exactly how he is going after them. His reasoning, his conviction, would be, "Well, they'll do it to me so I've got to do it to them first" And I think that should be a bit of a jolt.'

Subsequently, *Casino Royale* would be far more violent than any previous Bond movie. It was important to make the fight scenes more realistic than ever before. Daniel wanted to portray Bond as less of a cartoon superhero and more of a human being. 'There's a lot of blood,' he admitted. 'We wanted to use elbows and heads. Basically, if his gun runs out of bullets, he'll pick up a bottle. Most real fights last about thirty seconds or less, but they are exhausting to film. I had to make sure I was wincing when I got hit so it looks like Bond's in peril.'

Although Barbara Broccoli stressed the importance of making Bond a universal brand, she admitted the new film probably wouldn't be suitable for younger children. 'We talk about the level of violence all the time. You do see consequences of the violence all the time. In the last couple of films you would not necessarily see blood. You do in this film. We think that it is a responsible approach.'

As far as Daniel was concerned, EON had successfully restored relevancy to the character of James Bond. 'What's important, I think, is this: the world's in a mess at the moment and we really don't know who the good guys and the bad guys are. Now, it's not that he himself has relevance but the character of Bond is as ancient as they come – it's a character who's unflinching, who knows who the bad guys are and comes after them. And I think of that as refreshing at the moment. He represents honour.

'Look at the Middle East, what's going on at the moment. Who the fuck's right there? I mean, I have opinions about it but I don't know what the answer is as we never have – it's very fucking confusing. And I genuinely believe that that's the way we're supposed to feel at the moment: confused because then nothing's right or wrong. And if Bond represents something good, it's this: *he* would know the answer.'

Although scriptwriter Paul Haggis tried to remain faithful to Ian Fleming's book, there were several alterations. In the original story, a Russian agent squanders his bosses' money in an ill-advised venture and then tries to win it back in a game of baccarat. In the screenplay, the villain Le Chiffre (played by Mads Mikkelsen) is a money launderer for international terrorists who has blown millions of his clients' funds in several bad investments. In an attempt to recoup the funds, he organises a poker game for serious high rollers. Bond sits in, hoping to clear him out and force him into becoming an informer.

Daniel had first stumbled upon Mads Mikkelsen in a 1996 Danish thriller entitled *Pusher*, in which he played a small-time skinhead drug dealer called Tonny. 'I thought, "Wow – he's *seriously* hard!"' he exclaimed with wide-eyed admiration. 'I thought that was important. *From Russia With Love* (1963) is one of the best Bond movies because Robert Shaw looks like he could fucking take Bond out! And Mads has that quality!'

Martin Campbell clearly agreed with him and cast Mads as Le Chiffre without even an audition. He took to the role effortlessly. 'He's not the main character so we decided you don't need to know everything about this guy,' explained Mads. 'He's a young guy who turns up in the international chess arena at the age of sixteen or seventeen, according to the original book. He's probably an orphan and where he's from we're not sure – Algeria, Montenegro, we don't know. He's a professional chess and poker player but he's also in the business of laundering terrorist money, and he's good at it. He will do it for anyone – he doesn't care who they are.'

Defining the character was difficult but, together with the production team, Mads was left to draw his own conclusions from a skeletal outline in the original book. 'You have to make some specific choices when you do a character like that. And since he plays poker a lot and wears this poker face, we decided that Le Chiffre is a poker face. He doesn't let his feelings out and he's lived all his life like an iceman: in the shade, never outside, almost like a vampire. He's not an open, charming fellow; he doesn't use a lot of energy to get what he wants. It seems as if he almost doesn't care about anything.'

Careful not to fall into the trappings of cliché, Mads nevertheless embodied all the qualities of a classic villain. 'This is 2006,' he shrugged. 'I'm not out to rule the world, I'm not a mad scientist. I'm just an average villain who wants to make some money. He's a cynical bastard, for sure, but I'm still the baddie. I have the scar and all the baddie punchlines.'

As part of his preparation for the role, he undertook a crash course in poker. After all, the topic of gambling was central to the film's plot. 'I've played with friends for years in a friendly way – but we still try to take each other's money!' he chuckled. A professional teacher was hired on set to help Mads and Daniel learn the intricacies of the game. 'We also went to some casinos and some tournaments to soak up the atmosphere,' added Mads. 'It was very useful to pick up some of the movements with the chips. And, of course, once we would finish shooting, say at nine o'clock at night, we would then sit around for hours playing against each other.'

These impromptu poker games would usually involve members of the cast and crew who were at a loose end, and they quickly became addicted to the game. 'Daniel wasn't involved so much because he was working every single day,' revealed Mads. 'But we had a couple of days off, sitting around, so we played poker together.'

On most occasions Mads would emerge victorious. 'We had a great time!' he said, grinning. 'Mike Wilson [one of the film's producers] was playing with us and he is a very dedicated poker player. Barbara Broccoli didn't want to play because she wanted to be able to watch the drama of it without knowing anything about poker. And she did. So we'll play her later…'

When Daniel did have the opportunity to play, however, he usually gave Mads a run for his money. 'I hadn't played a lot before the shoot but I cleaned everybody out – twice. Once I'd done it the second time I said, "I can't ever play this game again," and walked away. There's a line in the film which goes, "You don't play your cards, you play your man opposite you," and that's what you do. And you fuck with them and, when you've fucked with them enough, you move on to the next person and fuck with them, fucking with people around the table. You don't ever give away what you're trying to achieve.'

Despite the rivalry both on screen and at the poker table, Mads had to agree his co-star was an appropriate choice for the role of Bond. 'It's not a great secret but Daniel is a fantastic actor,' he enthused. 'And not to diminish or comment on the other Bond films but I think this is more of an acting Bond than we have seen before. He is still very classical in the sense of his language and sophistication. But he is out of gadgets this time so you have to believe that he can kill people with his bare hands – he does have that presence and he is kind of scary.'

That much was true but the script also revealed a sensitive side to Bond. For the first time, he falls in love rather simply in lust with a woman. The lady in question is Vesper Lynd (played by French actress Eva Green), a treasury official sent by the government to ensure Bond doesn't squander public money. Unlike the womanising playboy characterised by Roger Moore and Sean Connery, Daniel Craig's Bond embodied a greater degree of vulnerability. At one point his desire is so great it almost destroys him. Particularly touching is a scene where Bond consoles Vesper by sitting next to her, fully clothed, in the shower, sucking her fingers one by one.

'When we meet him,' said Daniel, 'he's all the things that Bond is: he's selfish, an egomaniac, all the things that drive him on. He couldn't do his job without being single minded but this woman just knocks him for six. And that's very interesting.

'I approached the film with the idea that Bond's attitude to women is really just one of distrust,' he continued. 'That's why it's so fantastic that Judi is still playing M, because that female figure in the movie is so very important; that's what, hopefully, will let us get away with him being as sexist as he is. Having Judi in the film doesn't forgive it, but it gives it gravity. Because how could Judi Dench be wrong?'

In the run-up, the topic of Daniel's on-screen love interest was certainly a hot one. Who would be cast opposite him? Surely it was every young actress's dream to star as a Bond girl. Rumours ranged from the plausible to the ridiculous. There were whispers Daniel had urged producers to consider his old flame Sienna Miller. One story even suggested he was keen on the original Bond girl Jane Seymour. Now aged 57, she had starred opposite Roger Moore in 1973's *Live And Let Die*. One website suggested he was petitioning to bring her back. They quoted Daniel as saying, '*Casino Royale* was about early James Bond and I love the idea of him revisiting his past and meeting up with ex-loves. That has to include Jane Seymour. I'm a huge fan; I thought she was fantastic.'

Of course, there was no substance to these stories. Daniel agreed that Eva Green was perfectly cast as his love interest. 'I want to make it complicated,' he said of the love sequences. 'It was so important that Eva got the part because she was going to come along and do something that was unusual and equal to him.'

She was equally complimentary about her leading man. 'He's very professional and I learned a lot from him,' she beamed. 'He told me to take my time and be more assertive. He's just a beautiful, deep actor... He plays Bond as a real gentleman but he's also capable of being trashy and sexy and scary.'

The Italian actress Caterina Murino, who was cast in the role of Solange Dimitrios, also took the opportunity to enthuse about her co-star. The villain's wife would also seek revenge on her husband by sleeping with James Bond. A former Miss Italy finalist, she was the only Bond girl not to take part in an action sequence but was to wow cinema audiences by appearing on screen in a green bikini and riding a white horse.

Relatively new to the acting game, she felt intimidated at playing opposite an actor as accomplished as Daniel Craig. 'After seeing *Munich* I came out of the theatre and I was so scared!' she admitted. 'I thought, "How can I play with him? How can I rise to his level?" But he was such a professional and he helped me so much. I am very glad I worked with him.'

Proving all his critics wrong, she had to agree that Daniel was a fine choice of actor for the role. 'I am happy that people speak badly about Daniel. They are going to be so surprised,' she defiantly declared. 'Daniel Craig is such a great actor — he was the right choice. [His] James Bond is not as much of a cartoon. There's less special effects, more stunt scenes, to make the movie more real. Daniel is playing James Bond like a real actor, not just playful, like always. When Daniel kills somebody, he's a real killer. When he kissed me, it was so sexy and so real.

'You will see James Bond fall in love for the first time — unfortunately, not with me. For the first time, you will see James Bond with blood in his face. I don't remember Sean Connery or Pierce Brosnan with blood in his face when he came out from a fight. He's so violent, and we never see James Bond violent – so modern. It's completely different from the twenty movies before.'

Despite all the changes, Daniel was quick to point out that many of the traditional Bond elements would remain integral to the film. 'Let's not beat about the bush over this,' he said. 'It's a franchise that has been built on huge action sequences, beautiful girls and fast cars – and we have all of that.'

In fact, he had been bombarded by taunts from female friends. 'I get it all the time: "Is he still gonna be a sexist pig?" Well, yeah, he is still a bit of a sexist pig. But the fact is that the balance there is always through Judi. Because she's the one person that ever really keeps him alive. She's the one that protects him and looks out for his back. So I suppose that sort of gives us carte blanche to let him be a pig to women. Not that he needs to be a pig to women, but what I'm saying is that, hopefully, in *Casino Royale* we get this situation where we'll understand why he is the way he is.'

The dynamic between Bond and Judi Dench's M was vital to the film. Although some fans might argue that it undermined Bond's masculinity, Daniel believed it was important to be deferential to his commanding female boss. It revealed a lot about the new-age, 21st-century Bond.

'Look, maybe it will change but my root for Bond was always that he's a commander, and a commander aboard a ship is the second most important person on the ship. He's not the captain of the ship; he's a trained soldier. And M's the boss. And however much he's like, "Fuck it!" it's always, "Thank you, ma'am!" I mean, that's the way it has to be. I love the dynamic and I'm glad Judi has more of a part to play in this film. She's not mum exactly, but she kind of *is* mum, and that's what I want to fuck around with.'

The producers felt that it was time to explore the character of M in greater depth and give her a degree of humanity glossed over by previous films. In *Casino Royale* the viewer would be invited into her world and given details about her personal life and background.

'I love the flat Peter Lamont [set designer for *Casino Royale*] has designed for M,' praised Judi Dench. 'I think it will be a shock for people who might have expected her to have a little house in Kensington to see that she has this gorgeous penthouse in Canary Wharf. Of course, the exact address is a secret, except to me and now James Bond.'

The fact that one scene involved M in bed with a younger man especially appealed to Daniel: 'I think it's brilliant that we see her in bed with some young man. I was desperate to get someone like Brad Pitt or Keanu Reeves to do it.'

Although he undertook very thorough research, not all of Daniel's preparation for the film was intellectual. It soon transpired that this would be a very physically demanding film. If he wanted to carry off the death-defying character effectively, he would have to get in shape.

He started training almost immediately. Soon after being offered the role, he called up Barbara and told her of his plans. 'Look, I need to get in shape for this because I want to do as many stunts as I possibly can.' But fitness wasn't his only motivation. 'I also think that, if Bond should at some point take his shirt off, we should feel that he's physically imposing, that he's done the things he's supposed to have done, like being a commander in the Navy.'

But this was more than just a vanity project. 'I said, "Look, I've got to look like I can kill somebody." If I take my shirt off, it's not, "Oh, nice body!" It's got to be "Oh, fucking hell, he could do somebody!"' he explained. 'I wanted to look like I could do everything Bond does.'

Both Barbara and Martin agreed that Daniel should embark on a training programme. One of their only concerns in casting him was that he might not be physically up to carrying off an action film. It was a completely different discipline to the arthouse films he was used to. Although *Casino Royale* might never be a high-octane blockbuster along the lines of *Tomb Raider*, certain scenes would still be physically gruelling.

'Daniel had never done an action film before and you gamble that he is going to be able to deal with that,' admitted Martin Campbell at the time of Bond's casting. 'Action is difficult. There's a tendency to be dismissive and say, "Oh, it's just action." But it's tricky. And I'm talking about the kind of action that feeds into the character and narrative, not the sequences that are there for their own sake. Some actors you might expect to be very good but because of their image they turn out to be incapable of doing action.'

Daniel had always kept himself reasonably healthy but now he began to visit the gym more frequently, lift heavier weights and run more miles. Friends of the chain-smoking pint drinker were amazed by the transformation. 'I started training for the film when I knew there was a possibility I might get the part,' he revealed. 'And I thought, "Fuck it, I'll start trying to get myself fit anyway and even if it doesn't come off I'll live another year!" And if I hadn't done it, I don't think I would have survived.'

But his hard work paid off and he quickly developed muscles to rival the likes of Arnold Schwarzenegger! Daniel joked that he hadn't been this fit since the age of 16 when he was a keen rugby player, training twice a week. 'I went five days a week before the film started and every day while we were filming,' he said of his new training regime. 'I had a great trainer and I did a lot of work because that's what you do.'

Friends would tease him, joking that he was turning into a meat head or, worse still, a 'body-beautiful' obsessed A-list celebrity with an eating disorder. Rolling his eyes incredulously, he soon set them straight. 'I'm not obsessive about it!' he protested. 'I work out three or four times a week, but I take the weekends off and drink as much Guinness as I can get down my neck.'

Unfortunately, his training programme had been almost

too successful! His stunt advisor Gary Powell revealed the eager actor had built up too much muscle. 'He'd put a lot of muscle on in a very short period of time. Muscle can affect your flexibility and he needed to loosen up for a couple of the fight scenes. Halfway through he said, "I'm big enough now," and stopped bulking up.'

Now in much better shape, Daniel was keen to carry out as many stunts as possible. 'I wanted to look like Bond could kill someone,' he explained. 'I wanted to bulk up quickly so I did a lot of weights and had a high-protein diet.'

But on the eve of filming, there were rumours he had cold feet about the amount of action scenes required. It was completely understandable. 'Daniel's not a typical action man,' reiterated director Martin Campbell. Nevertheless, he was confident that his actor could overcome his nerves. 'To begin with, he buffed up and he trained and he looked great. I think there was a little bit of a learning curve in the way you do action and the way you shoot action.'

But Daniel had more than just a physical challenge to overcome. 'Action is not easy,' continued Martin. 'You know, you have to acquire a lot of technique to do it. It's not like playing the scene where the psychology and the subtext of the scene is everything. It's much more about applying yourself to the actual mechanics of action.'

Thankfully, any reservations were quickly eliminated and he tackled even complex scenes with ease and confidence. 'Once he was in the rhythm he was great,' praised Martin. 'I think audiences will be impressed with his fighting skills.'

Daniel himself revealed, 'I wanted to do as much of the action work as possible so that the audience can see that it's me, and that it's real. That meant acquiring injuries and carrying on, blasting through to the next level of action – and pain.' Although he wasn't allowed to do all the stunts, he featured in the majority. 'Obviously insurance wouldn't let me do all of them,' he shrugged. 'But at some point in every stunt it *is* me.'

An expert stunt team were drafted in to offer him assistance whenever it was required: 'Gary Powell and his stunt team did fantastic work to make sure that everything was safe – if you don't get bruised playing Bond, you're not doing the job properly.'

His first action scene was shot in Modrany Studios, just outside Prague. It was the pulse-pounding chase sequence in which Bond pursues the would-be bomber through the Nambutu Embassy and it proved to be a sharp introduction into the painful world of a stuntman.

'I had black eyes, cuts, bruises and muscle strain. We had a physiotherapist on the set and I took lots of painkillers, but it was part of the job. I'd get out of bed very slowly in the mornings. You ask a stuntman what it feels like to fall down a flight of stairs, and he'll tell you, "It's like falling down a flight of stairs." That's the simple answer. As much as I was hurt, the stuntmen were in much more pain than I was, so I had to just get on with it.

'Getting hurt wasn't fun, but pushing myself physically and mentally was great. There was this feeling of finishing a shot, breathing a sigh of relief and feeling so alive.'

Another complex scene involved terrorists storming a jet in a bid to send Boeing's share prices crashing, so that Le Chiffre could clean up on the stock market. During an attempt to ram a fuel tanker into the side of the plane, Bond leaps onto the roof of the vehicle. A terrorist swerves into baggage trolleys fitted with nitrogen and then a bus, in an attempt to shake him off.

An aircraft was specially flown in for the sequence. 'Amazing, eh?' said Daniel with a laugh. 'We've got our own fucking jet liner!' The unmarked Boeing 747 would later be transformed into an Airbus by the CGI post-production department. According to the script, the scene was supposedly set in a bustling Miami international airport. Instead of this, Daniel found himself in the middle of a private airfield in Surrey. 'Yes, rather surprisingly, they wouldn't let us film on a runway in Miami!' he admitted, with typical sarcasm. 'Fucking killjoys!'

Three tankers were also used for the shot – each fitted with 600bhp racing engines and pyrotechnic devices designed to send sparks flying on contact with any other vehicles. Explosions were created with petrol and a pulley system used to hoist one half of the bus into the air.

It was a difficult scene and, not surprisingly, it took a long time to get right. With every take there seemed to be a problem and, dissatisfied with the results, Martin would order his crew to reshoot. After the 30th take, everyone was exhausted. By then it was almost 3.30am – surely they could pack up and call it a day soon?

Sighing, Martin promised his cast that this would be the

last take. Suddenly there was an almighty explosion – but this time it was totally unscripted! Two vehicles had collided and the front wheel of a tanker blew. Sparks were flying everywhere. The ambulance team and fire brigade leapt into action, but they needn't have bothered as no one seemed particularly bothered. Daniel shrugged his shoulders – by now this was just another everyday occurrence.

Very soon it became apparent that he was more than capable of handling most stunts. Stunt co-ordinator Gary Powell was impressed by the actor's abilities. 'Daniel is extremely fit and strong and he's a hundred per cent up for it,' he praised. 'In the construction-site scene we had him ninety feet up on eight-inch girders. He had no problem with that.'

Daniel's co-star Sebastian Foucan, the French free-runner who played terrorist Mollaka, explained the scene. 'There were security systems in place but all the action is real. There was no point pretending the chase across the girders wasn't going to be dangerous – it was.'

'Daniel really took some hits on *Casino Royale*,' added Gary. 'I'd see him bruised and cut up fight after fight. And he'd just say, "Oh shit, that smarted a bit! Let's go again.'

As it turned out, though, he could give as good as he got. 'In stunt scenes you're not meant to connect but in the heat of the moment it happens,' revealed Gary. 'Daniel certainly accidentally lamped a couple of stuntmen!'

The son of famous stuntman Nosher Powell (who was stunt double for Sean Connery and George Lazenby),

Gary had a long-running relationship with the Bond franchise. His brother Greg doubled for Roger Moore and Timothy Dalton, while he himself worked as Pierce Brosnan's stunt double in *GoldenEye* and *The World Is Not Enough* (1999). He compared both actors in action. 'Pierce was a lovely man but he'd always emerge from a punch-up or a huge explosion with an unruffled tie and immaculate hair.'

Of all the Bonds, Daniel seemed by far the most adventurous. 'Someone told me recently, "Sean Connery sweated, Roger Moore perspired and Pierce Brosnan glowed,"' chuckled Gary. 'I don't agree but I'll add one thing – Daniel Craig *bleeds*. He did everything we asked of him and more.

'Without a doubt, Daniel is the toughest,' he continued. 'When you're constantly fighting, swinging your arms about, it's like playing tennis every day, all day, for six months. The effort takes a lot out of you.'

But the latest Bond never once relented. He was eager to undertake every challenge thrown in his path. 'He said to me, "Whatever you think I can handle, let me do it,"' recalled Gary. 'There's no ego there but he's up for anything. The chase along the crane was especially tough – running about a hundred and forty feet up is not for the faint hearted.

'And the underwater sequence at the end of the movie was impossibly hard. With thousands of tons of water being thrown about, you might as well be running a marathon every day.'

Unlike previous Bond movies, *Casino Royale* relied less on special effects and for that reason many of the stunts were real. 'Audiences are getting bored with computer graphics,' reasoned Gary. 'There's so much computer work in films, you may as well be watching *Shrek*! We use them to top up, but really as little as possible.' This was by far the most realistic Bond film yet. '*Casino Royale* comes closer to real fighting than any other film,' said Gary. 'You wouldn't mess with Daniel!'

By all accounts, it wasn't a safe set. But any sense of danger only added to the energy and excitement of the film. 'In one sequence, Bond's Aston Martin gets rolled after a chase with a Jaguar,' revealed Gary. The stunt showed Bond swerving to avoid his girlfriend Vesper Lynd, and flipping the car. 'We had four Astons and four Jaguars on hand. If something went wrong, we didn't waste time repairing it. We just kept the cameras rolling.'

On this particular occasion, Gary had to step in and take over from Daniel. 'I had to draw the line,' he said with a shrug. 'I'm sure Daniel would have been keen to give it a crack but that stunt was super-dangerous. We wrecked three BMW 5-series and two £150,000 Aston Martins in the process but our driver managed to beat *Top Gear*'s record for rolling a car – seven times to their five!

'It was incredibly difficult,' he added. 'The stuntman had to drive at seventy-five miles per hour, dodge the stuntgirl lying in the middle of the road, press a button to fire the cannon built into the car and survive the roll. The car ended up six inches from the camera. It was perfect.'

Daniel was under no illusions that this would be an easy ride. Bracing himself, he dived in headfirst and tackled every challenge thrown in his direction. 'I learned from day one that it was gonna hurt,' he winced. 'Just pain. But if I was hurting, the stunt guys were hurting ten times more than I was. They were going through pain levels that I couldn't even imagine, and carrying on. Compressed spines, all sorts of things. I just had to suck it up and get on with it. Now times that by ten, ten times an hour...

'No, actually, that's a fucking stupid way of putting it. It was like being beaten round the head and neck with a stick most days. I was in pain throughout the whole movie but you can't show pain around these guys because they're hard!'

Pierce Brosnan had given him forewarning that this would be the case. 'Pierce said it best: "If you're not getting hurt, you're not doing it properly,"' explained Daniel.

Unfortunately, that prophecy came true when Daniel suffered his first on-set injury while filming on location in Prague. 'I knocked a cap out,' he explained, pointing to his teeth. 'And that threw me a bit of a curveball.' The accident took place during a dramatic fight scene. Daniel and his assailant had rehearsed the sequence several times. However, when it came to the final shot, Daniel misjudged his footing and found himself on the receiving end of a painful blow to the face. He crumpled to the floor in agony, clasping his mouth.

As soon as the tabloids caught whiff of the accident, they published stories claiming Daniel had lost two teeth in a dramatic accident. Some cruel journalists used it as evidence to back up the claim that Daniel was too much of a wimpy thespian to carry off the role of hard man James Bond.

In complete exasperation, Daniel set the record straight. 'According to the tabloids, there was blood everywhere,' he sighed. 'But what really happened is that I knocked it out, gave it to somebody to hold and we carried on. I got it fixed that night, but I must admit it did freak me out. And then I thought, "Well, it's a fight scene, and they can CGI the cap back in if they really need to."'

Early reports suggested *Casino Royale* would be the most violent of the Bond movies to date. The film would open with an aggressive black-and-white sequence, cutting between Bond murdering two men – one in Prague and one in London. It's suggested these are his first killings as a secret agent. He would then embark on an adventure through several exotic locations, including Madagascar, the Bahamas, Montenegro and finally Venice. In contrast to previous Bond outings, the violence would also be far more realistic.

There was speculation that the film would even receive a 15 certificate. 'I don't know,' said Daniel, when asked about the likely classification. 'But if they cut all that shit out, there's not going to be much of a movie left!'

Although he was happy to participate in every scene, in real life he had never been an advocate of violence. He detested guns and had only ever been involved in one fight. 'I don't like it,' he shuddered. But in this instance he thought the violent scenes were an integral part of the film's plot. 'You get to see the consequence of violence,' he reasoned.

A scene in which James Bond kills a man in a bathroom turned out to be particularly violent. 'I watch the bathroom sequence and I wince,' admitted Daniel. 'All my knuckles spilt; my hands were in bandages after it. And I had a fight double, Ben. I did the bits that hurt. And he did the bits that *really* fucking hurt! But that's the thing with this Bond: he bleeds!'

Inevitably, guns featured heavily in the film. Daniel was even assigned an armourer to assist him in handling firearms. Ex-soldier Joss Skottowe quickly pulled the actor into shape. 'Daniel came in hating guns, but left rather keen,' he revealed. 'I've yet to meet a man who doesn't relish holding a Walther PPK – and Daniel is more man than most!'

Rather than use replica guns, it was suggested real guns were used for filming. Even though they were adapted to fire blanks, there was still an element of danger involved in using the weapons. 'Blanks can still hurt or kill you,' explained Joss.

But Daniel breezed through his training. 'I brought in some SAS pals to give Daniel some extra training and even they were impressed. One said to me, "That boy's a natural." And he was right! Daniel is the only Bond who in real life could pass SAS selection. He's fit, he looks like a killer and he's smart.

'I could never imagine Roger Moore or Pierce Brosnan doing any real damage to anything stronger than a vodka martini. But Daniel could really hurt you – with or without a gun.'

Along with learning how to use firearms, Daniel also had to become a proficient scuba diver in just a matter of months. Scuba specialist Dave Shaw prepared him for a scene in which Bond rescues Vesper Lynd from a house collapsing into a Venetian canal. 'Daniel really threw himself into training,' applauded Dave. 'Scuba is a dangerous sport. We were having to film six metres under water and even three metres can kill you. If you surface too quickly you can burst a lung.

'Daniel was having to hold his breath for up to a minute. He must have swallowed pints of water but he never whinged. And acting under water is tough – you can't see and you can't hear.' In fact, Daniel turned out to be a natural at the sport and Dave even joked that he might want to throw in the day job! 'I would be amazed if Daniel didn't take up scuba diving,' he chuckled. 'He loved being in the water – it's such a calming environment.'

Having worked with numerous Bonds in the past, Dave agreed that, in his view, Daniel was by far the most professional. 'Daniel was without doubt my favourite Bond to work with,' he beamed. 'Yes, he'll do whatever it takes but he's also very safety conscious.'

But if Daniel was playing safe off-screen, he didn't give that impression in front of the cameras. One of the most controversial scenes in *Casino Royale* involved James Bond being tied naked to a chair, while his testicles are whipped. It was an extremely humiliating sequence and one that inevitably aroused debate. The torture scene was translated almost verbatim from Ian Fleming's original novel.

'Le Chiffre's bad guy takes the bottom out of a chair,' explained Daniel, recalling the scene. 'I'm in the middle of the room and I'm thrown down on the floor and stripped. You see the henchman take a chair and cut the bottom out of it with a knife and then I'm sat in it naked and supposedly my nuts are hanging down there. Although I kind of think in that situation they would go north. In the book they hit him [under the chair] with a switch – a whip. In the movie we used a spliced ship's rope. The henchman swings it under the chair and does me with it.'

Mads Mikkelsen admitted there was a sexual aspect to the scene. 'The way he [Le Chiffre] enjoys the beating can be categorised as having sexual undertones,' he chuckled. During a playback of the footage, Daniel couldn't believe how realistic the sequence looked. He almost had to turn away as the whip cracked against his chair. Thankfully, he was sufficiently protected and on this occasion didn't suffer any injuries. 'It all had fibreglass protection but it did crack at one point and we stopped filming quite rapidly. I ran over the other side of the room. Woah!'

However, everyone had to agree that the final cut was impressive. It was a fine example of his excellent screen presence. 'Somehow, the way Daniel does that scene, he comes out as the winner,' Barbara Broccoli enthused. 'It's hard to articulate what he does, but he does hold the power in that scene, and he does it throughout the movie.

He has taken something that was really good on the page and made it even better.'

Typically modest, Daniel played down any praise. 'I don't think about whether I have a strong screen presence,' he claimed, shrugging his shoulders. So how did he carry off the scene? 'I just got myself angry. Bond thinks he's going to die – it's his last shout.'

It was unusual to see James Bond in the role of a victim and some fans were outraged at the idea. But Daniel disagreed. He believed it gave a vital new insight into the character – 007 was no longer a superhero, he was a regular human being and as fallible as the next man.

'I just wanted people to see him make a few mistakes,' he explained. 'I want to make the audience believe that it's all going to go wrong and then when it goes right it's much more exciting. I also want the audience to feel that this man might be in danger; that he's not infallible – because he isn't.'

But rather than weaken the character, Daniel believed such mistakes were a sign of Bond's strength. 'In *Casino Royale* Bond gets knocked down. I mean, he gets mowed down, but he always fucking gets up – *always*! And that's really fascinating.

'I suppose this film's about the reason he gets up. The reason he gets up is that there's a drive in him that makes him who he is when he's given a double-0 status. There's a reason that M trusts him; there's a reason [why] he's the top guy. It doesn't matter what you do to him, he's Teflon coated and he's gonna come bouncing back. But he does get fucking hurt. He gets damaged and in *Casino Royale* he gets damaged in the biggest way – he gets his nuts banged up into his throat.'

More than anything, Daniel wanted to entertain his audience. 'I'm a Bond fan. If I go and see a Bond movie, there are certain things I think should be in it. And they're there; we've got them in spades. Nobody knows more than I do how important this is and it's my job to get it right.' He also had a responsibility to uphold the James Bond legacy. It was a heavy weight to bear, but he was willing to take up the challenge.

'I accept the fact that there is this Bond history,' he proclaimed. 'I want to continue the tradition of parents taking their children to see the movie because they were taken by their parents. You could be critical of past movies, you can be critical of my movie, but it's a great cinema tradition and Bond is a great character. I want to appeal to everybody, but then I'm greedy.'

# CHAPTER 11

# LICENCE TO THRILL

Proving his critics wrong, Daniel would ultimately emerge triumphant from the filming of *Casino Royale*. Even prior to the film's release, early whispers suggested he had successfully resurrected the 007 brand and looked set to be the most popular Bond since the halcyon days of Sean Connery and Roger Moore. Not only was he commended for his fine acting, but he was also heralded as being a major sex symbol.

It wasn't the first time he had been a focus for adoring female fans. When *Our Friends In The North* first aired in 1996, numerous women's magazines proclaimed the rugged northern actor to be a major pin-up. Although this wasn't a title Daniel felt particularly comfortable with, over time he had learned to take the compliment graciously.

But when stills from *Casino Royale* were published in

the tabloids, female audiences appeared to be both shaken and stirred. Coupled with his manly good looks, Daniel's new ripped torso was attracting quite some attention! One scene in particular seemed to send cinemagoers into a flustered frenzy. Adorned in nothing more than a tight pair of swimming trunks Bond emerged from the water, his naked torso dripping wet and glistening in the sun.

Although James Bond had always been depicted as a womaniser, never before had he been quite so broody and sexually appealing. Former Bond girl Valerie Leon, who played opposite Sean Connery in *Never Say Never Again* (1983) and then Roger Moore in *The Spy Who Loved Me* (1977), couldn't believe her eyes when she stumbled upon the publicity shots. 'I'm just flicking through the *Radio Times* and there's his naked torso, his trunks and, dare I say it – they've cut him off just below the penis! And then there's some water.' she exclaimed.

It was quite some contrast to the Bond movies of the 1970s, where most semi-naked bodies belonged to women. A sexual revolution had blatantly taken place. Now Bond appeared to be the only veritable eye candy. 'You can't get away from his body,' cooed Valerie. 'And I'm not aware that there are any bare women in the film. There may have been, but it's not memorable to me at all. Whereas I really come out of that movie thinking about Daniel Craig's body. I just kept thinking, "*How* did he get it?"'

Rumour had it that Judi Dench was also impressed by Daniel's physique when she was lucky enough to receive an eyeful while filming on location. The tongue-in-cheek actress reportedly revealed intimate details of Daniel's manhood. While using a trailer opposite his, she was surprised to find the actor wandering around naked one day. 'It's an absolute m*onster*!' she gushed. 'Sorry, I shouldn't say that, should I? How uncouth of me – I'm old enough to be his grandmother!' However, she did add, 'He was divine to work with.'

When asked about her crude comments, Daniel turned uncharacteristically bashful and self-conscious. 'You have to ask Judi about that. I am not going to get involved with that question,' he said. But he protested that he had never set out to be a sex symbol – even though his new body would undeniably boost box-office sales. 'I got in shape because I needed to for the character,' he said with exasperation. 'But that was my only criteria. Look, I don't know what sexy is. I think if you go out and think you're sexy, then that immediately becomes not sexy.'

In fact, he hated the fact that his looks might be used as a means to promote the film. To him, this seemed like a cheap shot. 'There's this whole thing about demographics,' he complained. 'We're told, "OK, we're a bit low on twenty-two to twenty-eight-year-old women at the moment." What am *I* supposed to do? Go on telly and make bread?'

But although he vehemently denied any accusations of vanity, he had to admit that he was deeply concerned about the image of Bond that was portrayed to the public. When suggestions were initially made for the slant any advertising campaign should take, Daniel eagerly weighed in with his opinion. 'I've been a complete pain in the arse,' he later admitted. 'I've said to them, "You have to explain that to me. Why does the poster have to be a composite of explosions? Tell me why we need girls, tits, cars, explosions… Why can't we have something that's fucking cool?" And they've gone, "OK, let's try and work this out."'

After much protest, he eventually had his own way: the team decided to run with a poster of Bond in a tuxedo with a gun in his hand. It was the epitome of understated cool and exactly what Daniel believed was required to advance the brand.

As usual, he was keen to get his hands dirty both off and on screen. He even played a major role in selecting wardrobe items for the character and confessed the choice of tight swimwear had been his own. This was a situation he walked into with his eyes wide open. 'The trunks were my choice,' he later admitted. 'We discussed ten pairs. Bond shouldn't wear Bermuda shorts; it's just not right. Anyway, the ones I chose aren't that skimpy. I mean, they're not Speedos – that would have been wrong!' The trunks Daniel eventually settled on were made by designer label GrigioPerla. The £55 undies proved to be a great success and upmarket department store Selfridges sold out in days!

With baited breath, audiences waited to catch a glimpse of Daniel semi-naked on the big screen. The patience was finally rewarded on Tuesday, 14 November when *Casino Royale* premièred in London's Leicester Square, which was taken over completely for the royal première of the film. The gardens were shut to the public on the Monday and

Tuesday while frantic activity went on to dress the square in a *Casino Royale* theme. The three cinemas screening the film displayed different versions of the poster. The Empire featured the poster with Bond and Vesper (who was wearing a purple dress) and had a bridge from the gardens to the cinema entrance with purple carpet, while the Odeon West End featured Solange in a red dress and had a matching carpet. The gardens were surrounded with *Casino Royale* branded drapes and on the Tuesday morning an Aston Martin DBS was delivered to take its place on a stage towards one end of the garden.

Looking suave in a midnight-blue Dunhill tuxedo, Daniel was every bit the 21st-century James Bond and over a thousand adoring fans waited in the rain to greet the actor. He was joined on the red carpet by numerous Bond stars past and present, along with the Queen and the Duke of Edinburgh. It was unlike any film première he had ever attended in his life. 'It's fabulous,' he said with a huge smile. 'I didn't expect it, you know. It's wonderful. The thing to do is just enjoy it. These things don't happen very often and I'm just going to have the best time.'

Daniel's leading ladies, Eva Green and Caterina Murino, both looked spectacular. Eva had chosen an Alexander McQueen gown and £30,000 worth of Autore jewellery for the occasion, while Caterina looked demure in a pink silk dress and white faux-fur shawl. Judi Dench, meanwhile, opted for a glamorous floor-length Armani dress. Other celebrities in attendance included Sir Elton John, Shirley Bassey, Paris Hilton, Sharon Osbourne and Sadie Frost.

It was certainly a star-studded line-up. But despite the number of celebrities in tow, all eyes were set on a relative nobody. Daniel had taken the public occasion to introduce his girlfriend Satsuki Mitchell to the world. Fearful of any intrusion into his private life, he had taken some time to reach the decision but he was proud of his girlfriend and he no longer wanted to keep her hidden from view. Filming *Casino Royale* hadn't always been easy, but she had constantly been on hand to offer support. Now she deserved to share in the film's success.

'We're together, and she's been experiencing this whole situation with me,' explained Daniel. 'That's incredibly important.' Now confident their relationship was strong enough to withstand press intrusion, he was eager to show off his leading lady. 'She's been with me all the way through this and all the way through filming so why exclude her? She's up to it – she's an adult, I'm an adult.

'I'm not going out there purposefully holding her hand to say, "we're a couple", but Bond has been too big an experience – it might not come around again. We had to do that amazing thing in Leicester Square and walk round in all that craziness, just because it may never happen again.'

But he was aware that any public displays of affection might be noted down and used against him in the future. 'I knew what it might open us up to – God forbid we should ever split up!' he exclaimed. 'The response will be "Ah ha!" and there's nothing we can do about that. Now that we've appeared publicly, we've declared something or other. There is something out there,' he joked, in reference to the curse of celebrity magazine endorsements. 'There's an organisation where they sit in dark rooms with hoods on!'

Like any couple, Daniel and Satsuki had been through their fair share of ups and downs in the past year, but thanks to hard work and perseverance their relationship had survived. 'Any relationship needs a little love and care at least once a day,' he smiled. 'I don't want to get soppy about it, but you've got to put the time in. It doesn't matter who you are, you've got to keep putting it in.

'Relationships don't take care of themselves. Romance is fine but it's not about expensive hotels and beautiful locations – it's about being with the right person and feeling close to them. I have a huge respect for women, which I've learned from my mother and my sister, but that doesn't mean I haven't made mistakes. Being in love takes a lot of work and if you don't look after it, it will fall apart.'

Even though Satsuki had to watch Daniel cavort with beautiful women on screen, she never once showed signs of jealousy. It was testimony to the strength of their relationship that the beautiful American producer had invested so much trust and faith in her man. 'I don't have to reassure anybody about anything!' fumed Daniel. 'We have beautiful women in Bond movies because it's one of the elements, just like the explosions and cars. But that's my work. My girlfriend is my girlfriend first and foremost – she knows that.'

As a sign of his love, Daniel gripped Satsuki's hand tightly throughout the whole evening. The pair were inseparable. Even when Daniel stopped to sign autographs for fans, he refused to let go of his girlfriend. When asked by one journalist who his ideal Bond girl might be, he simply pointed at Satsuki and said, 'This one here.'

Once the film had finished, everyone adjourned to an after party in Berkeley Square. Daniel continued to sign autographs and leaned out of the VIP section to pose for photos – mostly with female fans. But he only ever had eyes for Satsuki. When leaving the party, he took a moment to prepare himself for the awaiting paparazzi. Pulling Satsuki towards him in a passionate embrace, he planted a kiss on her lips. It was full confirmation that he was very much in love.

Guests at the party took the opportunity to commend him for his fantastic performance. By all accounts, *Casino Royale* had been an overriding hit. 'Daniel is a great Bond!' said Mads Mikkelsen, holding aloft a flute of champagne. 'He's excellent, definitely the best,' agreed Judi Dench. 'Things are always loaded against whoever plays the new Bond,' she reasoned. 'People will resist him because they don't like change. They didn't want change from Sean Connery, then they didn't want change from Roger Moore and then they didn't want change from Timothy Dalton. But I think they'll be very pleased about Daniel, because he's frighteningly good.

'And he was lovely to work with too,' she added. 'Of course, so was Pierce Brosnan, although they're very different people. But I did have a wonderful time working with Daniel.'

'Daniel will be a revelation to the audience,' predicted director Martin Campbell. 'He combines toughness with charm and humour and, because this is a much more character-driven story, Daniel's gravitas is a perfect match for the role. At the same time, he's in great physical shape and proved himself to be excellent in the action scenes.'

In turn, Daniel repaid the compliment by praising the director for his motivating energy. 'Martin fires everyone up. You obviously need that level of energy in the action sequences, but it's equally valuable in quieter, dramatic scenes like the poker tournament.'

Early reviews of the film were positive and one newspaper even hailed Daniel as 'the best Bond since Sean Connery – perhaps the best ever'. By all accounts he had proved his critics wrong. Rather than be smug about it, he was simply relieved that the film had received the warm reception it so justly deserved. Everyone involved in the production had shed a lot of blood, sweat and tears in the process.

'Bond's a bad man and I wanted to bring that across,' he told journalists at the première. 'He kills people. The people he kills are bad people, and one of the things he is fantastic at is knowing who the bad guys are. But I think that a true good guy would definitely have to step into the dark side to get to do the job he does.

'The character of Bond is nothing new. In every culture there's a character like this; a lone warrior who goes after the bad guys. But he's a bad man too and that, I think, is part of his attraction. He burns brightly, both for men and for women.'

As with every role, Daniel invested all his energies into the role of 007. He employed 'the methods, the skills and all the things that I know how to do as an actor... It doesn't matter how big the movie is, there's got to be an element of truth in everything I do, because if *I* don't believe in it, nobody else will! All I can do is rely on my experience. I mean, I'm in the entertainment business and part of whatever job I do has to have an entertaining element because that's the art form.

'Maybe I'm not the prettiest Bond that's ever been, and maybe I'm not the suavest,' he added. 'All I can say is there are millions of fans, and I don't want to let them down. I've worked my butt off for this movie – I'm not going to foul it up!'

Deep down he had always known he was capable of doing a good job, but even he couldn't predict how successful the final cut would be. In the past he had never taken much notice of the box-office takings but now it was difficult to ignore the soaring figures. 'Watching the number coming in and steadily going up, I thought, "Okay, we've got away with it." It was like watching the fucking *Blue Peter* appeals!'

With the film now on general release, he was confronted with the full force of newfound fame. His face was plastered across billboards and along the side of double-decker buses. On the opening weekend alone *Casino Royale* grossed $417 million worldwide.

Overnight he became an even greater focus for media attention. From the very beginning he had known that the role of 007 would change his life for ever. But nothing could really prepare him for the reality. Fiercely protective of his private life, he now struggled to conduct his personal affairs behind closed doors. With photographers lurking at every corner, it seemed impossible for him to even breathe without it being documented in the press. All in all, it was an extremely frustrating time for him.

Every day a new story emerged in the press – DANIEL HAS GROWN A BEARD, DANIEL HAS PURCHASED A NEW SUIT. Generally, the stories were harmless but the suspicious actor was prepared for the tabloids to take a darker turn. 'If someone in my past decides they want to write about me, there's nothing I can do about it,' he sighed. 'It's their thing, it's what they're going through. But if it's to do with my present group of friends, my family, there is need for some control to be taken because that's private.'

He had thought long and hard about how he should deal with fame. It was something he had always avoided. He cited the *Harry Potter* author JK Rowling as someone who handled her fame with grace. 'She's kept her privacy,' he commended. 'I think she may have a child, but I don't know, which is good. Now she's using her money to fund things she believes in. But her charity is her own private thing, which I think is incredibly admirable.'

Highlighting Daniel's newfound popularity, the working-class actor was invited to appear on the chat show *Parkinson*. To many it was a benchmark of success, but Daniel disagreed. 'What does it feel like to be doing the chat show circuit?' one journalist enquired. 'Exactly what you think it feels like,' he deadpanned. 'Actually, I was reluctant to go on *Parkinson*,' he admitted, 'which was weird because when it came to America I was like, "Oh fine, I'll do *Letterman*, I'll do whatever."

'I had less fear about it because it was not my town,' he reasoned. 'But suddenly you're at LWT in London and you're at the top of the fucking stairs. The band's winking at you and all you can think about is not falling down those stairs.'

Fortunately, the experience turned out to be much more painless than he had anticipated. 'Parkinson is delightful, though,' he revealed, with some relief. 'He came and talked to me before the show and I thought, "Okay, I don't have an act; this is all I can do, this is it – sorry." I admire people who can go and just turn it on. But if I do that, I just look like a wanker so I try and talk normally with people.'

In the past, he had always been cast as the reluctant celebrity. 'I just don't pursue it for want of a better word for celebrity reasons. I've got nothing against it; it's just not for me. I've got other things to do. If I'm not working, I don't want to be sitting around talking about myself.'

Despite his reservations, though, he was savvy enough to realise he couldn't play the reluctant movie star any more. If he wished to advance his career then he would have to embrace this whole new area of the business. Otherwise he would risk allowing his career to stagnate and this would be a woeful loss of opportunity. 'At the beginning I said to the Bond producers, "I will do everything you want me to do to sell this film,"' revealed Daniel. 'Because I can't do this movie and go, "I don't talk to the press" – it defeats the object.'

Although now willing to speak with the press, he still preferred to avoid paparazzi encounters on the street.

Subsequently he tended to spend evenings indoors rather than out on the town. 'The truth is I can't really go out at the moment,' he shrugged. 'I can walk round Soho – *anyone* can walk round Soho – and it's OK in New York. But I get shouted at. It's not anything bad and it will die down eventually. And if it stops me walking into too many bars, that's no bad thing!' he smirked playfully.

'I think he can go wherever he wants from here,' said his friend, the director John Maybury. 'Bond can only empower him. He's the real deal. He's strangely ego-less for an actor, and able to distance himself from the rigmarole and the palaver of celebrity.'

Although adept at keeping his feet firmly planted on the ground, Daniel was the first to admit that playing James Bond had completely changed his life. 'The only thing that ever really changes is that some people suddenly think you're a millionaire,' he laughed. 'Some fans do think that I'm James Bond and that's even more worrying, and they write to me with plans of action. That is only a few, I should say. Most people are very nice about it. You just have to keep your friends close.'

With fame came inevitable exposure. 'My personal life will probably be picked apart,' he sighed. 'But my only concern is that my friends' and family's private lives are left alone.' Most notably, Daniel refused to discuss any personal relationships in public. The whole episode with Kate Moss had proved how difficult it was to conduct a high-profile relationship. 'It's not easy for two successful people to be together,' he admitted.

'I understand the interest, but I won't talk about any relationship in public because that's behaving like a prick. At the press conference they asked me questions that I wouldn't answer so they called me "James Bland". Well, fuck you, I don't care! The thing I'm most glad about is that people don't really know what I am.'

In practice, Daniel could handle himself in public but if anyone made an advance towards his family or friends he quickly lost his cool. One such instance occurred while he was on a shopping trip to London department store Harvey Nichols with his girlfriend Satsuki. Allegedly he lashed out at a fan for trying to take a picture.

According to a story in the *Daily Mirror*, Daniel apparently stormed over to the fan and screamed, 'What the fuck are you doing that for? You've got a fucking nerve! Can you delete that? Get the fuck out of my face!' The startled fan went on to say, 'He squared up to me and he's a lot bigger than me. I was really intimidated. It ruined my day – it was only a picture of his back.'

Allegedly, even Satsuki was stunned by Daniel's behaviour and ordered him to calm down. 'The only reason I'm fucking swearing is because I'm fucked off with you,' Daniel allegedly continued.

The ardent Bond enthusiast said that he was 'frightened out of my mind': 'I told him I was only taking a picture, that I thought he was a great actor and that I'm a huge James Bond fan.'

But Daniel remained tight lipped about the matter and refused to discuss it with the press. Some cruel papers suggested he had developed an over-inflated ego, but that seemed drastically far from the truth. 'Nothing has changed,' he insisted. 'I have very good friends and a very close family. They'll keep a watchful eye on me and knock me back into shape if I change too much.'

Some questioned whether he had ultimately compromised his credibility by accepting the role of 007. It was a concern that he himself had voiced in the very early days of casting but ultimately he was convinced there was nothing to worry about. He hoped the Bond experience would prove liberating rather than stifling: 'It's a high-class problem to have an actor typecast as James Bond, and I'm certainly going to try and get as much out of it as I can. I'm aware that it might limit what I do, but I shall approach that problem as it comes.'

Besides, in many ways he believed the idea of a Hollywood star was now a fading anachronism. 'There's no above-the-line British movie stars; there's no above-the-line movie stars, full stop,' he insisted. As far as he was concerned, the era of the Hollywood star capable of carrying a movie by name alone was dying out. 'Now more people are going to the cinema, there's a broader spread and people will go and see smaller movies. Potentially they won't make a lot of money, but they will take people away from other movies. And that's great, because suddenly you're not in the situation we had ten years ago when we had Stallone and Schwarzenegger earning ten to twenty million dollars. Those people are a dying breed because Hollywood is way too canny. If it can find one person who can do it then it'll fucking feed them, but they are going to be few and far between.'

On a more positive note, he hoped his newfound fame status might help fund the low-budget movie projects he adored: 'There are hugely positive things out there which I am going to grab with both hands.'

Ultimately, Daniel knew he would never win an Oscar for his portrayal of Bond, but it had still proven to be a pivotal moment in his career; it was a launching pad from which to bounce several new and exciting projects. Without wishing to be overly dramatic, he had to admit that being cast in the role of 007 had changed his life for ever.

But even though there were several more James Bond films in the pipeline, his ambitions didn't end here. 'The plan is to shoot another Bond movie by the end of next year,' he told journalists once filming for *Casino Royale* had wrapped. 'But we really have to get this one out first. We have to find out what the response is, which will affect where we take the next Bond picture.'

Although he hoped to continue the role of James Bond for quite some time, there were other projects on the horizon too. Offers of big-budget commercial work could never tempt him away from the arthouse projects he so dearly loved. More than anything, he still had his sights set on winning an Oscar. After all, wasn't that every serious actor's dream?

'When this came along I probably thought, "The Oscar dream will go away now." But for an actor to have an ambition, it has to be to win an Oscar. I have not taken my eye off that,' he admitted.

## CHAPTER 12

# NEVER SAY NEVER AGAIN

Even though it would have been easy to get carried away by the success of James Bond, Daniel was determined not to keep all his eggs in one basket. While it was probable that he never need work again, thanks to the success of *Casino Royale*, he wasn't about to slow down the workload just yet.

Small independent films were just as vital to his career as big-budget blockbusters. 'I mean, for me it's crucially important,' he explained. 'It's kind of like it's where you get... Independent movies are what shore up the film industry. It's where people get their experience as well. It's what I've done; it's what I've been doing for all of my career – it's where I learned my trade.'

Alongside *Casino Royale* he was also working on the Douglas McGrath film *Infamous* (2006). The movie was based on a true story about the writer Truman Capote and his 1966 novel *In Cold Blood*. Capote was inspired to write the book after reading a headline in the *New York Times*, WEALTHY FARMER, 3 OF FAMILY SLAIN. His investigations led him to Kansas and the Clutter family. The book would turn out to be a major success. Sadly Capote would spend the remainder of his career trying to emerge from its shadow. But the experience bore more than just literary fruits for he also embarked on a homosexual relationship with convicted murderer Perry Smith, played by Daniel Craig.

The part was a million miles from the overtly masculine character of 007. Daniel was almost unrecognisable in the role. He dyed his hair black, wore contact lenses to disguise those trademark blue eyes and used make-up to give his skin a sallow appearance. For the first 40 minutes of the film, he didn't even make an appearance. 'But boy, the minute he comes in, he sure grabs everyone!' praised director Douglas McGrath. He was instantly enamoured with the actor: 'I knew Daniel was right because he is very persuasive violently, very persuasive as a vulnerable person, but he is totally magnetic. As Perry, you think he is dumb, or much smarter than you thought, which keeps you on a knife edge.'

Critics appeared to agree and singled out Daniel's performance as particularly worthy. 'Craig goes bravely where no previous 007 has gone before with Perry, oozing menacing sexuality,' said *Rolling Stone* magazine. And when it premièred at the Venice Film Festivals, the film received rave reviews. Daniel was even nominated for Best Supporting Male at the 2007 Independent Spirit Awards in Santa Monica. 'It means a tremendous amount to me,' he said of the nomination. 'I'm very proud of the movie we did and hopefully we can share it about a bit with everybody who was involved in it.'

But some childish critics couldn't let go of the idea that James Bond would be embroiled in a gay embrace. Several American journalists even hounded Toby Jones (who played Capote) about what it was like to kiss the new 007. 'What's he supposed to say?' scoffed Daniel. 'Very dry? Anyway it's all over the internet now… BOND HAS GAY KISS.'

There was only one major problem with the movie. Unfortunately, just 12 months previously, another film about Truman Capote had been released. Directed by Bennett Miller, it dealt with the same period in the author's life. Actor Philip Seymour Hoffman was even awarded an Oscar for his portrayal of the troubled writer. So how on earth could the production team persuade audiences to see a film they might think they'd already seen?

'My feeling all the way along was I wish they had put the two bloody films out together! I wish they'd had the balls to do that,' insisted Daniel. 'I love Truman Capote, and I love *In Cold Blood* so much, I thought, "You know what, whatever happens, this is worth telling." It's worth seeing another interpretation of that character.'

As far as he was concerned, it had never been a question of competition. As he saw it, there was enough room in the film industry for two films about Truman Capote. 'We made, I think, a very beautiful movie. We made them at the same time and they both turned out.'

He particularly loved the fact that *Infamous* was about a writer, rather than a celebrity. 'Some of my greatest heroes are journalists,' he said with a grin. 'I genuinely believe getting to know people, going out and looking people in the eye and understanding the situation, like war reporter Robert Fisk does, that's proper journalism. Maybe that's just a dinosaur way of looking at things, but I don't believe anything that I read on the internet.'

Comparing the two films, McGrath's felt more light-hearted. Sigourney Weaver, who was cast as Babe Paley, one of Capote's swanky Manhattan friends, made the following comparison: 'If the other film is like a shot of bourbon, then this is a glass of champagne.'

But *Infamous* was far from light and fluffy. As the plot unravelled, tensions between characters began to develop – most notably when Capote and Perry Smith meet for the first time. The artist and murderer appear to be a mirror image of each other; both had mothers who committed suicide, both were sensitive kids who dreamed of creative pursuits.

Daniel approached the love tangle between his character and Truman Capote with great sensitivity. 'There was never anything self-conscious about it,' he shrugged. 'I always think that's how a love story needs to play out anyway, because it's this friendship that starts growing, and if it turns into sex, it turns into sex. But it's not like two young men meet in a bar, go back and fuck. This is about two human beings really sitting down and trying to figure each other out.'

He was extremely passionate about the film and proud of his performance. Although he would have liked to give the project 100 per cent support, prior commitments prevented him from attending the première in Venice. 'I had this whole awful debate going on with myself,' he recalled. 'I thought, "I can't go because otherwise it will be all about the new Bond being in town."'

Fortunately, he was able to pledge his support from afar. Although it occasionally presented difficulties, he enjoyed the contrast between making two different types of movie. 'I like working so I don't really make that comparison. You do have more freedom in movies like that because there are less constraints. You can tackle difficult subjects and that, I think, is important.'

Without wasting a minute, Daniel eagerly moved on to his next projects. He had two more films due out in 2007: *The Golden Compass* (based on the first installment in Phillip Pullman's *His Dark Materials* trilogy) and *The Invasion* (a modern version of the sci-fi classic *Invasion Of The Body Snatchers* (1956). In both movies he was to star alongside Nicole Kidman.

A fantastical tale of witches and warlocks, *The Golden Compass* centred round one girl – Lyra's – quest to find a miraculous particle capable of uniting whole universes. Along the way she meets all manner of creatures and monsters. But what starts out as a magical children's tale soon becomes a complex philosophical epic.

Daniel was cast in the role of Lord Asriel. His character was both a hero and a villain. 'It's complicated,' he explained. 'He's Lyra's father, but he's sort of given his child to this college in Oxford, which is in a parallel universe to ours, but very similar in lots of ways. He has a desire to open up the heavens so that knowledge and understanding can float between the worlds and we'll understand the world sort of scientifically.'

For the part, he wore brogues and corduroy and even grew a beard. Daniel referred to it in jest as his 'explorer's look'. 'I grew it for the beginning of the film because Asriel is holed up in a prison cell, so shaving it off symbolises his freedom,' he explained.

Once again it was a completely different experience to anything he had been involved in previously. 'It's the first time I've worked with so many special effects,' he told journalists at a press conference. 'I've not actually done very much but I mean, there's always a certain aspect in big movies that you're going to do, but not like this. It's been a great experience; but I've been lucky enough that my character's quite aloof. He doesn't have to have major conversations with his daemon. I have a connection with the bears… It's an acting job; I've been doing it a long time – imagining people who aren't there has never been particularly difficult for me. I don't know whether that's a good thing.'

The film was thankfully also much less physically demanding than James Bond. 'It's a great relief,' said Daniel, smiling. 'Well, except we've been up in

Switzerland doing these extra scenes. I've been sliding down my arse on a glacier for the past week and it's been fantastic. We were literally helicoptered up there and spending the day up on a glacier filming some chase sequences. We're using it as being the North Pole and around northern Scandinavia.'

Although working on *The Golden Compass* was child's play compared to the dangerous stunts in *Casino Royale*, the Bond production team was still anxious about Daniel's trip to the arctic. 'I guess they were a little concerned that, having discovered their new James Bond in Daniel, we then headed to the Arctic Circle where polar bears were a constant and deadly threat to the crew,' revealed *TGC* director Chris Weitz.

Daniel confessed that he had been a fan of fantasy novels as a child. 'I read Tolkein when I was a child and I still read *Lord Of The Rings* occasionally. It's one of the books that I revisit. You have a holiday and you have two weeks, they're kind of easy books to pick up and just plough through.' He drew comparisons between the two trilogies. 'Like with Tolkien, there's something about these books that's beyond fantasy. It's not just about witches and elves. It's a story about true feelings.'

Already a fan of Philip Pullman's work, Daniel was happy to be involved in the project. 'He's [Pullman's] a very subversive human being – a very intelligent, lovely human being, but he's got a big subversive streak; very appealing. It's the debate the books raise that I find so interesting. And I know they've been accused of being anti-religious. I don't actually agree with that – I think it's quite the opposite really; they believe in faith and they believe in all the original Christian ideas of love and charity. If it [the film] raises a debate about organised religion, that can't be a bad thing.'

There was also the risk that religious topics might be off-putting to an American market. Daniel disagreed. 'I don't think we should worry about it,' he said, shaking his head. 'I really don't, because actually that's not the central theme of the books. The central theme of the books is the journey of this young girl and how she deals with the problems of going there. I really don't think there's a problem with this debate. I think it's a very healthy thing to talk about and if we do raise controversy in the States then we should deal with it.'

He even had the opportunity to spend some time with Phillip Pullman and discuss the different subject matters considered in the book. 'We've had a couple of – fairly – sober evenings. I was a big fan of his obviously because I'd read the books. He's got a lot of energy and desire, and feels very passionately about what he writes about.'

Working alongside Nicole Kidman also made filming a pleasurable experience. Daniel admitted, 'She turns me on. Not in a sordid, horrible way… well, come to think of it…' Nicole was equally fond of Daniel. She even asked him for his autograph! Her son Conor was a big Bond fan. She also praised his acting ability, referring to him as 'an actor's actor'. 'Stephen Daldry [who directed Nicole in *The Hours* and Daniel on the London stage] said to me, "He is the best actor in England, and if you get a chance to work with him, do it."'

Daniel enjoyed taking a break from filming James Bond, but he was still fully committed to the franchise. Once filming of *The Golden Compass* was complete, he set to work on *Bond 22*, due for release in November 2008. 'He has these gaps between the Bonds,' explained the producer Kevin Loader, who had worked with the actor on numerous occasions. 'We did float a little script past him the other day and he did consider it extremely seriously. I think he'll go where his curiosity and his sense of value takes him.'

Although everyone involved in the Bond project had a feeling that it would be successful, no one could have quite predicted just how popular the brand would become. Barbara Broccoli and her production team understood Daniel had to have the freedom to work on various other film productions, but ultimately he would need to work around the schedule for filming James Bond. He had signed up to work on two more films. It was a huge commitment but one that he felt comfortable in keeping. If several projects had to go on the back burner, then so be it. 'There's time,' he shrugged. 'And if there isn't, there isn't. I love going to work. I mean, as long as I'm not doing too much that it becomes a bore. What's great about it is that these films will be spaced and there's going to be time to work on other jobs. We'll figure it out.'

There were also several more projects scheduled for 2008. Baille Walsh's *Flashback Of A Fool* told the story of a fading Hollywood star who looks back at the days of his youth after returning from his best friend's funeral. Cast in the lead role, Daniel filmed in London and Cape Town. Satsuki accompanied him for part of the trip and the pair enjoyed a few days of rare and well deserved holiday, prior to filming.

*Defiance*, directed by Edward Zwick (*Blood Diamond* – 2007) was based on a true story about a band of Jewish resistance fighters, while *I, Lucifer* (based on Glen Duncan's bestseller) followed the implications of giving Satan a human existence for a one-month trial period.

By all accounts, his diary was looking extremely busy. 'Bond's six months of shooting so that's half the year. And then another three months at the end of the year to advertise the movie,' said Daniel, doing the calculations. 'There's a couple of months in there to squeeze in something.'

As was to be expected, the new 007 movie was shrouded in secrecy. Given the working title of *Bond 22*, it would be the 22nd official film in the James Bond franchise. Pre-production work on the movie was already underway before *Casino Royale* was completed. Barbara Broccoli confirmed that the new film would be a direct continuation. Daniel also hinted that events in *Casino Royale* would spur Bond on to 'go out for revenge'. Discussing the final scene of the film where Bond shoots Mr White (Jasper Christensen) in the leg, he said, 'This is the last scene in the movie and I wanted to show that Bond means business. We don't know if he kills the guy. We certainly expect that he is going to extract some information from him.'

In an interview with the magazine *Entertainment Weekly*, Eva Green suggested that Vesper Lynd's French–Algerian boyfriend, mentioned in *Casino Royale*, would be the villain in *Bond 22*. Giancarlo Giannini also revealed to the Italian newspaper *Il Giornale* that he would be taking on the role of Rene Mathis for a second time. He said that Mathis would be an ally of Bond and would use his status as a double agent to help him find out who it was that Mr White and Le Chiffre worked for.

The director Roger Mitchell, who worked previously with Daniel on *Enduring Love* and *The Mother*, was initially drafted in to work on the project. However, due to several complications, he soon walked out. 'We couldn't find a way of making us all happy with the script,' he told reporters. 'It's been through various drafts, but I just decided to say no before I got too far into it. In the end I didn't feel comfortable with the Bond process and I was very nervous that there was a start date but really no script at all.' Daniel confirmed that the script was yet to be completed. 'We have to make the next one, I think, better than the last one to keep people happy.'

Although details of the actual plot were kept under wraps, scriptwriters Neal Purvis and Robert Wade suggested that *Bond 22* would feature untapped elements from the original Ian Fleming short stories (originally published in 1960). 'There's a few morsels but you'd have to say that the carcass has been pretty stripped. There are still a few details from the short stories that it would be nice to use.'

Rumours about the project ranged from plausible to ridiculous. The singer Amy Winehouse revealed that the producers had approached her to sing the main theme for *Bond 22*. Unfortunately, due to prior work commitments, she was unable to take them up on the offer. It was also unlikely that Aston Martin would supply the new car for Bond this time, due to Ford selling the company in March 2007. Instead it was speculated that Jaguar would provide a replacement.

After a 12-month break, Daniel was very much looking forward to reprising the role of James Bond. But he admitted there was a lot of preparation work to be done – principally in the gym! 'I had some down time and got to enjoy myself a bit,' he said. 'I'm getting back in shape now; I'm building myself up again.'

Some tabloids reported that Daniel had requested Bond bosses keep him covered up in the next movie, fearing fans were more concerned with his physical prowess than his acting talents. 'Daniel was uncomfortable with the amount of nudity he had to do,' an undisclosed source told the *Daily Mail* newspaper. 'He appreciated that a lot of it was to win over the female fans, but it's not something that he wants to make a habit of, no matter how good he looks in his trunks.'

But the man himself refused to shed any light on the matter. Whether Bond would be featured in any further states of undress was almost as tightly guarded a secret as actual details of the film's plot. Initially frivolous stories had irritated the serious actor, but over time he had grown accustomed to dealing with tabloid speculation.

As anyone who knew Daniel Craig well would testify, never once did he allow success to go to his head. Hailing from humble beginnings, he had learned to patiently hone his craft over time. With hindsight he was glad to have enjoyed that period of gradual development. 'I got a lot of work quite young, but nothing that you'd call success,' he admitted. 'The experiences I've gained made me a happier person. If I had been successful when I was younger, I would have blown it.'

Now older, wiser and a little more rugged round the edges, he was ready to take on the world. At last it appeared the 'actor most likely to' was finally realising his dream and, by all accounts, he was ready to tackle every challenge head on. 'Completely,' he said with a mischievous grin. 'There's no point in turning up unless you're ready to rock and roll!'

# CHAPTER 13

# FINDING SOLACE

Having proved himself a worthy heir to the 007 title, Daniel Craig's career path was firmly mapped out. Once known only as Kate Moss's rugged arm candy, the tabloids now deemed Daniel worthy of his own column inches.

While the attention was flattering, it wasn't always welcome. Daniel found himself in a difficult position: at heart he was still just a simple actor, but his ambition and huge success had thrown him into the limelight. It wasn't a place where he felt entirely comfortable.

In a bid to redress the balance in his career, Daniel opted to take part in several smaller-scale productions. One particularly close to his heart was Baille Walsh's *Flashbacks of a Fool*. Daniel described Baille as his 'closest male friend' and was overjoyed to be cast in the lead role of Joe, a lonely washed-up movie star, and then called upon to be the film's executive producer.

Walsh had written the script six years previously, specifically with Daniel in mind. 'We've had an on-and-off goal of trying to get it off the ground ever since,' admitted Daniel. There were some eerie parallels between Daniel and the main protagonist.

'The premise was always about a big Hollywood actor who's had a huge amount of success,' said Daniel. 'It just so happened that I did become James Bond – though that has helped a little bit in other ways.'

In contrast to the staggering £60 million production budget of Bond, *Flashbacks of a Fool* was made for just £5.5 million. Daniel hoped to use his newfound success and status to help fund the film and drum up interest among investors. 'You can be very embarrassed about asking people to spend money and you're putting your neck on the line, so if I'm going to ask people to spend money, it has to be something I believe in,' said Daniel. By adding a big name to the bill he hoped to raise the movie's profile: 'If being famous means I can make films like this, if I can be responsible – even slightly – for getting movies I can be proud of off the ground, I am going to get a huge amount of enjoyment out of it.'

Daniel felt immediately drawn to his character: 'When we meet Joe he has lost everything, not just interest in his business but his interest in living. And that for me was what drew me to the story. I think you have to work hard at not becoming disillusioned about what you do for a living. If you have any success you have to maintain an energy and a love for it. If you can that is a great thing.

'But it is less to do with whether he is successful as a businessman or as an actor – he has failed as a human being and I wanted to explore that.'

*Flashbacks of a Fool* opens with Daniel's character Joe receiving some bad news that casts his mind back to an event from one summer in his childhood. 'There are things in the film I relate to very directly,' said Daniel. 'I hit 40 this year, but I still think about being a teenager, and hopefully I will for the rest of my life.'

Exploring his character's childhood led Daniel to revisit certain aspects of his own past. The young Joe (Harry Eden) falls for a girl his own age (Felicity Jones) but also has a disastrous relationship with an older woman, and the scenario stirred up Daniel's memories of teen romances and first loves.

'It's supposed to look like that endless summer we all had when we were kids,' he explained. 'But with that much sex though? I don't know? I don't think that ever happened. Maybe in my mind ...'

Those early yearnings and awkward pangs of passion reminded Daniel of his first kiss. 'You can remember those feelings of thinking, Oh my God, we're touching! You'd read about it in magazines but nothing could prepare you, and then suddenly, Oh my God, I'm doing it!

'Those moments at 15 define the rest of your life. Everything starts firing – suddenly the electricity starts, the connectors start happening ... you might be going to have sex at some point. And it's a huge emotional turmoil. It certainly was for me.'

Daniel was joined by a strong British cast including Helen McRory, Olivia Williams and Harry Eden, and a soundtrack of vintage David Bowie and Roxy Music. Set in an English seaside town, the film was actually shot in South Africa.

Once again, Daniel dazzled critics with his performance. Female fans paid particular attention to a scene where Daniel saunters into a shower naked. Given his past resumé, Daniel had absolutely no hesitation about filming a revealing scene. He prepared by putting in a few extra hours at the gym.

'Obviously, when I came to do the movie I knew that I was going to have to take my clothes off – so I might have worked a little bit harder to keep myself fit,' he confessed. 'But it doesn't matter if you look a million dollars, everybody has their flaws.'

Thanks to Daniel's involvement, *Flashbacks* received a great deal of media attention. Celebrities such as Noel Gallagher, Lily Allen, Sharlene Spiteri, Boy George, Rupert Everett, Claudia Schiffer and Donna Air all turned out for the premiere in London's Leicester Square.

Daniel was chuffed: 'It was a good way to launch it. Every movie I get involved with, I do it at as deep a level as I possibly can. But this has been a much more personal journey for me. I just feel amazed because it has been a struggle.'

While he enjoyed the diversion of working on *Flashbacks*, Daniel was looking forward to reprising his Bond role. As a date for filming drew closer, the frenzy – which had never really died down – started to build.

Filming finally began on 3 January 2008. Daniel felt strangely relieved and comfortable to be back on set with his 007 cast and crew. Even though they hadn't been in touch much in previous months, Daniel felt instantly at home.

'When you first walk onto a film set, it's the most wonderful thing, like running away to the circus. You feel like you've gone to a special place, because everybody works very intensely and parties very hard and gets on with each other because they have to.

'On the whole, people are genuinely nice, and you end up with a million phone numbers that you don't call. It's kind of sad, but when I arrived on the set for the Bond movie, I knew at least 80 per cent of the crew – I had worked with them before on other jobs over the years.

'It was kind of reassuring that I knew all these people. But when you finish a job, you say goodbye to each other, and you give each other a big hug, and you go, "I'll see you on the next one." Because everybody's got a life, and you realise you've got to go back to that life.'

It didn't take Daniel long to get back into his role. He teased the public with tasters of plot lines for the as yet untitled movie.

'It's a completely new story,' he said, 'and it does go straight on from the end of the last one. We've picked some themes that come up in the last movie. They are pretty fundamental ones, and they're good fun to do.'

He promised there would be more action, more humour and – much to the pleasure of his female fans – a little bit of nudity. Speculation about the film was finally put to rest in January 2008 when the production team held a press conference in London. They took the opportunity to announce the title – *Quantum of Solace*.

Even Daniel admitted it was a curious choice. 'It has grown on me,' he told reporters on the film's set at London's Pinewood Studios. 'It doesn't trip off the tongue. But why should it?'

According to producer Michael Wilson, the title (chosen only a few days earlier) was taken from a story by Ian Fleming that appeared in the collection *For Your Eyes Only*. It translated roughly as 'a measure of comfort'.

'[It's] that spark of niceness in a relationship that if you don't have, you might as well give up,' explained Daniel. 'In this film Bond is looking for a quantum of solace. He wants closure.'

The film would be a direct sequel to *Casino Royale*, beginning with Bond devastated by the betrayal of his true love Vesper Lynd. 'He had his heart broken at the end of the last movie and that certainly is a spur for him in this one,' revealed Daniel.

'I'd be lying if I said there wasn't revenge in his heart. But it's more than that. That spurs him on, but that's not what the movie is. It's not a revenge movie. It's about him figuring a few things out.'

Producer Barbara Broccoli said the film mixes Bond's 'inner turmoil' with action and, of course, plenty of gadgets. Michael Wilson confirmed Daniel's earlier claims by promising the film would have 'twice as much action' as its predecessor.

'It's pretty jam-packed,' he told reporters, going on to say that even Judi Dench's character M would be 'kicking some ass'.

A new addition to the cast was Mathieu Amalric, cast as the villain, Dominic Greene. The French actor had recently starred in the Oscar-nominated *The Diving Bell and the Butterfly*. Mathieu joked that he'd modelled his character for the Bond film on the former Prime Minister Tony Blair and the French President Nicolas Sarkozy. 'I've been taking details,' he said. 'The smile of Tony Blair, the craziness of Sarkozy, he's the worst villain we've ever had.'

Upping the glamour stakes were two new Bond girls – Ukrainian Olga Kurylenko as Camille, a feisty Bolivian, and Gemma Arterton as an MI6 agent named Fields. Producers hinted that Bond may find his solace with one of these two beauties.

'In the movie, he is obviously still attached to his past,' revealed Olga Kurylenko. 'The appearance of this new girl might divert him. Or, it might not.'

Made famous by the 2007 remake of *St Trinian's*, 21-year-old Gemma was still incredulous at having landed her new role. Up until a year ago the beautiful brunette was just a budding drama student. Now she was filming love scenes with one of the most sought-after men of the big screen. 'I still feel like I shouldn't really be here,' she said. When asked about a kissing scene with Daniel, she confessed to being reduced to a 'giggly girl'.

'It's insane,' she admitted. 'To be working with Judi Dench and Daniel Craig – I feel so young and inexperienced and green.'

Luckily Daniel offered her some helpful reassurance. He admitted that even he felt nervous about shooting the new film. 'All the fear I felt before is still there,' he told her. 'This is a $200 million movie, and it's James Bond. We have to make it great.'

As with previous Bond movies, *Quantum of Solace* would be shot on location all over the world. Destinations included Italy, Austria, Chile and Peru. Daniel flew out to Chile to film his first scenes. The film would open with a mammoth chase scene – the longest ever opening sequence of any Bond film – lasting 30 minutes.

Travelling the world and visiting exotic locations was one of the biggest perks of the job, Daniel admitted. For this particular film, he would be accruing quite a few additional stamps in his passport. He was particularly impressed by northern Chile.

'It's an extraordinary place,' he mused. 'A shingled desert, high plains and nothingness, and we were up at 10,000 feet and the sky is beyond big. It's horizon to horizon, uninterrupted, and the stars - just a complete canopy of stars, and you can watch them move over as the night goes on.'

In Italy, the Bond crew was lucky enough to have a

private viewing of the Sistine Chapel, and in Panama they went to Colón on the Caribbean side. 'It's an incredibly poor city with all this crumbling deco architecture and no running water, and shit running in the streets, gunfire going off at night, and all the kids are wearing perfectly pressed white clothing – I don't know how they do it.'

Daniel vividly recalled the first night when he arrived. 'A thousand people came out with their families. I got out of the car and they all said, "James Bond!" It was the last place on earth I was expecting it.'

Daniel loved to travel, and wished it was something he could do more often.

'I'd love to travel like Ewan McGregor and Charley Boorman, just get on a motorbike and take off but unfortunately I've become a bit of a commodity and I've got security guys around me most of the time.'

'I do try to slip the net as much as I can and get out and see places. Otherwise you're getting the big gate up and hiding behind it and losing touch with reality. I say that but actually I think by doing Bond I've lost touch with reality quite a lot.'

Producers had warned Daniel that filming *Quantum of Solace* would be both physically and emotionally demanding. It was a challenge he relished. He coped by setting himself a disciplined timetable: he would get up at 5am, be in make-up by 6am, and on set by 7am. After a quick run-through of the day's scenes, he would then be shooting for up to twelve hours. The day would end with a session in the gym, some stunt practice, and a very light dinner. By 10pm, Daniel would be tucked up in bed and fast asleep.

'That's my life six days a week, six months a year,' he sighed. 'I don't just do the five or six days of filming on set. I also have meetings and training. I have stunts to work on and scenes to figure out with the director. That is my job for six months. And it is a good job.'

But Daniel wasn't completely monastic about his schedule; he did factor in some time to relax – after all, he was only human. 'Maybe on Saturday night I'll get shitfaced and sleep it off on Sunday, because if I didn't I'd go insane,' he smiled.

'That's the way he works,' said one of the Quantum producers, Michael Wilson. 'I've never known an actor to be that focused.'

It quickly became apparent that Daniel had taken on more than just an actor's role; he was also becoming increasingly involved in the film production. He was forever tinkering with the script, or embellishing stunts.

'Now, when I go and get involved with a movie, I have to apply this experience,' he admitted. 'I have to do those same things. I can't just sort of turn up anymore.'

Now comfortable in the character of Bond, Daniel was keen to give his portrayal of 007 even greater depth and complexity.

'The question I keep asking myself while playing the role is, 'Am I the good guy or just a bad guy who works for the good side?' he told journalists. 'Bond's role, after all, is that of an assassin when you come down to it. I have never played a role in which someone's dark side shouldn't be explored. I don't think it should be confusing by the end of the movie, but during the movie you should be questioning who he is.'

Daniel was determined his Bond should have a softer, more empathetic side. 'There are people on this planet where you go, 'Oops, no, I don't even want to look that person in the eye. But that real scariness is not something I'm capable of. That's something maybe De Niro is capable of at his best. But that's not me. As tough a role as I have to play, I'm always just me. It's good to be in touch with as much of yourself as possible. Otherwise, you're a rather one-note performer. Who wants to be the tough guy and nothing else?'

Feeling more relaxed in the role, Daniel agreed with producers that it was also time Bond dressed more comfortably, too. American fashion designer Tom Ford was keen to lend a hand. He admired the way Daniel Craig had shaped Bond into a sophisticated 21st century man. 'James Bond is, for me, an international character,' Tom Ford gushed. 'One of the things that makes Daniel's Bond fresh and relevant is that he does not play up the clichés or mannerisms of English style.'

He described the suits he designed for Daniel as being 'global', blending English cuts with Italian flair. The suits were a big hit, with up to 300 made for the film. 'Daniel knows exactly what works on him,' said Tom Ford. 'Really, the simpler the clothes, the more handsome he looks.'

Daniel was even spotted wearing them off screen. He

would arrive at magazine photo shoots wearing Tom Ford, firmly believing the suits were a far superior fit to anything the stylists could provide.

Daniel was reportedly nervous about one aspect of the filming. Given the commotion caused by his "trunks" scene in *Casino Royale*, Daniel was prepared for more nudity to come. After all, the Bond producers knew they had an eager audience of women to please.

Although he'd buffed up for *Casino Royale*, Daniel admitted to letting himself go once filming was complete. 'I went on holiday and I let myself go in a lot of ways,' he confessed. 'But that was just because we were in France and eating good food and drinking a lot of wine.'

Besides, he'd never been a gym freak. Life was too short to spend it sweating on a treadmill. 'I've kept up going to the gym, but not quite as intensely as I was doing before. Frankly, it's nice to just sit back for a minute and just enjoy your life.'

Daniel had made his feelings clear to producer Barbara Broccoli, insisting she go easy on any nude shots. Unfortunately for the reluctant pin-up, the savvy businesswoman had other ideas.

'I think Barbara is going to have a word to say about that,' he said of his reluctance to film nude scenes. But he refused to give away any details when he said, 'We'll see. Bond might have to take a shower.'

Despite her plans, Daniel insisted he wouldn't be hitting the gym quite as hard as he had done for *Casino Royale*. 'I'm probably not going to bulk up as much as I did last time. It was an exercise that worked and I'm very happy we did it.'

Tabloid reports emerged that Daniel had ditched his dumbbells in favour of a far more meditative form of exercise – yoga. His girlfriend Satsuki was already a big fan and had been attending classes for years. She encouraged Daniel to experiment with calming exercises such as Pilates and yoga.

There was also a rumour that Daniel had developed an interest in girly cosmetics. A lorry load of products was allegedly delivered to his on-set trailer. 'As well as fake tan, bronzer, eye cream, cleanser, toner and moisturiser, Daniel's been having regular manicures,' reported an insider.

'He uses eye drops to make the whites of the eyes appear brighter and has been told to splash his face with ice-cold water before filming to close the pores and make him look younger.'

Daniel was even billed as the first 'metrosexual' Bond, thanks to his popularity with both men and women. When asked to comment on such reports, Daniel simply raised his eyebrow.

Another source at Bond production company Eon confirmed that Daniel was having trouble getting back into the fitness swing. 'His only comfort is a post workout pint of Guinness!' they joked. 'He says it's all part of his regime and reckons it's good for the heart.'

Given Daniel's love of a drink, it was totally conceivable. Another vital exercise aid was Daniel's iPod. He often used music to help him train. 'I have about 5,000 songs on my iPod. It's very eclectic – anything from Kate Bush to the Raconteurs,' he said. 'I love it on shuffle. But it can be nerve-racking if anyone is around. When something dodgy comes on, like *Grease*, you're like, 'Nooo!' and dive to switch to the next tune.

'I also quite like German heavy metal – like the band Die Toten Hosen,' he added.

Once again, Daniel insisted on doing his own stunts wherever possible. 'We're going from stunt sequence to stunt sequence. We did a body flight thing where you are free-falling in a wind tunnel. That was tough.

'I did a two-day fight sequence which we had been rehearsing for two months. That was physically very hard; getting hit, basically."

This was the kind of physical workout Daniel enjoyed. 'Until my joints go, I will keep going as Bond,' he joked. 'I love having that adrenaline rush. It makes you realise that you are mortal and that life must be enjoyed.'

He also strongly believed that doing his own stunts was beneficial to the success of the film. 'I really think it makes a huge difference. No matter how good the CGI is, however good the double is, if the audience can see it's you, and they have that moment of, "F*** me, it's him!" they get more involved in the movie.'

His commitment was commendable, but enthusiasm did nothing to diminish his fear. 'I'm not good with heights. I'm not an athlete, although I've always enjoyed keeping fit in between bouts of minor alcoholism. So it's a big challenge. You're up there on top of a building and it's a long way down, and the explosion is going to go off, and you have to go on "Action" and look cool while you're doing it. I go for it because I'd be pissed off with myself in the future if I didn't.'

But as for undertaking dangerous sports in his spare time, Daniel was quick to point out that quite the opposite was true. 'I read books, go to the pub and drink.'

But he wasn't prepared to take any chances. According to newspapers Daniel had insured his body for £5 million. 'Daniel's insurance premiums have gone through the roof!' revealed an on-set spy.

More confident than ever, Daniel attempted even more dangerous stunts. It felt almost inevitable that he would experience an accident at some point. During one scene Daniel cut his face, which then required eight stitches. A week later he suffered a minor hand injury and was sent to hospital.

'There was a minor incident on set,' Columbia TriStar Motion Picture Group spokesman Steve Elzer said in a statement. 'Daniel injured his hand. He sought medical attention. He was back on the set within a matter of hours and production went on.' Daniel simply put his injuries down to occupational hazards.

It wasn't the first accident to occur during filming. Stuntmen were injured while filming an action sequence on winding lakeside roads in Northern Italy, and a fire had broken out at Pinewood Studios. Such incidents gave rise to a rumour that the film was jinxed.

Fortunately, Daniel came out of the filming relatively unscathed. Now he was preparing to enter the real lion's den – the media circus. 'I love acting,' he smiled. 'It's the whole bollocks that comes along with it that I'm not sure about. You are judged, and the way people perceive you suddenly becomes an issue.'

Playing the world's most famous spy had changed Daniel's life considerably. 'I was at a stage of my career in which things were going pretty well,' he admitted. 'I was making plenty of money, relatively speaking – enough to live on. But when this opportunity came along, I knew it would turn everything upside down. It wasn't about the money. It was about changing things up and seeing what would happen.'

But there were some inevitable downsides. Daniel was still uncomfortable with fame. 'I can't go out without being recognised,' he complained. 'It's a pain in the ass.'

He could no longer, for instance, spontaneously meet up with friends in the pub. These days he had to be a lot more careful. 'I have learnt to drink faster and duck out before I'm surrounded by a mob,' he laughed. 'I'm not moaning, but I have had to reassess the way I look at the world, the way I live my life. I knew I would, I just didn't have a plan for it.'

Daniel knew he had a reputation for being difficult in interviews, but he put any perceived difficulties down to lazy journalism. The press was particularly interested in Daniel's relationship with Satsuki. It had been reported that the pair would marry after filming for *Quantum of Solace* was complete.

Daniel had reportedly presented Satsuki with a Cartier ring – a large diamond solitaire with a platinum setting –

during a romantic holiday in Italy. She was seen sporting the rock on the red carpet for the premiere of *The Golden Compass*. When quizzed about any marital plans, however, the pair denied they would be tying the knot anytime soon.

He had always been extremely protective of his close friends and loved ones. He not only wanted to shield them from the glare of the public eye; he was also worried that being too vocal could, somehow, jeopardise his happiness. 'If you go, "This is my life, this is my beautiful family, these are my beautiful children, my beautiful mother, my beautiful father, my beautiful house, blah blah, blah," then it all goes tits up, and they go: "It's not so beautiful, now is it?"

'I would kill for my family. But this is not their world, and they have to be kept separated. I can't take the risk of opening that door.' Daniel's family played a vital role in helping him to keep his feet on the ground. He claimed he found it much easier to escape the crowds when he was in America. 'I get in a car with my girlfriend, I pick a direction and go that way, because you can go that way for a very long time. And once you get away from the cities and into the middle of nowhere, even if people recognise you, they've got more important things to think about, like getting on with life. If I didn't have that, if I couldn't escape, I'd go insane.'

Once filming of *Quantum* had finished, Daniel rewarded himself with a well-earned holiday. 'We,' he told journalists, referring to Satsuki, 'are taking a holiday ... It's a military operation to remain private.'

He travelled to Italy for two weeks to relax, read books and watch films. 'I just did all those things I hadn't been able to do for six months because I'd been working so hard,' he grinned. 'It was glorious.'

Spending time with Satsuki really helped Daniel to keep his priorities in check. The couple had been together for many years and their relationship had weathered a number of storms.

'I couldn't get through it without her,' Daniel admitted. 'You've got to have a sense of perspective and she gives me that. Being an actor does put a strain on a relationship because I'm never in one place, and there's never seems to be a lot of time. I have to fight for that, and for my family. I need that balance; it's crucially important.'

Like Daniel, Satsuki was also a keen traveller. They both loved to compare notes on the wonderful places they'd visited. 'We've been to some amazing places,' Daniel recalled. 'I remember one night when we were in China. We were in this sky bar, at the top of a beautiful hotel, having a drink looking out over Beijing, and we were just blown away. You have to have someone to share this stuff with. In Italy, we even had a private viewing of the Sistine Chapel. A fantastic guy took us around and explained the history of all the paintings. How cool is that? I said to Sats, "We have to remember this."'

When Daniel returned to London to promote *Quantum*, journalists were surprised to see him wearing a sling. He was still recovering from injuries sustained on set. Some journalists joked that now Daniel Craig looked even more of a hard man, but the actor was quick to play down any damage done.

'It's exactly what happens every time you do something like this,' he shrugged. 'You get your finger trapped or your face split open. I had a boo-hoo, but it's amazing how the human body can repair itself. I have very little of the fingerprint left on this finger because I ripped the pad off ... I also had stitches in my face and shoulder surgery but that was more of an old injury that I needed to get fixed.'

'A lot was made of the injuries. I am not trying to be macho I promise you. It is just that I work with stunt guys and those guys are working through pain barriers that I couldn't even imagine.'

Looking back at the previous few months, Daniel was satisfied with his achievements. 'I think James Bond has changed,' he mused. 'He's not a shallow brute. It's no good if Bond is a cocktail-swigging sexist pig with no interior struggle. Bond is often p****d off or upset and I wanted to bring that out.'

When *Quantum of Solace* finally opened in cinemas, it received glowing reviews. The box office figures were also proof Daniel Craig had finally been accepted as James Bond: pulling in £15.4 million, it was the biggest movie opening in British history.

When informed about the hit figures, Daniel responded with typical nonchalance. 'I know that, when it comes down to it, these films are about box office, but the moment I start thinking about the figures, I'll be stuffed –

though maybe I won't be saying that in a year's time, when I've spent everything,' he joked.

At last, fans had accepted the blond-haired, blue-eyed actor as 007. When asked how he's managed to charm his audience, Daniel lay credit partly with the fact he'd managed to shift Bond into the 21$^{st}$ century without losing any of the character's quintessential Britishness.

'We've taken the chin-chin out of it but I love the Bond-isms. I love all the lines. I love all the quirkiness about it. Like, the martini scene in this movie is him drinking six of them, getting pissed and being thoughtful about the woman he loved. But it is important that he does drink martinis because they are part of him.'

But right now, Daniel was just looking forward to a break. Although he was contracted to do two more Bond films, for the next few months he would probably turn his attentions to arthouse films and his personal life.

# CHAPTER 14

# ACTION
# HERO

Ever since Daniel first set foot on a stage, he'd always been driven by a commitment to his art. Of course he enjoyed earning money, but he wasn't about to stop working just because his pay packet was now considerably larger. Even before *Quantum of Solace* had hit cinema screens, Daniel was already busy working on his next film project, directed by Ed Zwick (*Blood Diamond*, *The Last Samurai*).

In *Defiance*, he would play another action hero. But the character was quite a leap from James Bond. The film followed a band of Jewish partisans who held their own against the Germans in the forests of Belarus during the World War II. Daniel would play the hard-ball leader Tuvia Bielski, and was joined by co-stars Liev Schreiber and Jamie Bell.

250

The film was based on a true story about a group of farmers who managed to keep more than 1,200 Jews alive by refusing to surrender to the Nazis. The story only came to light after a book was published in 1993. Daniel was immediately drawn to the script and his character.

'What I find fascinating was that this normal man, a farmer, was thrust into the role of leadership and somehow figured out these great moral questions. That really made the story interesting for me. It was just literally one of those situations that I sort of looked at, read it and thought that it was an amazing story.'

Whenever he was presented with a new script, he would always ask himself – does this story actually work? 'Everything falls into place around that. And, really, I try to keep it as instinctual as possible, because if you start thinking, I must do a romantic comedy now, because I've just done a psychotic, you're stuffed. It would seem the antithesis of art.'

Daniel's co-stars quickly warmed to him on set. Live Schreiber recalled meeting him for the first time. 'I was in Lithuania wondering what I had gotten myself into,' he said. 'Then I see Daniel running toward me with open arms. He gave me the biggest bear hug, and I thought, Okay, this is going to be okay. I'd follow this guy anywhere.'

Alexa Davalos, who played Daniel's love interest, was equally complimentary. When preparing for a sex scene in a chilly tent, Daniel did everything to make her feel as comfortable as possible. 'He's obviously a handsome creature, but it's who he is generally that comes through. There's a strength and a calm that's very attractive,' she swooned. 'He's comfortable in his skin.'

On set, Daniel made an effort to be friends with everyone – from co-stars to production crew. He was known for his on-set playfulness and was always cracking jokes. Although he was extremely disciplined about his work, he would never take himself too seriously. He also remained extremely humble, and few would guess he was an international movie star.

'Daniel comes to know people,' said director, Ed Zwick. 'He's very able and interested in connecting. There are other actors whose process forbids that, who need to be isolated.'

However, it wasn't all plain sailing on the set of *Defiance*. Daniel did run into difficulty learning Russian, a necessary part of his role. 'It was a nightmare for me. I'm just the worst student in the world. I left school at sixteen. I literally cannot conjugate a verb in English! I really did screw up there because I actually don't really know what a verb is.'

Instead, Daniel had to learn the language phonetically. Although he often felt like giving up, he persevered for the good of the role. What's more, he was stubborn and refused to be beaten. 'I've tried to learn languages and I know there's a certain stage that you get to where you have to make that sort of leap of faith and go, 'Okay, I know how to put this accent through my mouth. It's a really hard process to go through. As an actor you have to try and make that leap because you're trying to communicate and communication is the name of the game. If you're not doing that you're kind of failing.'

Another aspect of training for the role involved meeting family members of the Jews who had survived in the forest. Daniel admitted it was a very strange and quite awkward situation. The hardest thing, he said, was how to start a conversation. Looking for a way to break the ice, he disappeared to find some vodka for his guests. 'We all sort of toasted and then they came out of their shells. By the end, we had to be told to leave because they were making so much noise. We connected and they're full of life. They're full of energy.'

Once again, Daniel found himself fully absorbed in a film role. While filming on location in Lithuania, he worked for six long days a week. 'We stayed on set literally constantly and we'd be under tents, tarps, sort of watching the scenes. That made it very immediate. It made us all feel involved with everything and it gave a community feeling to us which was kind of essential for the movie, giving it that life.'

Once *Defiance* was done and dusted, Daniel moved swiftly on to his next film project, *Cowboys and Aliens*. A sci-fi Western set in the mid-19th century, the film also starred Harrison Ford, Olivia Wilde and Sam Rockwell. There were also some nig names behind the scenes: the film was directed by Jon Favreau (*Iron Man*) and produced by Steven Speilberg, Brian Grazer and Ron Howard.

Daniel would play Jake Lonegan, a mysterious cowboy and wanted fugitive who wakes up in the desert with no memory of the past and only an alien device attached to his wrist. He realises the town is under attack by aliens, and that he may hold the key to saving his fellow citizens. However, first he must persuade them not to hand him over to the Federal Marshall.

The film was based on the 100-page graphic novel created by Scott Mitchell Rosenberg and written by Fred Van Lente and Andrew Foley in 2006. Expectations were high, and it was tipped to be one of the biggest films of 2011. The script was quite a departure from Daniel's usual film fodder. Unlike *Defiance*, there was a big budget involved – reportedly $100 million. But that didn't put Daniel off.

'I'm a great fan of popcorn movies when they're done right, and it's hard to get them right,' he admitted. 'With this, we looked at *The Searchers* and *Close Encounters* – classic, serious films from both genres, because we wanted to get the feel absolutely right.'

The script also appealed to Daniel's more playful side. After all, alongside the serious stuff there had to be some fun and humour. 'I get to play a cowboy,' he smiled. 'Then, I get to play a cowboy who battles aliens.'

One of Daniel's favourite aspects of filming was getting to ride a horse every day. 'Whether you came to work with a bad head, or just in sort of a bad mood, getting on a horse was just sort of like, "Oh okay, here we go."'

On set, he made sure he had a laugh with his co-stars – particularly Harrison Ford. He would forever crack jokes about seeing Han Solo on horseback. 'It was the only way I could stay sane working with him,' he joked in defence.

Sharing a wicked sense of humour, Harrison and Daniel became good friends on set. Daniel said of the veteran actor: 'He came powering in with lots of ideas, but also with humour and grace and all those things you'd hope in somebody, but you can't expect.'

Director Jon Favreau also had first-hand experience of Daniel's good sense of humour. 'He likes to laugh. He's not dour by any stretch. His persona onscreen tends to be reserved and calculated, but he's a good host. Gracious. He's very smart. Very. He has a quiet facade, comes across as reserved, but the minute you break bread with him he's full of observations and conversations.'

Actress Olivia Wilde, who played Ella Swenson, was also fortunate enough to share some intimate scenes with Daniel. She had nothing but praise for his kindness, acting ability and – most importantly – good looks. 'There's nothing quite like staring into Daniel Craig's eyes,' she told one journalist. She also recalled her most challenging scene in the film, which involved stripping off for the cameras. 'It was really exciting because we knew we were creating something kind of spectacular in that scene. It was a really cool effect happening, as people will see. It was kind of strange because I was half-naked in front of about a hundred people, including the crew, a bunch of Apache warriors, a bunch of cowboys, and Daniel Craig, who I had to stand in front of basically naked. And he had to take a moment to sort of look me up and down before covering me in a blanket. And I was, like, this is crazy.'

While working on *Cowboys and Aliens*, Daniel also landed to further major film roles. The first would be another Steven Spielberg production, *The Adventures of Tintin: The Secret of the Unicorn*. The second would be David Fincher's adaptation of Stieg Larsson's best-selling book, *The Girl With the Dragon Tattoo*.

In *Tintin*, he would once again star alongside Jamie Bell (who would take the lead role). Daniel would play villain Red Rackham. Simon Pegg, Nick Frost and Mackenzie Crook will also appear in the film.

In *The Girl With The Dragon Tattoo*, Daniel would play the hero's role of journalist Mikael Blomkvist. It was a prestigious role to land; apparently, Brad Pitt, Johnny Depp, George Clooney and Viggo Mortensen were all considered for the part. A Scandinavian version of the film had already been released in UK cinemas, but this would be a much bigger-budget affair.

Adding a further string to his bow, Daniel was also invited by the BBC to do a natural history voiceover for documentary film, *One Life*. It would feature footage from TV series *Life On Earth*, originally narrated by Sir David Attenborough.

Daniel was extremely proud to be involved in the project. 'The BBC Natural History Unit have proven, year after year, that their documentary skills are second to none,' he said. 'For the filmmakers who spend their entire lives recording beautiful images of dwindling wildlife, I have only a sense of awe and a deep rooted respect.'

With so many film projects on the horizon, it looked as

if Daniel would barely have a minute to himself. And the work couldn't have come at a better time. Due to financial difficulties at MGM, production for the next Bond movie had temporarily been put on hold.

Reports suggested MGM was up to $4 billion in debt. Production company EON confirmed in a statement: 'We do not know when development will resume and cannot comment further at this stage.'

However, Daniel remained optimistic. 'I'm ready and willing, and if I get the call, I'll be there... I'm really keen to get going, it's as simple as that. And I'm hoping that, in a while, we will.'

Besides, Daniel had plenty to occupy him for the time being. While his professional life was even busier than ever, there were also important developments taking place in his personal life.

# CHAPTER 15

# A NEW ROMANCE

Remaining true to his word, Daniel was steadfastly tight-lipped about his love life. But it emerged that the Cartier ring he'd bought Satsuki back in 2008 was, in fact, an engagement ring. Describing the willowy film producer as the only person who could keep him grounded, Daniel had decided to make her a more permanent fixture in his life.

The world wondered how the publicity-shy actor might celebrate the big day. Lavish celebrations were unlikely, and he probably wouldn't be selling his story to the glossy magazines. With no immediate plans for a wedding on the horizon, Daniel and Satsuki took another step in consolidating their relationship – they bought a penthouse suite in New York's trendy Tribeca district. The $1.9 million one-bed loft conversion – with 20-foot ceilings, floor-to-ceiling windows and three terraces – was just the sort of place where 007 would have felt at home. It even had a private lift that opened onto one of the terraces. 'It's a very Bond apartment,' estate agent Fredrik Eklund told the press.

There had been a furious bidding war for the apartment, situated close to homes owned by Justin Timberlake, Jessica Biel, James Gandolfini and Mariah Carey. Despite the high price tag, Daniel had no plans to sell his £4million London apartment. But when quizzed about a wedding date, he refused to reveal any plans. He maintained that it was better to keep his private business to himself.

'Nobody's private life is anyone's business, even if you are in the public eye. There should be a clearly defined line and I don't think it takes brain surgery to try and figure that out. It's fairly simple. There's privacy and then there's public life. If you choose to be in the public eye, then maybe you open yourself up to all sorts of rubbish. But if you don't then I think that should be respected. I've had various members of the press knocking on my family's door at various hours of the morning.'

He was especially protective of his daughter. 'I don't really talk about her, because – well, she can't defend herself. But she's fantastic. Fantastic, and she's – you know, she's doing something. She's finishing her education in the States.'

Unlike other celebrities, he wasn't a fan of promoting his career on social media sites such as Facebook and Twitter. 'I'm not on Facebook and I'm not on Twitter either! "Woke up this morning, had an egg"? What relevance is that to anyone? Social networking? Just call each other up and go to the pub and have a drink. I hope the generations to come learn to be a little bit cynical and learn how to mess it up a bit.'

Although Daniel claimed to despise all the 'extraneous stuff' that comes with acting, he did once confess to searching for his name on Google. 'The truth is that I mistakenly go online occasionally and Google my name. It's worse than smoking crack. And, oh man, the hating on the internet. It feels like that's the norm, that the internet has licensed this vitriol.'

While plans were still on hold for the next Bond movie, Daniel set his focus on new film project, *Dream House*. Featuring Naomi Watts and Rachel Weisz, the film was a horror about a family who discover a brutal crime was once committed in their idyllic new home. Daniel would take the lead of Will Atenton, a successful publisher in New York who quits his job to relocate his wife Libby (Rachel Weisz) and their two daughters in a pretty New England town. However, as he starts to uncover the mystery of a mother and children who died, supposedly at the hands of the husband, he realises his own family may be in trouble.

The film was shot on location in Canada, which meant that once again Daniel would be working away from home. Fortunately, he was in good company. He and Rachel Weisz had been friends for about ten years. They moved in the same London theatre circles and had several mutual friends. They allegedly met in 1994 when they appeared together in a workshop play at the National Theatre Studio about French courtesans of the 19th century called *Les Grandes Horizontales*. 'Of course, neither of them was famous then so their first meeting went unrecorded,' said one of the production crew. 'The plot put them into a number of amorous clinches and there was a lot of faked sexual congress and "tasteful" nudity.'

Both actors went on to become extremely successful and their paths would intermittently cross in recent years at film premieres and parties. While not quite as a big a name as Daniel, Rachel had appeared in a number of successful films such as *The Mummy* and *About A Boy*. Her role in 2005 film *The Constant Gardener* earned her an Oscar for Best Supporting Actress.

The daughter of a Jewish/Hungarian medical inventor father and Viennese psychotherapist mother, Rachel was born on 7 March 1970 and brought up in leafy Hampstead, North-West London. At the age of 13, after her picture was featured in society magazine *Harpers And Queen*, she landed a modelling contract. She was then offered a role opposite Richard Gere in the 1985 Hollywood movie *King David*.

But keen to carry on with her education, she turned it down. Instead, she went to read English at Trinity College, Cambridge. She was a particularly active student and became known as a radical feminist. She also founded an award-winning student theatre group, which she later took to the Edinburgh Festival.

She was linked to several high-profile names – including

TV star Neil Morrissey, comedian Ben Miller, American actor Alessandro Nivola and film director Sam Mendes – but for the previous nine years had been living with director, Darren Aronofsky. Responsible for directing Oscar-winning film *Black Swan* Darren was himself quite a success story.

But when Daniel and Rachel started to spend more time together on set, rumours started to fly that they may be more than just good friends. Some members of the film crew even went so far to say Rachel had fallen head-over-heels in love with Daniel. Both camps vehemently denied the rumours. But when Rachel announced that she would be ending her relationship with Darren Aronofsky the rumour mill went into overdrive.

Filming for *Dream House* had ended months previously and Daniel was now in Sweden filming *The Girl With the Dragon Tattoo*. Rachel and Darren issued a statement saying: 'Rachel Weisz and Darren Aronofsky have been separated for some months. They remain close friends and are committed to raising their son together in New York.' Another source claimed the couple had simply grown apart.

The separation came as quite a shock. Only a year earlier, Rachel had gushed about how watertight her relationship was, and she even mentioned the possibility of marriage. 'Funnily enough, just recently I suddenly felt like I really would like to get married. It's just a feeling. I know it's a funny thing,' she told journalists.

Of course, given their busy lives it wasn't easy to have a

relationship, but she worked hard to make sure they spent as much time together as possible. 'I have to consider where I'm travelling to if Darren's going to be working at the same time. I filmed *Agora* in Malta for four months and Darren edited there. I started and he came out two weeks later with his editor. Before that we were both at home in New York, so we've managed to keep the family together and it works.'

But just 12 months later, Darren had packed his bags and moved out of the couple's five-storey townhouse in the East Village. However, he remained on friendly terms with Rachel for the sake of their four-year-old son Henry, of whom they agreed to share custody.

Daniel, in many ways, was an extreme opposite to Darren. 'Darren's such a good and responsible man, but Daniel's brooding and mysterious,' revealed a source. Perhaps he was just what Rachel needed. With a history of working at the RSC, and a number of intellectual interests, it was also extremely conceivable that Daniel should be attracted to the beautiful and intelligent actress.

When it emerged Daniel had also ended his long-term relationship with Satsuki Mitchell, it seemed something must be going on. Rachel was stopped by reporters as she left her home and asked about her relationship with Daniel. She smiled and refused to comment. Reports about the couple started to emerge. One source claimed to have seen Rachel and Daniel kissing in a New York grocery store. 'They looked like the world's hottest couple.'

Then, just before Christmas, the tabloids printed

pictures of Daniel and Rachel enjoying a romantic break in the countryside. The pair were photographed holding hands and laughing. They were reportedly staying in a £1,000-a-week cottage near Yeovil in Somerset. According to local sources, they spent Christmas Eve cuddling up to one another in the local pub.

'Daniel and Rachel looked like a romantic couple in a film,' said one unnamed source. 'They were laughing and hanging on to each other's words and stopping to take photos of each other.'

'They were clinging to each other like honeymooners,' added another customer in the pub. 'The chemistry was obvious.'

A few months later, they were spotted shopping together in the Louis Vuitton store in London's Mayfair. Once they realised photographers were waiting outside, the low-key couple made a dash for their car. Daniel left first, while Rachel cowered behind the shop door.

Rachel was in London working on her new film *360*, in which she stars alongside Jude Law. The cast also includes Sir Anthony Hopkins, Maria Flor and Karl Markovic.

Jude and Rachel had worked together previously on *Enemy At The Gates*, where they shared an on-screen romance. Although she was snapped cuddling up to Jude on set, it was obvious Rachel had eyes only for one man – Daniel. But still the couple stayed silent about their fledgling romance.

Then, after six months of speculation, the shock news broke that Rachel and Daniel had actually tied the knot.

Daniel's publicist released a statement, but refused to elaborate on any details. Reports suggested the simple ceremony had taken place at a friend's house in New York, with only four guests in attendance. These were said to include Daniel's 18-year-old daughter, Ella, and Rachel's son, Henry, plus two family friends who acted as witnesses.

One source was reported as saying: 'Daniel and Rachel insisted on having a small, quiet wedding. They are madly in love and couldn't wait to be husband and wife – but they wanted minimum fuss.'

However, some reports suggested that friends of Daniel at home weren't quite so happy about the event. They were allegedly disgruntled to hear about the wedding through the tabloids, and were hurt Daniel hadn't chosen to invite them.

One actor friend who had worked with Daniel in the past told the papers: 'Frankly, I think it's a bit much he couldn't let his old pals know. I really don't understand why he feels the need for all this cloak-and-dagger silliness.'

Given that Daniel and Rachel had both just come out of very long-term relationships, the whirlwind nature of their romance was quite surprising. However, it did in some way explain why they had chosen to keep the ceremony so small and quiet and it was rumoured they had done so out of respect for their respective past partners. Since splitting up with Daniel, Satsuki had kept away from the public eye. However, when news of the wedding broke, her father reported to the press that she was 'absolutely bewildered'.

He told the *Daily Mail* that the producer has banned all mention of Craig's name after reading about his nuptials in the press.

'His sudden marriage came out of nowhere,' her father Christopher said. 'We heard about it like everyone else, by reading the newspapers. She doesn't mention his name now and tells me off if I do.' But he insisted the break up had been for the best. 'Satsuki has only just reached a happy place. She has since said, more than once, that the break-up was the best thing for her. She knew he was not the man she wanted him to be and there was something wrong in the relationship.'

However, this recent news had obviously caused a setback. Already very slim, Satsuki had reportedly lost even more weight. Her father even expressed concern that she might have an eating disorder. 'I have suggested to her on a number of occasions that she might have one. Yet whenever we're together she eats like a horse.'

Daniel, however, had most certainly moved on. There were reports suggesting he and Rachel might be setting up home in London. Workmen had apparently been seen refitting her £3 million North London home. It was also suggested Daniel and Rachel were looking at a six-acre property on the south coast as a holiday retreat.

It seemed that all the pieces in Daniel's life were falling into place. The only element missing was a start date for the next Bond film. But when Judi Dench let slip in a press conference that she would be starting work on the film very soon, it became clear the ball was definitely rolling.

Bond producers Michael Wilson and Barbara Broccoli confirmed that 007 would be back in November 2012. Even though there had been a considerable gap, Daniel felt confident the film would be a success. 'The hiatus may prove to be a good thing,' he said. 'I'm itching to have another crack at it.'

He complained that the writers' strike, which took place during the filming of *Quantum of Solace*, had inevitably had detrimental impact on the finished product.

But this film would be different. His old friend Sam Mendes (ironically once romantically involved with Rachel Weisz, before he left her for Kate Winslet) would be taking the directorial reigns, a decision Daniel very much approved of. 'All the things are in the right place,' he said confidently. 'Sam's on board and we have the bones of a really good script.' When asked what this involved, he joked, 'I want to spend the first 40 minutes of the next movie on the beach, with a cocktail, just relaxing.'

Having settled comfortably into the role of James Bond, it was hard to imagine anyone else would ever play the part. But, being typically non-committal, Daniel refused to be complacent. 'I take it one job at a time,' he shrugged. 'If we mess it up, I won't be asked to do another. The contract goes both ways. I can walk away from it or they can sack me.' Given the rate at which Daniel's star had been in ascendance that was extremely unlikely. It was more likely Daniel may tire of the dangerous stunts and high-octane action scenes. For now, he felt sufficiently challenged. What's more, just like Bond he'd got his girl.

Whatever the future held for Daniel, it definitely looked exciting, and with so many ambitious film projects on the go his mission, for now, was only half accomplished.

# CHAPTER 16

# BOND AND BEYOND

To the frustration of journalists worldwide, Daniel had developed a skill for steering clear of the limelight despite his rapidly growing fame. Details of his personal life were often left to speculation, with journalists desperately attempting to piece together a story from fragmented information.

In the few interviews he did give, Daniel proudly defended his refusal to share information about his private life. On the topic of his low-key marriage to Rachel Weisz, he told GQ magazine: 'We got away with it...We did it privately. And I've got a lot of people to thank for that. But that was the point. We did it for private reasons.

'Because we didn't want it fucked up, because that

would be sharing a secret. And the whole point is that it was a secret. A secret is a secret in my mind.'

According to friends, Daniel and Rachel were madly in love, but neither was keen to discuss their new marriage with the press. When asked if he had been attracted to Rachel when they first acted on stage together in 1994, Daniel replied: 'I'd rather not say. But we're together, so maybe there's a clue in that.'

Rachel though would later reveal that she had noticed a spark during those early encounters. She recalled having to 'literally spend the whole day' trying to seduce Daniel's character in *Les Grandes Horizontales*. 'It was really hard work, as you can imagine!' she laughed.

While he bristled suspiciously at the mention of Rachel's name during interviews - he believed talking about friends and family was like stabbing them in the back - Daniel did admit that he was happier than he had been in a long time. 'I'm in love. I'm very happy. And that is as far as I'm prepared to go. Life is long and I am hopefully in this for the long run.'

For her part, Rachel said marriage had made her a better person and mother. 'I love it,' she said of married life. 'It's different being married than living with your partner. There is a contract. You don't necessarily have to think about respecting the rules, but it is just there. It's in your heart, it's not like a piece of paper.'

Despite being one of Hollywood's most attractive actors, Rachel would later admit to *The Mirror* that she'd often felt alone in her twenties. 'I'd eat pizza at home by myself, rent movies, all the clichés... It was hard sometimes but you hope eventually you'll find the right partner.'

Now, in later life, she'd discovered greater contentment and happiness, and Daniel Craig was largely to credit for that. 'When I was younger, I worried about so many things and it was hard for me to feel happy or understand what made me happy. Once you reach your forties, you know where to look.'

She would go on to say that she and Daniel enjoyed life's simple pleasures, conjuring up images of domestic bliss. 'I love to cook. Daniel is also very good at it. We always enjoy trying out different kinds of cuisine and having fun with that.'

Despite the media interest in his marriage, Daniel didn't really need to worry about intrusions into his private life. People were more interested in the latest Bond film, *Skyfall*, when cameras started rolling in 2011.

The film would be released in 2012 to coincide with the 50th anniversary of the franchise, and high-profile director Sam Mendes was doing a good job to ensure this Bond movie would be a box-office smash. In an interview just before the film's release, Daniel admitted he had been instrumental in hiring the *American Beauty* director. 'He's English, he's Cambridge-educated, he's smart. He's lived with Bond all his life, he grew up with Bond the way I did,' said Daniel.

The conversation about Bond started during a party at Hugh Jackman's house in New York. After 'a few too many drinks', Daniel said he approached Sam and asked him if he'd like to direct the next film. 'I went, "How do you fancy directing a Bond?" And he kind of looked at me, and he went, "Yeah!" And it snowballed from there.' Both men discovered their mutual love of Bond and discovered they were fans of the same scenes.

The next day, Daniel mentioned the conversation to the film's producers Barbara Broccoli and Michael G Wilson. They were both keen on the idea and soon Sam Mendes was signed up to do the project.

It had been four years since *Quantum,* during which time MGM (the studio that co-produced the films) went into and came out of administration. But Daniel had enjoyed the break; a lot had happened in that time. 'I'm a different person now to who I was then,' he said.

Daniel felt confident that *Skyfall* would mark a return to form for the Bond movies. He told press that the film 'made me remember why I do it'.

Hoping to avoid the accidents that had beset *Quantum of Solace,* many of *Skyfall's* stunts were planned far in advance. Yet Daniel still managed to sustain several injuries. 'I tore a muscle right at the beginning of this one, crazily, in a kind of warm-up for something, which is what happens,' he said.

During the filming for a hair-raising fight scene on the roof of a train travelling at 30mph, he also recalled fearing he might fall off. Despite being secured by a 3ft wire, he remembered thinking: 'If I fall, it'll hurt…but I won't die.'

Although reprising the role of Bond had thrown Daniel back into a world of physical challenge and danger, he was quick to point out that he was no longer the hard man he had once been. 'I know I play a tough guy, but that's genuinely, genuinely not me,' he told *Rolling Stone* magazine. 'I've always been very good at avoiding fights, having worked in pubs and seen pools of blood everywhere.'

He admitted that the only thing that could still cause his blood to boil was 'someone looking at my girl the wrong way'.

'I still get jealous now, but not the way I used to. These days I'm much more happy to have a quiet word with somebody.'

With *Skyfall*, Daniel said he was keen to resurrect some of the humour that had made James Bond so popular in the first place. He joked to *The Telegraph* newspaper that he'd like to see the return of 'a submarine base and 20 karate-kicking girls'. But he went on to say that: 'Certainly the humour has come back in. It's got some fun in it, but it's not forced. I'm not winking at the camera. The writing's really good, and I think that lends itself to humour, because most of life is fucking funny.'

That humour clearly extended off set when Daniel agreed to film a spoof opening sequence with the Queen as part of the London 2012 Olympics Opening Ceremony. During the five-minute sketch, seen by 900 million viewers, Daniel collected the Queen from Buckingham Palace in a helicopter, then parachuted with her into the Olympic stadium. The sketch, masterminded by Danny Boyle, was shot on one of Daniel's days off from *Skyfall*.

Although he didn't really have time to speak to the Queen, he described her as being enigmatic and professional. He also praised her acting skills and claimed, 'she completely got it'.

He recalled a moment when she started improvising at her desk. 'She sat down at the desk and said, "Would you like me to pretend to be writing something?" Took out a piece of paper. Did some business.'

Public frenzy surrounding the release of *Skyfall* had been building for some time, and a teaser photo had been released at the beginning of 2012, showing Daniel with his top off. 'They wanted a picture of me with my shirt off,' said Daniel. 'And I said, "You can have the one with my back turned." That's as simple as that.'

When the 23rd Bond movie was finally released in cinemas, it was met with rapturous reviews. Along with Daniel, Judi Dench, Javier Bardem (as the villain Silva) and Naomie Harris (as field agent Eve) were all commended on their roles. The film would go on to become the highest-grossing film of all time at the British box office (according to figures released in July 2013), earning nearly £103 million. At the worldwide box office, the film made more than $1.1 billion.

Daniel's drive and commitment had clearly paid off. 'He wants to be the engine room, he wants to be the motivating factor, he wants to be the person trying the hardest,' Sam Mendes later told *The Telegraph*. Javier Bardem also told reporters that he would frequently arrive on set at 7am to find Daniel had already done a session in the gym.

But despite his success, Daniel confessed he was still not completely satisfied with his career. In particular, he still struggled to cope with fame and the demands of being a Hollywood star. He compared interviews to being like 'a trip to the dentist' and avoided TV talk shows whenever possible. 'I always forget verbs,' he complained. 'I'm not good at that tits and teeth thing.' Performing was still something he could only do as an actor.

He was typically publicity-shy when it was announced he would be starring alongside his new wife, Rachel, in a Broadway adaptation of Harold Pinter's play *Betrayal* (running from October 2013 to January 2014). Daniel was cast in the role of Robert, playing alongside Rachel as his cheating wife Emma. He said they had both been keen to work on a play together for some time and had been searching for the right project.

It was by no means a publicity stunt and he quickly dismissed any suggestion that the pair might consider themselves a 'power couple' or, worse still, 'Hollywood's hottest couple'.

'I think there are far hotter couples out there than Rachel and I,' he laughed, before adding, 'not putting Rachel down in any way, shape or form.'

Keen not to 'expose our marriage on stage' they avoided sitting next to each other during press junkets, and when being photographed together made a conscious effort not to look lovingly into each other's eyes. He told reporters that although the play was very intense, he and Rachel still managed to switch off at home. 'We don't talk to each other about it, no. She gets on with her thing, and I get on with my thing. We decided to do that because it's important to be separate entities when you're at work.'

Rachel confirmed this, telling the *Sun*: 'I don't talk about my work, and nor does he. It's very private. There is nothing worse than two actors getting together and talking about acting. It's like the end – it's the worst.'

Daniel also revealed that one of the secrets to their successful marriage lay in banning technological devices in the bedroom. 'If the iPad goes to bed, I mean, unless you're watching porn on the Internet, it's a killer. We have a ban on it,' he joked to *The Telegraph*.

At the end of 2014, Daniel started work on the next highly-anticipated Bond film, *Spectre*, due for release at the end of 2015. Once again director Sam Mendes was at the helm, and Daniel teased the script would be 'better than we had last time'.

'We've got an amazing cast,' he said. Ralph Fiennes (M), Naomie Harris (Miss Moneypenny), Ben Whishaw (Q) and David Bautista (Mr Hinx) had all signed up.

After a draft script was stolen and leaked, producers were forced to change the plot, which Daniel hinted would be building on some of the themes explored in *Skyfall*. 'We started something in *Skyfall*, it felt like a beginning of something. This feels like a continuation of that. We're going to put all of those elements in, and much more.'

An official plot teaser revealed a cryptic message from Bond's past would lead him on a trail to uncover a sinister organisation. Although filming was based at London's Pinewood Studios, location shoots also took place in Mexico City, Rome and Morocco. Daniel described Mexico City as 'being one of my favourite cities I've ever been to...But you can get into an awful lot of trouble there!'

Many other details were kept under wraps, but Daniel did talk openly about the thrill of driving an iconic Aston Martin DB5 on set, though he admitted he preferred it when the professionals took over. 'I giggle like a girl the whole way round!' he confessed.

True to form, Daniel managed to sustain injuries while filming stunts and even ended up in hospital needing knee surgery. Although he agreed to use a stunt double for several sequences, he always insisted on doing his own daredevil scenes wherever possible. 'I don't do all my stunts - I'd be lying if I said that. But I like the fact that occasionally you'll see on screen that it's my face and it's me,' he told late-night talk show host Jimmy Kemmel. 'And I think audiences hopefully appreciate that. At least, I really hope they do.'

Websites were buzzing with rumours about the film, which looked set to be another blockbuster hit. Daniel Craig had clearly made the role of Bond his own but he wasn't ready to take all the credit just yet. Ian Fleming's classic character had an enduring appeal greater than any actor, and Daniel wasn't about to steal that thunder. Attempting to explain the popularity of the Bond franchise, he said the stories revelled in 'darkness with a sense of humour – a black humour'. But most tellingly of all, in some ways revealing his own enduring attraction to the role, he admitted: 'It's about danger, but good danger, because you're in the hands of somebody who's saying "Fuck you" to risk and "Fuck you" to dying.'

It was also revealed that the actor would end up seducing one of his oldest bond girls yet – 50-year-old Monica Bellucci – who played the role of Lucia.

Monica described her character as 'an Italian woman with secrets. She watches her Mafioso husband get killed and she risks the same thing happening to her.'

'Lucky James!' his wife Rachel told journalists. 'She's one of the most beautiful women in the world. It's not her that's lucky, it's him.'

Director Sam Mendes also dropped several hints about the film's carefully guarded content. 'This is only the beginning of the story,' he told the *Independent* newspaper once filming had wrapped, later declaring that *Spectre* would be his final outing as a director for the Bond franchise. He went on to suggest that the film would finally provide some background on 007's character. 'The Bond creation myth never happened,' he said. 'I felt there was an opportunity there: What made him? And who were the people who affected him along the way? You're sort of telling the story backwards of how Bond became Bond.'

'A lot of the film is a celebration of what it is to be Bond,' Daniel added. 'But it's not retro. Hopefully it's not just classic Bond but a classic thriller.'

Amusingly, Sam Mendes also admitted he had originally dismissed the casting of Daniel Craig as 007. 'I had cast Daniel Craig in this film I made in Chicago called *Road To Perdition* about 15 years ago and it was his first big American film.

'Then the role of Bond came up years later and I was called by Entertainment Weekly, a showbiz publication, and they said your old friend and collaborator has been suggested as Bond, what do you think? I said "terrible idea - he shouldn't do it."

'Because for me at the time I thought Bond had become the opposite of what Daniel is - a slightly disengaged, urbane, jokey, eyebrow raising, you know, a pastiche in a way and I feel Daniel's reality, passion and sort of honesty as an actor would not work.

'But of course the franchise adapted to work with Daniel and when I saw it at the cinema I thought it was a fantastic piece of casting. And it was that that got me reinterested in Bond as a movie.'

Daniel was rewarded for his efforts with an enormous paycheck, propelling him into the Forbes list of the world's highest paid stars – the only British actor to do so. He came 15th on the list, having netted earnings of £17million in the previous year.

Daniel provided some irresistibly quotable sound bites to *Esquire* magazine at the beginning of September 2015 about his most famous role: 'He's misogynistic, sexist and very lonely... I am certainly not that person. But he is, and so what does that mean? It means you cast great actresses and make the parts as good as you can for the women in the movies.'

This does not mean that Daniel is foolish enough to disrespect the character who has brought him fame and considerable fortune: 'I used to get asked all the time, "Don't you worry that you're going to get typecast?" "And?" I mean, talk about a high-class problem.'

A further indication of his growing star status, Daniel was cast as a waxwork figure at London's Madame Tussauds. He was put on display alongside the other five actors who had played 007 throughout the years.

It was the first time the stars had been seen together; previous attempts by producers to reunite the actors at the 2013 Oscars ceremony for the Bond franchise 50th anniversary had failed. Roger Moore, who had played Bond seven times, was cast in the guise of his 1977 film *The Spy Who Loved Me*; Timothy Dalton appeared as he had done in *The Living Daylights*; and Pierce Brosnan was cast in the style of his *Tomorrow Never Dies* character.

The Omega watch brand also announced plans to produce a limited edition Omega Seamaster 300 'Spectre' watch in honour of Ian Fleming's famous character. Daniel would wear the watch, which featured a 007 gun barrel logo on the strap holder, on screen. It would be the first time a watch from the movie would be made available to the general public for purchase.

Unfortunately for Daniel though, his star status did prohibit him from doing some things. Rugby player Mike Tindall had approached the actor to take part in a charity rugby match at Twickenham, after hearing the star had played for Hoylake RFC when he left school. But insurers had banned him from taking part. With the cinema release of *Spectre* approaching, they were concerned 007 might end up looking bruised and battered on the red carpet.

Instead, Daniel took the opportunity to get some rest and relaxation once filming had completed. He knew very well that Bond fever was already beginning to grip the nation in anticipation of *Spectre*'s release. Even though he didn't necessarily enjoy it, he was ready to be pushed into the media spotlight once again.

A family holiday in Menorca with his wife Rachel and her son Henry was just the tonic he needed. Rachel was photographed on the beach in a black bikini and the 45-year-old was applauded for her stunning figure. Unlike Daniel, who had been known to spend hours in the gym when filming, Rachel was far from being an exercise addict. 'I eat well, I exercise, but I'm not hysterical about it. I'm just healthy,' she said. 'Being an actor is like being an athlete. I have to be somewhat in shape because this [my body and face] is all I've got.'

But just like her husband, she had dabbled in doing some of her own stunts in films. She told one tabloid journalist about her experience of shooting a dangerous sequence in *The Bourne Legacy*. 'I found all the physical work quite scary and exciting at the same time - it toughens you up. There was a great deal of running and lots of stunt work I didn't expect to do. You feel like you can handle yourself in difficult situations after doing a film like this one.'

Credit to her general health and fitness, she hadn't needed much preparation to meet with the film's physical demands. 'They (the producers) took me as I came. I'm quite fit and I can run, but I didn't have to get into extra shape for it. I'm not Lara Croft. I didn't have to be all biceps. I can climb trees and run and jump. I'm not too girlie.'

Even before *Spectre* had hit cinemas, there was the usual speculation about whether this would be Daniel's final outing as Bond. Celebrities worldwide shared their opinions about who might play 007 next.

Rapper A$AP Rocky told *NME* news that he thought it was time for a black Bond. 'I'd get the job done, and I'll look better than any other Bond that has ever lived. All I need is a six-pack,' he said, adding that he could easily use his street skills to bring the role to life.

'I've been in group fights before,' added A$AP Rocky of understanding what goes on in a real fight. 'This kid pulled out a gun and was hitting people with the butt of it.'

Former 007 star Pierce Brosnan also waded into the debate about how a modern Bond might take shape, backing Idris Elba as a possible candidate. 'He has the physicality, the charisma, the presence.'

In fact, a previous leaked email from Sony Pictures had revealed the studio would be keen to see the British actor as the next incarnation of Ian Fleming's seductive spy. Idris had responded with a Tweet saying 'Glad you think I've got a shot!' and confirmed that he'd most likely accept the role if it was offered to him.

Pierce Brosnan also discussed the possibility of a gay Bond, an idea in principle he'd support, although he didn't believe the producers would ever go along with it. 'I don't think Barbara [Broccoli, producer of every Bond film since 1993's *Octopussy*] would allow a gay Bond to happen in her lifetime,' he told *Details* magazine. 'But it would certainly make for interesting viewing.'

Overall though, he believed Daniel still had more to offer the role. Indeed, newspaper reports suggested the actor had signed up to do one more movie after *Spectre* – even though he'd repeatedly been quoted as saying he'd like to leave the franchise after fulfilling his contract. No matter how hard he tried to resist, there was something that kept drawing him back to the role. It was just the fame side of things that he never seemed to feel comfortable with. While he was happy to meet and greet fans, he still found the whole obsession with Bond – and Daniel Craig – to be overwhelming. 'Bars are hard [for me to go to], but that's more because of mobile phones,' he told American magazine *DuJour*. 'I'll do autographs all day long, and I'll even do a picture at the end of an evening. But if I'm being photographed all night long in a bar, that pisses me off.

'If you ask, I may say yes, but come up to me and say, "Would you like to take a photograph with me?" If you're fucking sneaking photographs of me... it's human nature, you're sneaking something! I'm being fucked with! But people don't see it as a problem. Maybe I'm delusional.'

Social media and rapidly developing technology meant that finding privacy was even harder than ever before. The actor recalled that a few years ago when *Casino Royale* was released, he'd never experienced problems to the same degree. 'There were phones back then, but nobody used the cameras.'

As far as he was personally concerned, he could never imagine indulging in such behaviour – he didn't have a Twitter account and refused to read gossip on the Internet. 'On a flight to New York recently, Alicia Keys and Desmond Tutu were on the plane. I didn't go up to them. I smiled at Alicia Keys, but I couldn't look Desmond Tutu in the eye. I wanted to go up to him and fall at his feet. It was one of those situations where I blew it completely.'

His wife though had developed a successful method for dealing with persistent fans. 'My wife is the best in the world at all that, she'll just turn to them and go, "No, thank you very much," and they're like, "Okay".'

The frenzy of public attention did mean that Daniel's social life had become much more limited. 'I like to have a drink, and I love pubs and I love finding new pubs and places to socialise. But that has a limit on it now.'

Daniel had never shied away from his love of alcohol, and admitted he enjoyed playing drunks. 'I love playing drunks…Drunk, damaged people: it's like, bring them on!'

In the coming months, Daniel would no doubt be nursing a few hangovers. With *Spectre* set to propel the actor into even higher echelons of stardom, there was plenty of reason to raise a toast to the future.

# FILMOGRAPHY

*Spectre* (2015), as James Bond
Directed by Sam Mendes
Screenplay by Neal Purvis, Robert Wade, John Logan, Jez Butterworth
Released by MGM
Cast Christoph Waltz, Ralph Fiennes

*Skyfall* (2012), as James Bond
Directed by Sam Mendes
Screenplay by Neal Purvis, Robert Wade, John Logan
Released by MGM
Cast Javier Bardem, Naomie Harris

*The Girl with the Dragon Tattoo* (2011), as Mikael Blomkvist
Directed by David Fincher
Screenplay by Steven Zaillian
Released by Columbia Pictures
Cast Rooney Mara, Christopher Plummer

*The Adventures of Tintin* (2011), as Sakharine/Red Rackham (voice)
Directed by Steven Spielberg
Screenplay by Steven Moffat, Edgar Wright, Joe Cornish
Released by Columbia Pictures
Cast Jamie Bell, Andy Serkis

*Dream House* (2011), as Will Atenton
Directed by Jim Sheridan
Screenplay by David Loucka
Released by Warner Bros.
Cast Rachel Weisz, Naomi Watts

*Cowboys & Aliens* (2011), as Jake Lonergan
Directed by Jon Favreau
Screenplay by Roberto Orci, Alex Kurtzman, Damon Lindelof, Mark Fergus, Hawk Ostby
Released by Paramount Pictures
Cast Harrison Ford, Olivia Wilde

# FILMOGRAPHY

*Quantum of Solace* (2008), as James Bond
Directed by Marc Forster
Screenplay by Robert Wade
Released by MGM
Cast Mathieu Amalric, Giancarlo Giannini, Judi Dench

*Defiance* (2008), as Tuvia Bielski
Directed by Edward Zwick
Screenplay by Clay Frohman, Edward Zwick
Released by Grosvenor Park Productions
*Flashbacks of a Fool* (2008), tbc
Directed by Baillie Walsh
Screenplay by Baillie Walsh
Released by Left Turn Films
Cast Harry Eden, Olivia Williams, Helen McCrory

*The Golden Compass* (2007), as Lord Asriel
Directed by Chris Weitz
Screenplay by Chris Weitz
Released by New Line Cinema
Cast Nicole Kidman, John Hurt, Eva Green,
   Kevin Bacon, Eric Bana

*The Invasion* (2007), as Ben
Directed by Oliver Hirschbiegel
Screenplay by Dave Kajganich
Released by Oliver Pictures Inc.
Cast Nicole Kidman, Jeremy Northam,
    Jackson Bond, Q-Tip

*Casino Royale* (2006), as James Bond
Directed by Martin Campbell
Screenplay by Neal Purvis, Robert Wade, Paul Haggis
Released by MGM
Cast Eva Green, Mads Mikkelsen, Judi Dench, Jeffrey
Wright, Caterina Murino, Giancarlo Giannini

*Infamous* (2006), as Perry Smith
Directed by Douglas McGrath
Screenplay by Douglas McGrath
Released by Jack and Henry Productions Inc.
Cast Sigourney Weaver, Toby Jones, Gwyneth Paltrow,
    Juliet Stevenson

*Renaissance* (2006), voice of Barthélémy Karas
Directed by Christian Volkman
Screenplay by Jean-Bernard Pouy, Patrick Raynal
Released by Onyx Films
Cast Patrick Floersheim, Catherine McCormack,
    Laura Blanc

*Munich* (2005), as Steve
Directed by Steven Spielberg
Screenplay by Tony Kushner, Eric Roth,
Released by Dreamworks SKG
Cast Eric Bana, Ciaran Hinds, Mathieu Kassovitz

*Sorstalanság* (2005), as US Army Sergeant
Directed by Lajos Koltai
Screenplay by Imre Kertesz
Released by EuroArts Entertainment
Cast Marcell Nagy, Bela Dora, Balint Pentek

*The Jacket* (2005), as Rudy Mackenzie
Directed by John Maybury
Screenplay by Massy Tadjedin
Released by Mandalay Pictures
Cast Adrien Brosy, Keira Knightly, Kris Kristofferson,
    Jennifer Jason Leigh, Kelly Lynch

*Enduring Love* (2004), as Joe
Directed by Roger Mitchell
Screenplay by Joe Penhall
Released by FilmFour
Cast Samantha Morton, Bill Weston, Jeremy McCurdie,
    Rhys Ifans, Bill Nighy

*Layer Cake* (2004), as XXXX
Directed by Matthew Vaughn
Screenplay by J.J. Connolly
Released by Columbia Pictures Corporation
Cast Tom Hardy, Jamie Foreman, Sally Hawkins,
Burn Gorman

*Sylvia* (2003), as Ted Hughes
Directed by Christine Jeffs
Screenplay by John Brownlow
Released by BBC Films
Cast Gwyneth Paltrow, Jared Harris, Blythe Danner,
    Michael Gambon
*The Mother* (2003), as Darren
Directed by Roger Mitchell
Screenplay by Hanif Kureshi
Released by BBC Films
Cast Anne Reid, Peter Vaughn, Anna Wilson-Jones,
    Danira Govich

*Ten Minutes Older: The Cello* (2002), as Cecil (segment
Addicted to the Stars)
Directed by Michael Radford
Screenplay by Michael Radford
Released by Odyssey Films
Cast Charles Simon, Roland Gift

*Occasional, Strong* (2002)
Directed by Steve Green
Screenplay by Steve Green
Released by Rogue Films
Cast Ella Jones

*Road to Perdition* (2002), as Connor Rooney
Directed by Same Mendes
Screenplay by David Self
Released by Dreamworks SKG
Cast Paul Newman, Tom Hanks, Jennifer Jason Leigh

*Lara Croft: Tomb Raider* (2001), as Alex West
Directed by Simon West
Screenplay by Patrick Massett, John Zinman
Released by Paramount Pictures
Cast Angelina Jolie, Jon Voight, Iain Glen, Noah Taylor

*Hotel Splendide* (2000), as Ronald Blanche
Directed by Terence Gross
Screenplay by Terence Gross
Released by Canal+
Cast Toni Collette, Katrin Cartlidge,

*Some Voices* (2000), as Ray
Directed by Simon Cellan Jones

Screenplay by Joe Penhall
Released by Dragon Pictures
Cast David Morrissey, Kelly Macdonald, Julie Graham

*I Dreamed of Africa* (2000), as Declan Fielding
Directed by Hugh Hudson
Screenplay by Paula Milne, Susan Shilliday
Released by Columbia Pictures Corporation
Cast Kim Basinger, Vincent Perez, Liam Aitkin,
    Garrett Strommen

*The Trench* (1999), as Sgt Telford Winter
Directed by William Boyd
Screenplay by William Boyd
Released by Arts Council of England
Cast Paul Nicholls, Julian Rhind-Tutt, James D'Arcy,
    Danny Dyer

*Elizabeth* (1998), as John Ballard
Directed by Shekar Kupar
Screenplay by Michael Hirst
Released by Channel Four Films
Cast Cate Blanchett, Geoffrey Rush, Christopher
Eccleston, Joseph Fiennes, Richard Attenborough

*Love Is the Devil: Study for a Portrait of Francis Bacon*
(1998), as George Dyer
Directed by John Maybury

Screenplay by John Maybury
Released by BBC Films
Cast Derek Jacobi, Tilda Swinton, Anne Lanbton

*Love and Rage* (1998), as James Lynchehaun
Directed by Cathal Black
Screenplay by Brian Lynch
Released by Nova Films
Cast Greta Scacchi, Stephen Dillane, Valerie Edmond
*Obsession* (1997), as John MacHale
Directed by Peter Sehr
Screenplay by Marie Noelle, Peter Sehr
Released by high Speed Films Paris
Cast Heike Makatsch, Charles Berling, Seymour Cassel

*Saint-Ex* (1996), as Guillaumet
Directed by Anand Tucker
Screenplay by Frank Cottrell Boyce
Released by BBC Films
Cast Miranda Richardson, Janet McTeer,
    Ken Stott, Katrin Cartlidge

*A Kid in King Arthur's Court* (1995), as Master Kane
Directed by Michael Gottlieb
Screenplay by Michael Part, Robert L.Levy
Released by Tapestry Films
Cast Joss Ackland, Thomas Ian Nicholas, Art Malik,
    Kate Winslet

*The Power of One* (1992), as Sgt Botha
Directed by John G. Avildsen
Screenplay by Robert Mark Kamen
Released by Alcor Films
Cast Nomadlozi Kubheka, Agatha Hurle, Nigel Ivy

*The Adventures of Young Indiana Jones: Daredevils of the Desert* (1992) (Video), as Schiller
TV dramas
*Archangel* (2005) – Fluke Kelso
*Copenhagen* (2002) – Werner Heisenberg
*Sword of Honour* (2001) – Guy Crouchback
*Shockers: The Visitor* (1999) – Richard
*The Ice House* (1997) – D.S. Andy McLoughlin
*The Hunger* (1997) – Jerry Pritchard
*The Fortunes and Misfortunes of Moll Flanders* (1996) – James 'Jemmy' Seagrave
*Kiss and Tell* (1996) – Matt Kearney
*Tales from the Crypt* (1996)
*Our Friends in the North* (1996)– Geordie (George) Peacock
*Heartbeat* (1993) – Peter Begg
*Between the Lines* (1993) – as Joe Rance
*Drop the Dead Donkey* (1993) – Fixx
*Sharpe's Eagle* (1993) – Lt Berry
*Genghis Cohn* (1993) – Lt Guth
*Boon* (1992) –Jim Parham
*Covington Cross* (1992) – the Walkway Guard